Praise

"Yes, universities may produce assemblies which serve the people. So, in 2012 at Grahamstown, South Africa, did Rhodes University (despite the name), and in that service produced a people's knowledge to transform the economic, material, social, family, political, educational, and spiritual institutions of capitalism at their core, without hierarchy, racism, oppression, or chauvinism of any kind. With sober care, practical acumen, and passionate eloquence the knowledge from that assembly is presented here. Absorb this knowledge and sense the future!"

—Peter Linebaugh, author of *The Many-Headed Hydra: Sailors, Slaves, Commoners and the Hidden History of the Revolutionary Atlantic* (with Marcus Rediker)

"Capturing state power is regarded as the dominant means to achieving social transformation. This excellent collection challenges this prevailing perspective through examining societal and social movements in South Africa and Zimbabwe that have advocated and achieved tangible change from below without seizing state power. Kirk Helliker and Lucien van der Walt offer a compelling counternarrative that is indispensable to the literature on social movements."

—Immanuel Ness, City University of New York, author of *Organizing Insurgency: Workers' Movements in the Global South*

"Moving beyond the disillusion and cynicism engendered by liberation movements of the global South which 'triumphed' and then betrayed everything they professed to hold dear, the contributors to this volume explore what could happen when and if 'bottom-up' labor, gender, and livelihood social movements stop lusting after the capture of state power. Mainly based in South African and Zimbabwean studies, the authors construct an exciting dialogue with the ideas of Mexico-based sociologist and philosopher John Holloway. Can there really be independent survival strategies against the twin malignancies of late capitalism and state turgidity? This is a must-read about the scope and health of 21st century social formations, trying to walk new paths of equitable human flourishing."

—Teresa Ann Barnes, University of Illinois at Urbana-Champaign, author of *Uprooting University Apartheid in South Africa: From Liberalism to Decolonization*

"In the 1980s and '90s, people who sought a world of equality, liberty, and socialism looked to Zimbabwe. In the late 1990s and early 2000s, after the fall of apartheid, even more looked towards South Africa. Tragically, the ruling parties in both countries—and which had led the liberation struggles in each—have proven epic failures and profound disappointments. Hence, it is high time to revisit historical social movements and more fully analyze recent ones that never placed their hopes in state power. This collection brings together fascinating research on the history of anarchist, community, rural, and worker movements from the early 20th century into the 21st that believe another world is possible."
—Peter Cole, author of the award-winning *Dockworker Power: Race and Activism in Durban and the San Francisco Bay Area*

"In the light of the unfulfilled expectation of overcoming class and race inequality through state-centered national liberation movements and African state socialism this book edited by Kirk Helliker and Lucien van der Walt offers a fascinating insight into the seldom told history of alternative socialist currents in Southern Africa."
—Dario Azzellini, Autonomous University of Zacatecas, Mexico, author of *If Not Us, Who? Global Workers against Authoritarianism, Fascism and Dictatorships*

"A must read for all people-centered movements aiming to transform society. This book could not have been written at a more opportune time, as 'socialism' returns to the world stage after a period of much disrepute and gross misinformation. It introduces us to past and present struggles in Southern Africa that do not see the capture of the state by vanguard parties as an adequate form of struggle., and that devise new ways to deal with the changes in capitalism.
—Zarina Patel, is editor of *Awaaz* magazine and author of *The In-Between World of Kenya's Media: South Asian Journalism, 1900–1992*

"Time and again socialist movements have debated how best to achieve change. Some, like the anarchists and syndicalists, argued that it could only come from below, by means of working-class direct action, solidarity, and self-organization. The majority, with mainstream Marxists at the fore, argued that workers should take part in state politics and stand in elections. The judgment of history is clear: the former were right and, as predicted, rather the conquer state power, it conquered them. This excellent collection of essays brings a welcome South African and Zimbabwean perspective on this debate and will be interest to all those seeking to learn from history rather than repeat it."
—Iain McKay, editor of *Direct Struggle against Capital: A Peter Kropotkin Anthology*

Politics at a Distance from the State
Radical and African Perspectives

Edited by
Kirk Helliker and Lucien van der Walt

Preface by John Holloway

The first six chapters previously appeared in the *Journal of Contemporary African Studies*, volume 34, number 3, under the same authors and titles, Holloway at pp. 309–311, Helliker and van der Walt at pp. 312–331, Neocosmos at pp. 332–347, Byrne and Nicole at pp. 368–387, Naicker and Bruchhausen at pp. 388–403, and Alexander and Helliker at pp. 404–418 in that issue. They are reprinted by permission of Taylor & Francis Ltd, http://www.tandfonline.com. The final chapter and dossier by van der Walt first appeared in the Routledge hardcover of this book in 2018 and are reprinted by permission.

Politics at a Distance from the State: Radical and African Perspectives
Kirk Helliker and Lucien van der Walt © 2022
This edition © PM Press

ISBN (paperback): 9781629639437
ISBN (ebook): 9781629639574
LCCN: 2021945078

Cover design by John Yates/www.stealworks.com
Cover photo by Wendy Shwegmann

10 9 8 7 6 5 4 3 2 1

PM Press
PO Box 23912
Oakland, CA 94623
www.pmpress.org

Printed in the USA

Contents

Notes on Contributors

Tarryn Alexander is a lecturer in the Department of Sociology at Rhodes University in South Africa and is currently completing her doctoral studies in the field of decolonisation and curriculum development.

Sarah Bruchhausen is completing a PhD through the NRF SARChI Chair in "Local Histories and Present Realities" at the University of the Witwatersrand, South Africa. She worked for the Rivonia Trial archives at Lilies leaf Farm, after completing her MA degree in the History Department at Rhodes University, South Africa, in conjunction with UHURU (Unit for the Humanities at Rhodes University). Her work has examined the democratic and egalitarian nature of rural resistance in 1950s and 1960s South Africa, and its links to contemporary worker struggles. She is particularly interested in reconceptualising notions of emancipatory politics.

Sian Byrne is an industrial sociology PhD candidate at Rhodes University, South Africa, and a guest researcher at the Berlin Social Science Centre (WZB), Germany, with the Globalization, Work, and Production Project Group. She is interested in studying work and labour, with a specific focus on labour politics from comparative and transnational labour histories perspectives. Her PhD is a comparative historical study of labour politics in FOSATU (South Africa) and Solidarność (Poland) in the early 1980s.

Kirk Helliker is a research professor in the Department of Sociology at Rhodes University in South Africa, as well as founder and director of the Unit of Zimbabwean Studies in the department. His main research interests are land reform, civil society and political transformation with particular reference to Zimbabwe. His books include the edited volumes *The Political Economy of Livelihoods in Contemporary Zimbabwe* (2018) and *Everyday Crisis: Living in Contemporary Zimbabwe* (2021), and the authored *Fast Track Land Occupations in Zimbabwe in the Context of the Zvimurenga* (2021), all in collaboration with Sandra Bhatasara and Manase Kudzai Chiweshe.

John Holloway is a professor of Sociology at the Instituto de Ciencias Sociales y Humanidades in the Benemérita Universidad Autónoma de Puebla, Mexico. He has published widely on Marxist theory, the Zapatista movement and the new forms of anticapitalist struggle.

Camalita Naicker lectures in the Department of Historical Studies at the University of Cape Town, South Africa. She holds an MA in Politics and African Studies from Rhodes University, South Africa. Her work focuses on labour and popular struggles, examining how people use different forms of political practice, often outside of the state and institutional structures, to organise and to resist domination. She has written on the trade union movement, the 2012 Marikana massacre of miners, land occupations and student movements in South Africa.

Michael Neocosmos recently retired from his positions as professor of Sociology and Director of the Unit for the Humanities at Rhodes University (UHURU), South Africa. He is the author of *Social Relations in Rural Swaziland* (ed. 1987), *The Agrarian Question in Southern Africa* (1993), and *From Foreign Natives to Native Foreigners: Explaining Xenophobia in South Africa* (2006 and 2010). His latest book is entitled *Thinking Freedom in Africa: Toward a Theory of Emancipatory Politics* (2016).

Nicole Ulrich is a labour historian based at the University of Fort Hare, South Africa, interested in the organisation, political ideas and identities of the labouring classes in Southern Africa. She has been involved in the Workers' Library and Museum, the History Workshop at the University of the Witwatersrand and the Centre for African Studies, University of Cambridge. Her work has been published, inter alia, in *African Studies*, the *International Review of Social History*, the *Journal of Southern African Studies*, *New Contree* and the *South African Historical Journal*.

Lucien van der Walt is professor of Industrial and Economic Sociology at Rhodes University, South Africa. A prize-winning scholar, his research areas are anarchism and syndicalism, labour and the left, and the political economy of neo-liberalism. He has taught at the universities of Witwatersrand and Rhodes University (South Africa) and Kassel (Germany), and for the DITSELA Workers Institute, the Global Labour University/ ENGAGE, and the National Union of Metalworkers of SA (NUMSA). His books include *Anarchism and Syndicalism in the Colonial and Postcolonial World, 1880–1940* (2010/2014, edited with Steven Hirsch).

Preface: at a distance from the state

The state closes. Kills hope. Probably nowhere more clearly than in South Africa, but every-where: the state is disillusion; pushes us into cynicism; makes us die before we are dead.

South Africa was a symbol of hope in all the world for many, many years. A symbol of dreadful oppression it is true, but this very oppression was always linked to hope. The hope that one day, the dreadful, hateful system of apartheid would be defeated and every-thing would be different. Certainly that was the image for so many of us outside South Africa, but I imagine it was even more so for those who lived there; who breathed the oppression and fought for a better country.

Where did this hope go? And where is it now, after Marikana? Is this the country every-body wanted to see? What happened?

I would argue that the state killed hope, and that it always does. I do not say 'the ANC', or that it was the fault of Mandela, or Zuma. One could explain it in personal or local terms, of course (and yes, certainly Mandela and Zuma and the African National Congress (ANC) are somewhat to blame), but when one looks at one country after another and sees similar things happening (sometimes better, sometimes worse, always disappointing), one has to look for a more general answer. There must be something about the state as a form of organisation, as a way of operating that systematically destroys hope.

The most obvious thing about the state is that it sends us home. In situations of intense struggle for change, such as South Africa, or Bolivia, or Russia, once the old regime falls, the new regime sends everyone home. Thousands of people have devoted their lives (and often their deaths) to struggling for change, and once it seems to be happening, and the movement has conquered control of the state, the state says in effect: 'thank you very much, you can all go home now, we'll look after things. You can show your support for this arrangement by voting for us'. This is not necessarily said with malice: it is just the way that the state works. The state is, in its most obvious sense, a number of paid officials charged with governing. By assuming responsibility for the running of society, the state excludes society from self-government.

One obvious effect of this is that it weakens the capacity of those officials to do any-thing very meaningful. The fall of the old regime in each case mentioned seemed an impossible task, but it was achieved by the combined efforts of millions. And when the millions are sent home, the full-time officials who remain, no matter how strong their com-mitment to radical change may be, cannot have the same force to bring about change.

The exclusion of the people implicit in the existence of the state is just the opening into another problem. It is not just the state that is the problem, it is that all states are embedded in world capital, and are obliged to do everything possible to promote the accumulation of capital in their territories. If not, capital will move elsewhere, the state will lose its own revenue, and the material welfare of the population will suffer as invest-ment and employment fall. Any state, however radical the proclamations of its leaders (at least initially), is confronted with the fact that, in a capitalist world, access to material wealth depends on subordination to capital. Money rules: the state is trapped in this reality, and does not have the strength to break it, since it has already sent everybody home.

Yet hope arises, again and again. Perhaps it would die, if capital could just let us stew quietly in our dull conformism, having lobotomised all hope of a radically different world. But capital is incapable of doing this: it cannot stay still. Capital has the constant drive to expand itself through accumulating profit, and to achieve this it must attack us again and again: telling us in the universities that we are not working hard enough and not making an adequate contribution to the system; attacking us in the factories, urging us to work harder; telling peasants on the land that the world has no place for them, besides the slums of the cities; telling whole communities they must be destroyed to make way for mines and dams.

Capital is constant aggression, and against this aggression springs resistance, and often this resistance spills over into rebellion, and fills us with the hope that we can construct a world that is not based upon subordination to the state and capital.

Rebellion then faces a dilemma. It can take the obvious path of turning to the state. However, while it is possible to achieve small changes through the state, it is not possible to break from the rule of capital, to break the destructive dynamic that is capital.

This is why more and more movements throughout the world have been turning away from the state, and the idea of changing the world through the state. More and more movements of resistance and rebellion have been developing various forms of politics at a distance from the state. A difficult and uncertain path, but there is no other way to go. Or rather: difficult and uncertain paths, because there is no one path. And while there are definitely paths in the plural, these are not paths that we can follow: they are paths that have to be created, paths that are made by walking on them. And they are paths that go away from, that reject, the current destructive organisation of society, and say 'No! Enough!' to the deadly logic of capital.

But paths that go away from have to go somewhere. So where do they go? Here are four suggestions. Firstly, a path away from has a direction. The impulse is 'No! Enough! We do not accept this system that is attacking us personally and destroying the preconditions of human existence. Therefore, we do not accept the forms through which this system exists, such as the state and money.' This initial 'No!' is very important, if we are to avoid the danger that confronts any struggle: being sucked back into the system.

Secondly, our paths may have no definite goal, but they have a method. 'Asking we walk', say the Zapatistas. We shape our path through a process of asking, a constant process of discussion to decide which way we go. This already involves the rejection of hierarchy and alien determination, the rejection therefore of the state as a form of organisation. By the way we walk we are already creating the world we want to go to, a world of self-determination.

Thirdly, we may not have a pre-defined goal, but we do follow a utopian star. Our 'No!' to the violence of capitalism draws strength from the dreams of the ages, from our practices, imaginings, projections and longings for a different society in which we determine our own activity, a world based on the mutual recognition of ourselves as humans striving for our own humanity. This is no blueprint, but a movement towards the overcoming of that which negates us.

Fourthly, this utopian star is not outside us, but simply the recognition of the rebellion within us and an understanding of that rebellion as a historical and social reality. To explore a politics at a distance from the state is to open our eyes to our own traditions. The movement of resistance-and-rebellion against capitalism has always had its own political forms, its own forms of organisation far removed from the state: the tradition of councils, communes and assemblies that arises again and again as each new movement tries to find ways of articulating its anger and its dreams.

It is a great pleasure, then, to take part in this exploration and rediscovery of a politics of resistance-and-rebellion at a distance from the state, both during the initial 'Politics at a Distance from the State' conference in which I was honoured to be a participant, along with various academics, activists and movements, and in this special issue, which was inspired by that conference.

The repudiation of the state as a form of political organisation, the recognition that the state is part of the deadly dynamic of capital, moves with different rhythms in different parts of the world. The particular history of South Africa, the uniquely intense way in which the hope for radical change was concentrated on the state, gives a particular significance to this special issue and to its opening on to a different politics. It is an honour, and an excitement, to take part.

John Holloway

Politics at a distance from the state: radical, South African and Zimbabwean praxis today

Kirk Helliker and Lucien van der Walt

ABSTRACT
For decades, most anti-capitalist and anti-imperialist movements identified radical social transformation with the capture of state power. The collapse of supposedly enabling states led recently to a crisis of left and working class politics. But this has also opened space for the rediscovery of society-centred, anti-capitalist modes of bottom-up change, labelled as 'at a distance' politics. These modes have registered important successes in practice, such as the Zapatistas in Mexico, and have involved strands of anarchism and syndicalism, and autonomist Marxism. This article, an introduction to a collection of papers emerging from a 2012 conference of academics and activists in South Africa, aims to help articulate an understanding of social transformation from below that has been analytically and politically side-lined not only in South Africa (and Zimbabwe), but globally. In doing so, it provides a preliminary attempt to map and create a dialogue between three major positions within the broad category of 'at a distance' politics.

Challenging state-centric change

For much of the 'short twentieth century', the dominant sectors of anti-systemic movements focused on winning state power, seeing an enabling state as the essential means for social transformation (Taylor 1991, 214–215). This drive for state power was 'phenomenally successful', in that, post-1945, social-democrats, Marxists and anti-imperialist nationalists headed most states, their rule corresponding, to a large extent, with what came to be called the 'First', 'Second' and 'Third' worlds, respectively (216).

Thus, over time, radical social transformation had come to be identified with wielding a supposedly 'enabling state': this outlook was shared by ever-increasing sectors of the anti-capitalist left, of workers' movements, and of national liberation forces. Seen in this context, the historical trajectory of South Africa's leading nationalist formation, the African National Congress (ANC, formed 1912), from a popular movement that united a diverse range of forces, to a governing party deeply intertwined with the capitalist state apparatus and various forms of elite accumulation, is not unusual. Even relatively sympathetic commentary on ANC history notes that 'the utopian element' of its 'non-racial nationalism' always 'envisaged a state-centric developmental project: either social democratic, revolutionary nationalist or Soviet socialist'. The 'state loomed large' despite the 'various ideological inflections' of the ANC's project (Satgar 2012, 37). The ANC thus needs to be located in a larger rise of statist and hierarchical models of national liberation.

Possibilities for more democratic, bottom-up and radical models of transformation in South Africa (and elsewhere) were effaced by state-centric struggles and the project of capturing state power. But, within anti-apartheid organisations of the 1970s and 1980s, there was also an implicitly anti-statist tendency which sought to build a different form of politics, often consciously opposed to the top-down logic of state hierarchies and governance. For instance, the declared aim of the United Democratic Front (UDF, formed 1983) of constructing 'people's power' and the stress by many black-centred trade unions, notably those in the 'workerist' tradition of the Federation of South African Trade Unions (FOSATU, formed 1979) on 'workers' control', were indicative of a vision of an incipient politics of transformation that – despite ambiguities, contradictions and limitations – simply did not place the state centre-stage in liberation.

Unbanned in 1990, the ANC de-mobilised anti-apartheid struggles and structures in the early 1990s. The process was exemplified by the closing of the UDF in 1991 and the transformation of many UDF structures into ANC branches or affiliates, and the formation around the same time of the ANC-headed 'Tripartite Alliance' with the Congress of South African Trade Unions (COSATU, which replaced FOSATU in 1985), and the South African Communist Party (SACP, formed 1921 as the Communist Party of South Africa, CPSA). This was followed, in short order, by a technocratic, neo-liberal programme pursued vigorously by the ANC party-state formally inaugurated with the 1994 non-racial elections in South Africa, which entrenched core inequalities and devastated industry (e.g. Siedman-Makgetla 2004). In this process, it has sought to use formations like COSATU and the SACP to dampen popular opposition. The UDF's decline and the ANC's rise marked a shift in national liberation from 'people's politics' to 'state politics' (Neocosmos 1996). To reiterate, the ANC's evolution since taking state power in 1994 is not aberration, capitulation or abdication: it is the logical outcome of its nationalist project, and of a view of politics that declared (with Kwame Nkrumah) 'Seek ye first the political kingdom and all things shall be added unto you' (quoted in Biney 2011, 2). The ANC's evolution was quite typical of the fate of nationalist movements aiming at state power.

By the 1990s, however, state-centric models, whether social democratic, Soviet-Marxist, or anti-imperialist nationalist, were widely regarded as failing. They were marked by economic failures, goal-displacement, an inability to sustain themselves in the face of an increasingly internationalised capital structure, a deep crisis of accumulation and a shifting geopolitical order. Always marked by endemic inequality, they all faced popular unrest and dissatisfaction with their top-down, bureaucratic and statist approaches (van der Walt 2015), with some of the most trenchant critiques coming, not from the right, but labour and the left (e.g. Ascherson 1981; Larmer 2007; Wilks 1996, 97–98), and it proved impossible to co-opt or pacify the popular classes (e.g. Larmer 2007).

Multiple crises, including legitimacy crises, ended the era of the 'three worlds', and the absence of a clear labour and left alternative at the time opened the door to the victory of global neo-liberalism, marking the end of the era of state-led models of capitalism. The end of the enabling state disabled anti-systemic movements enamoured of states. Neo-liberalism centres on free markets: the state is not gone but is manifestly an agency for massive interventions to subsidise capital, expand commodification and disci-pline the popular classes.

Rather than an 'end of history' marked by the 'unabashed victory of economic and political liberalism' (Fukuyama 1989, 3, 4, 12), the end of the 'three worlds' opened a present marked everywhere by malaise, crisis and turmoil and deepening inequality, following the fault-lines of class, nation, gender, ethnicity, race and economic and political instability. In its 'golden age' (roughly from 1950–1973) capitalism 'appeared to achieve the impossible', but since then, it has staggered from crisis to crisis (Hobsbawm 1992, 59). Further, while parliamentary democracy now exists worldwide on a scale unmatched in previous eras, public scepticism of its value is equally widespread and unprecedented.

The question though is not *whether* people will resist, but *how* the forces of popular dissatisfaction will develop now and in the future. Of significance is that state-centric left politics continues to retain substantial support, despite its manifest impotence and declining credibility. Globally, there has been some revival in the fortunes of left-of-centre parties, like the Communist Party of India (Marxist) (CPI-M), the Social Democratic Party (SPD) in Germany and the Workers' Party (PT) in Brazil, as well as the formation of various new left parties during the 2000s. But these parties have failed to revive the old statist projects, and have, despite some reforms, embraced in large part the status quo of neo-liberalism. Dramatic examples are provided by the experiences of Zambia in the 1990s, Brazil in the 2000s and Greece in the 2010s.

The old options simply do not and cannot work anymore, given the deep structural changes in economy and politics that have taken place (Satgar 2012; Wilks 1996). Firstly, while social democratic *proposals* remain surprisingly widespread, social democratic *systems* like the Keynesian welfare state have failed. Rather than seeking to govern capitalism, social democracy today involves effectively, minimalist welfare and tax reforms. Secondly, rather than creating egalitarian 'new nations' against imperialism, 'third world' nationalism increasingly reveals political and cultural intolerance, and elite enrichment. This includes the deliberate promotion of ethnic, racial, regional and religious divisions (Ake 1983), and the rise of right-wing parties like the Bharatiya Janata Party (BJP) in India. And, thirdly, most of the mainstream of Marxism – Communism – has moved from revolution to a modest social democratic outlook such as Eurocommunism, CPI-M-led Kerala in India, COSATU and the SACP in the Alliance (e.g. COSATU/SACP 1999; SACP 1995) or an outright embrace of neo-liberalism (e.g. China and Vietnam). Today, 'there are only a few places left where seriously communist parties still exist' (Anderson 2014, xiii).

This is part of a general labour and left retreat from projects of deep change to a narrow focus on immediate grievances and vague demands for 'democracy', disarticulated from clear alternatives and strategies for transition. The global working class is larger than ever, labour movements remain resilient, but, while even capitalists despair in capitalism (e.g. Foroohar 2016), radical left politics is impoverished. If the radical left remains wedded to the failed statism of the three worlds, it will disintegrate, and the forces of the right will fill the gap it leaves. The discrediting of secular, progressive alternatives leads directly to the rise of religious fundamentalist and ultra-nationalist currents (Taylor 1991, 216–217; also Hobsbawm 1992, 64). This is borne out, in recent years, by developments in Egypt, India and the United States, where right-wing figures ride the tides of popular misery and disillusion.

Towards a 'politics at a distance from the state'

But this second round of failures – the failure of state-centred revolts against neo-liberalism, which emerged against the backdrop of the failure of the 'three worlds' – has not, in itself, foreclosed progressive, secular options. This is because left theory and practice has always included both state-centred and society-centred models of change. State-centred positions, which stress capturing the state, have been widely challenged by the failure of the old statist models, the failure of attempts at reviving them and the failures of left and workers parties, old and new. Society-centred positions involve a politics of anti-capitalist transformation that question fundamentally state-centred change. This may seem counter-intuitive, given that anti-statism has been widely appropriated by the neo-liberal right, but, as we will show, there is a rich and varied left anti-capitalist anti-statism that bears closer examination. This should not be confused with liberal-pluralist conceptions of 'civil society' as a counter-balance to the state, precisely because its radical outlook amplifies the deep social antagonisms obscured by the notion of civil society, and aims at far more than moderating state excesses.

Society-centred models have revived and registered some important successes. Alain Badiou provides a useful means of framing society-centred politics in its many possible, varied and heterogeneous forms (Badiou, Del Lucchese, and Del Smith 2008, 647, 649–650). Stressing the need to 'keep alive' the 'idea that there is a real alternative to the dominant politics' of capitalism and parliamentarism, he also argues for the need to reject the Marxist–Leninist vanguard model, and its party-state, which had secured, not emancipation, but 'a new form of power that was nothing less than the power of the party itself'. While the 'organisation of the masses is still the fundamental issue', a real 'politics of emancipation' has to take place at a 'distance from the state', because the capture of state power is not likely or desirable, and also because the standard party form, which is 'entirely articulated with the state', is not and never will be desirable: a historical failure, it does not deserve repetition.

When Badiou (2006, 270) calls for a politics 'outside the spectre of the party-state', he is also emphasising a practice of '*thinking* politics outside of its subjection to the state', which invariably involves 'a rupture with the representative form of politics' (289, 292, our emphasis). This means moving from the politics of representation by others, to a politics of presentation, of experiences, concerns and aspirations outside of rigid hierarchical arrangements, in formations like assemblies. Other writers suggest this entails an autonomous politics with 'self-established rules, self-determination, self-organisation and self-regulating practices particularly vis-à-vis the state' (Böhm, Dinerstein, and Spicer 2010, 6).

'Politics at a distance from the state' does not signify, in other words, a unified perspective, but rather encompasses a range of positions, not all of which are – as we will show below – altogether anti-statist either. It is a 'descriptive, negative, characterisation' signifying a break with the 'subordination' of politics to the 'question of power and the state and parties' (Badiou, Del Lucchese, and Del Smith 2008, 649–650).

In recent years, a variety of alternative approaches, broadly 'politics at a distance from the state', have been devised, revised, revived or reinvigorated. Notable moments have included the public emergence of the neo-Zapatista movement in Chiapas, Mexico in 1994, which explicitly rejected vanguardist conceptions of armed struggle, and initiated global 'encounters' against neo-liberalism; innovative developments in political philosophy that, starting from a broadly Marxist and anti-capitalist foundation, have sought to reframe the notion of revolution, including works by Badiou, John Holloway and Jacques Rancière; and a growing literature on the history and politics of non-Marxist left radicalisms (e.g. Linebaugh and Rediker 2000).

The debates these works have helped reignite also take place in the context of a revival of anarchism and syndicalism, an anti-statist left current dating back to the 1860s. A small 'avalanche' of publications on the topic (Anderson 2014) is matched by, for example, its notable role in the 'anti-globalisation' movement, including the 'black blocs' (Dupuis-Déri 2015), Occupy Wall Street (Bray 2013) and unions, including important anarcho-syndicalist currents in Spain and the Italian 'committees of the base' (Ness 2014). The most radical attempt to change society in the wake of the Arab Spring has been in parts of Turkey and Syria, notably the Rojava region, where the Kurdistan Workers Party (PKK, formed 1974) now defines its aim as a 'democratic system of a people without a State', a stateless 'democratic confederalism', with a strong emphasis on women's emancipation (Hattingh and van der Walt 2015, 72).

The same engagement with alternative political forms taking place globally is also taking place in South Africa, where ongoing economic crisis, racial inequality, political corruption and disenchantment with the ANC and other parties has, for many, generated deep disillusion. It is possible to identify currents that question the South African state's claims to represent the nation or the working class, by trying to build participatory democratic movements 'at a distance from the state'. Current schisms in the ruling ANC, SACP and COSATU alliance are symptomatic of an opening period of turbulence in which radical alternatives could gain real traction. For example, mass strikes took place in commercial farming, mining and postal services during 2012–2014, while student protests in higher education from 2014 onwards have raised demands around the abolition of tuition fees and support staff outsourcing, and a radical transformation of university curricula, symbols and roles. Scattered but endless township-based protests around a range of issues, including demands for greater popular control of 'development', are a daily occurrence.

In this context, for example, the Durban-centred shack-dwellers' movement *Abahlali baseMjondolo* (formed 2005) has been identified as one site of a democratic urban movement outside mainstream politics and fighting against evictions, political repression and patronage politics. At the end of 2013, COSATU's then-largest affiliate, the National Union of Metalworkers of South Africa (NUMSA), decided, at a special congress, to reject the ANC, and not to campaign for any political party. NUMSA has subsequently initiated a 'united front' of popular movements against neo-liberalism and is involved in efforts to form a new labour federation, NUMSA being expelled from COSATU in November 2014. Small radical groups, like local anarchists / syndicalists, also advocate the formation of a 'counter-power' to the state and capital (Maisiri 2014).

Such developments should not be exaggerated. Given the centrality in South Africa of nationalist and Marxist–Leninist traditions, a major outcome of growing unrest have been calls for a new, better nationalist or socialist party. For example, an ANC breakaway, the Economic Freedom Fighters, embraces militaristic themes and takes as an inspiration the 1921–1928 New Economic Policy in the Union of Soviet Socialist Republics (USSR) (Shivambu and Smith 2014). Sectors of the country's Trotskyist left, active in formations like the Workers and Socialist Party, formed in 2012, and the emergent United Front, continue to see the major task as the formation of a new socialist workers' party and the capture of state power (Maisiri 2014; WASP 2015). Substantial sectors of NUMSA, and the NUMSA-initiated United Front, formed in 2014, clearly see running a political party in state elections as the priority (Mngxitama-Diko 2016). There have been a range of debates around *Abahlali baseMjondolo*, including its controversial decision to support a centre-right political party, the Democratic Alliance, in the 2014 local government elections.

The contribution of this volume

This volume, with reference to South Africa, but also in relation to developments in Zimbabwe, and in engagement with larger theoretical questions, brings together a range of articles that highlight moments and currents in anti-apartheid and earlier movements, as well as more contemporary attempts at building alternative forms of politics that are explicitly or incipiently 'at a distance from the state'. Almost all the contributors are South Africans.

The immediate origin of this volume was a conference of radical academics and activists held on the 29–30 September 2012 at Rhodes University, Grahamstown, in the impoverished Eastern Cape Province in South Africa. Entitled 'Politics at a Distance from the State', this event was arguably the first of its kind in post-apartheid South Africa. It brought together a diverse range of people and formations interested in exploring, debating and understanding 'politics at a distance from the state', in terms of both theory and practice.

Besides inputs by academics, it involved inputs from movement activists from the following: *Abahlali baseMjondolo*; the Church Land Programme (formed 1996) in Pietermaritzburg; the Mandela Park Backyarders from Cape Town; various farmworkers committees, linked to the Eastern Cape Agricultural Research Project (formed 1993); the Landless People's Movement (LPM, formed 2001), from Soweto; the Unemployed People's Movement (UPM) (formed 2009) from Grahamstown; the anarchist-influenced hip-hop collective Soundz of the South (founded ca. 2010), from Cape Town; and the Zabalaza Anarchist Communist Front (ZACF, formed 2003), from Johannesburg, Khutsong and Sebokeng in Gauteng. Also present were veterans of the anti-apartheid UDF, which ran from 1983–1990. Finally, the Mexican-based John Holloway, a leading global theorist identified with a strand of autonomist Marxism, who questions the feasibility of meaningful transformation through the state, was also an active participant in the conference.

Two publications have been generated. The first, online, is a substantial dossier of interviews, texts and talks from a number of movements and activists from the gathering, along with a substantive introduction and notes. Material is included from *Abahlali baseMjondolo*, the Soweto LPM, the UDF, the UPM, Soundz of the South and the ZACF. Contributors include Murphy Morobe (UDF), Thapelo Mohapi, T.J. Ngongoma and Zandile Nsibande (*Abahlali baseMjondolo*), Lekhetho Mtetwa (LPM, ZACF), Ngcwalisa Maqekeza and the late Mkhululi 'Khutsa' Sijora (Soundz of the South) and Warren McGregor (ZACF). *From Below: A Dossier on South African Politics at a Distance from the State* can be freely accessed online, at https://politicsatadistance.wordpress.com/. It was compiled and edited by Lucien van der Walt, a co-organiser of the conference, who works on the history of labour and the left.

The second outcome is this academic volume, which has several main aims. Firstly, it aims to help recover an understanding of social transformation *from below* that has been analytically and politically sidelined not only in South Africa, but globally. It aims, secondly, to locate past and present South African debates and initiatives that engage, implicitly or explicitly, with a 'politics at a distance from the state', within broader discussions and developments about the politics of transformation which fundamentally question state-centred change yet reject market-based solutions. And thirdly, it provides a preliminary attempt to map, create a dialogue between, and critically assess, some of the major positions within the broad category of 'politics at a distance from the state'.

The contributors to this volume have divergent views on 'politics at a distance from the state'. Michael Neocosmos, now at the Unit for the Humanities at Rhodes University (UHURU), argues that 'politics 'at a distance from the state' should not be read 'as anti-state politics', but instead as conceptualising politics 'outside state parameters of thought' and 'identities'. Rather than 'oppose the state a-priori', it can involve different 'orientations to specific state forms and politics'. His paper, drawing heavily on Badiou and Rancière, and reflecting critically on African national liberation movements, argues that political emancipation must be 'conceived and achieved through establishing a "distance" from the state and its practices', 'subjective distance', expressed through collective subjectivities that develop a lived politics, 'movement communism', beyond the boundaries of the state, its norms and its impositions. This is inexplicable to formations steeped in statist nationalist and Marxist traditions, like the ANC and SACP of the 1990s, which found the emergent politics of 'people's power' and 'workers control' 'unrecognisable'. In office, for example, the ANC has increasingly viewed popular agency as illegitimate, and the masses as, variously, victims in need of aid, as spectres to be feared, or as dupes of "outside" forces.

On the other hand, and in response, Holloway defends an explicitly 'anti-state' outlook: there are no 'problems with "anti-state"' formulations, because the state is 'a way of doing things' for capital that must be opposed by 'a way of organizing that is asymmetrical to the state's organization'. In his preface for this volume, Holloway stresses a version of 'politics at a distance from the state' that locates it firmly in a project of anti-capitalist *and* anti-statist revolution that aims at changing the world without taking (state) power. (We revisit this project more fully below).

Van der Walt's paper follows a parallel approach to Holloway's, with a historical and theoretical account of anarchist and syndicalist politics. He outlines the tradition's perspective of accumulating class-based counter-power and counter-hegemony outside and against the state and capital, as the means to unite the popular classes, resist oppression and exploitation, and build forms and ideas that prefigure a radically democratic, libertarian communist society, providing the means for a revolutionary rupture. His article seeks to recover the variant of 'politics at a distance from the state' expressed by historical anarchism/syndicalism, including its theoretical and programmatic scope, and its enormously significant historical role, including in mass movements.

This tradition and history is elided by the tendency to collapse socialism into Leninism or social democracy, as well as by, for example, Badiou's stereotypically Marxist charge that anarchism lacks any clear mechanism for change, supposedly rendering it 'never ... anything else' than a 'vain critique' (2006, 126, 321). Van der Walt argues that anarchism/syndicalism has never ignored politics, or the state, the winning of reforms or the differences between types of state: rather, he suggests, it has stressed the importance of popular autonomy, direct action and empowerment as the heart of move-ment building, winning gains and pushing back and defeating capitalism and the state.

Important historical reflections are provided by Nicole Ulrich, a radical historian of popular struggles, and Sian Byrne, a researcher with a union background, who recover the story of the 'workers' control' tradition in the independent non-racial trade unions that emerged from the 1970s in apartheid South Africa. 'Workers' control', understood as a project of autonomy from the apartheid state as well as from nationalist and Marxist–Leninist parties, as direct democratic control over mass industrial unions, and as the foundation of a profoundly transformed South Africa, was central to the new unionism that laid the basis for the 'workerist' FOSATU, in 1979, the largest union centre by the mid-1980s. At the same time, tensions and ambiguities within this project also enabled its decline, the authors stressing the importance of a clear strategy if a radical project of 'workers' control' and autonomy is to be sustained, consolidated and generalised across society.

Camalita Naicker and Sarah Bruchhausen, both linked to UHURU and involved with student movements, bridge past and present to discuss the radical 'subaltern sphere of politics' seen in the 1950s in Mpondoland, a major reservoir of mine labour in the Eastern Cape, and again on the Platinum Belt mines in the 2010s. Struggles in Mpondoland in the 1950s, culminating in armed revolt from 1960–1962, and the mass miners' strikes of 2012 and 2014, were linked not just by actual migrant workers resident in both sites, but by the historical memory and political culture that linked the mine battles to Mpondo-land's traditions of bottom-up democratic revolt.

Moving slightly northwards, the article by Tarryn Alexander, who has worked on 'post-anarchism', and Kirk Helliker, whose work draws on autonomist Marxism, examines the dynamics of the land occupations and subsequent Fast Track Land Reform (FTLR) in Zim-babwe from 2000. In doing so, and in engaging forcefully with the work of Holloway, they seek to contribute to the further development of an 'autonomist feminist' perspective which is able to offer a critical appraisal of what might first appear as progressive anti-statist processes of 'commoning', but which, in fact, reproduce patriarchal practices (as hierarchical arrangements) in new forms. In this regard, though the Zimbabwean state subdued, subordinated and co-opted the land occupations through FTLR, there were marked patriarchal tendencies within the occupations themselves.

Mapping: modes of 'at a distance' politics

An important concern of this introductory article is to provide a framework for categorising and understanding these multiple tendencies of 'at a distance politics' and to suggest both their strengths and limitations. It is possible to distinguish analytically, we would suggest, at least three modes of 'at a distance' politics: 'outside-but-with' the state; 'outside-and-despite' the state and 'outside-and-against' the state. We stress that these modes do not always take the form of carefully articulated ideologies, but express a praxis, more or less identifiable, and associated with particular lines of argument and influ-ential in particular moments and movements. What they have in common is (to recall Badiou), a break with the 'subordination' of politics to the 'question of power and the state', and a stress on 'political organisation (whatever form it may take) in political processes that are independent' of 'the power of the state' (Badiou, Del Lucchese, and Del Smith 2008, 649–650). Here it is important to reiterate, with Neocosmos in his contribution, that politics 'at a distance from the state' does not necessarily mean 'anti-state' politics.

'Outside-but-with' the state

Although Leninist and social democratic solutions have provided unsatisfactory models, these does not exhaust the possibilities of using the state. An alternative approach has gained popularity in recent years (Satgar and Williams 2013; Satgar and Zita 2009). This is the notion that radical change should not centre on the state: rather, popular initiatives, movements and autonomy should have maximum scope, but should be *combined* with transforming and democratising the state. In place of a statism that supplants popular self-activity, and a politics that rejects the state in all instances, this mode involves a synergy (or at least a creative tension). It seeks to move beyond the traditional social democratic stress on parliament and corporatism, by complementing these with popular mobilisation (Wainwright 2004). Although often presented as new, these ideas had earlier incarnations in, for example, Guild Socialism (Masquelier and Dawson 2016).

This is certainly 'politics at a distance from the state', since it neither reduces politics to the state, nor seeks to subsume popular struggles into the state apparatus, yet it is also *not* anti-statist: it is a 'politics at a distance' that is 'outside-but-with' the state. There have been a wide range of efforts to implement it, and a range of possible modalities for its operation. For Morobe (1987), for instance, the UDF built 'active, mass-based democratic organisations and democratic practices within these organisations' as both a means of resisting apartheid and as the emergent core of 'a future, democratic South Africa' wherein 'all South Africans, and in particular the working class, [have] control over all areas of daily existence', 'on a daily basis'. Mass-based organs of 'people's power' would complement representative democracy, and legal and economic reforms in a new South Africa. He cited, as a reference point, the 'popular' structures linked to Marxist-leaning governments like that of the Sandinista National Liberation Front in Nicaragua (established 1979).

The CPI-M in Kerala, India, has taken a somewhat different approach. It used its electoral victories to institute land and other reforms, and also fostered – through the state – participatory democratic structures and collaborations with social movements (Williams 2008). On paper, at least, the SACP from the late 1990s (SACP 1995; Williams 2008), and COSATU, until the present, advocate something similar (COSATU/ SACP 1999). While the South African Students' Congress (SASCO) is allied to the ruling ANC, it has also continually exhibited a substantial degree of autonomy, including a key role in the 2015 university protests (Corke and Nicolaides 2015).

Another key example is the Landless Workers Movement (MST) of Brazil. It remains autonomous of the PT, has shown itself willing to confront the PT since that party came into office in 2002, and faces ongoing repression by sections of the state (e.g. MST-Goiás 2016). Yet the MST also relies on state aid, including contracts to supply state facilities with food from MST settlements, and access to state credit (Branford 2015; Gilbert 2015). The MST has consistently provided the PT with electoral support and has recently thrown its weight behind PT leaders facing attacks by the judiciary (MST 2016).

While models like Holloway's (discussed below) tend to view efforts to capture the state as at odds with a transition to a genuine communism, on the grounds that the state is subordinate to the logic of capital, the politics of 'outside-but-with' the state, posits that the state is a contested terrain, susceptible to popular demands and anti-capitalist policies. The problem is not that the state is intrinsically capitalist and anti-popular, but that it has been *contingently* captured by capitalist and anti-popular forces. Pressure on the state from without, contestation of the state from within, including through the use of electoral mechanisms, and alliances between movements and states are seen, implicitly or explicitly, as means of pushing back capitalism – with capitalism seem as external to, and only sometimes joined to, the state.

The core obstacles to social change, from this perspective, are posed in terms of illegitimate state capture (by domestic or international capital, political machines, predatory elites, etc.), the subversion of democracy (by corporate funding, financial markets, politicians from elite groups, etc.) or the loss of state sovereignty to capitalist globalisation: 'representative democracy', argues MST leader João Pedro Stédile, 'has been kidnapped by capital' (in Gilbert 2015, 78–79). The state is not the problem, in itself.

The radical project is then presented as a reform of existing states and multi-lateral institutions, involving alliances between movements and parties, and between progressive states, and steps to roll back corporate power (Brecher, Costello, and Smith 2000).

Although this approach has obvious similarities to standard liberal-pluralist theories of the state, it converges with a strand of radical (including Marxist) thinking that insists that transformation in, and through, the state cannot be ruled out a priori: its possibility is contingent upon the prevailing balance of social forces. The 'pull of the state away from the people is not inscribed in the state's character' but subject to 'historical transformation' (Wainwright 2004). Such ideas, as Byrne and Ulrich note in their article, had an influence on a strand of South African 'workerism'. In Eurocommunist Nicos Poulantzas' famous formulation, the state in capitalist society supposedly reflected contradictory social relations and was thus itself an 'arena' of class struggle (1979).

The record of such approaches is, however, far from positive. The MST's alignment to the PT in Brazil has, for example, posed serious challenges (Branford 2015). Despite rising electoral fortunes, the PT in government has conciliated with capital, and compromised its principles and programmes; land and agrarian reform has stalled; and MST support for the PT rests on 'fear of the alternatives' and appreciation for state funds (Gilbert 2015, 67, 76–77). MST land and agrarian reforms are carried out *despite* the state, while reliance on state funds potentially makes the MST vulnerable to patronage relations.

In South Africa, COSATU's strategy has been aimed at expanding popular control of the economy, through corporatism, co-determination, union investments and cooperatives, and by campaigning for progressive state policies: influencing the ANC-led alliance is seen as integral to this strategy (COSATU/SACP 1999; Satgar 2012). However, COSATU's corporatism has, by most accounts, failed to achieve much beyond bureaucratisation (Dibben, Klerck, and Wood 2014). The alliance with the ANC has tied COSATU politics to ANC neo-liberalism and political corruption, crippling the vision and power of the federation (Pillay 2012) with the state's factionalism and intolerance being echoed in union leadership battles.

'Outside-and-despite' the state

Holloway's work, as his preface to this volume shows, stresses the politics of refusal: ordinary people create and recreate capitalist social relations on a daily basis, through alienated wage labour, and through institutions like political parties and the state (Holloway 2014). While Holloway identifies with the Marxist tradition, he rejects its historic mainstream, which centred on the capture of state power by a vanguard party. He articulates, we suggest, a mode of 'at a distance politics' that can be called 'politics outside-and-despite the state', for reasons that will be outlined below (we focus here on Holloway's account, but stress that his is not the only voice that articulates this mode).

Emancipation requires, for Holloway, a rejection of the logic of capital and its categories: it begins, he argues, with 'a scream of sadness, a scream of horror, a scream of anger, a scream of refusal: NO' (2005, 1). The logic of capital is presented, in his work, as the core logic to overcome if humanity is to be freed, and as the basic logic driving a range of forms of oppression in a 'world of injustice, of war, of violence, of discrimination, of Gaza and Guantanamo', environmental destruction relentless commodification and alienation (Holloway 2012).

It is in the very process of 'refusal' and self-activity that 'a new wave of theory' and 'experimental communism' emerge (Bonefeld and Holloway 2014, 214–215). The process itself involves self-determination and rejection of alien determination. A 'We' free of narrow identities can develop new social relations with new logics, a new world – even if these are not necessarily intentionally counter-hegemonic, they are everyday practices contrary to imposed logics, hierarchies and subjectivities (2005, 62, 156). None can individually exit capitalism, but each can widen the cracks in it (Holloway 2014). Like Badiou, Holloway also rejects 'identitarian' modes of struggle that centre on a sole authentic subject of history.

While it 'becomes clearer every day that capitalism is a catastrophe for humanity', 'we do not know how to get rid of it' (Holloway 2005, ix). A project of consciously and programmatically building towards single decisive revolutionary rupture is viewed as dogmatic: since 'no one has the solution' the project must be experimental and based on dialogue (Holloway 2014), embracing the neo-Zapatismo injunction 'Asking, we walk'. Social transformation is envisaged as an open-ended indeterminate process. Building for a decisive revolutionary rupture is viewed with suspicion, as translating all-too-readily into a scheme for state power. The state is seen as following the dictates of capital, and therefore unable to negate it, thus the history of failed anti-capitalist revolutions. Since the state also involves the alienation of people from self-determination, the notion of an enabling, emancipating state is an illusion (Holloway 2014). The disastrous and futile quest for state power explains why socialist movements, both social democratic and revolutionary Marxist, have failed.

A key point here is Holloway's stress on prefiguration: forms of struggle shape the outcomes of struggle, and forms that emulate the state, like the classic Marxist–Leninist party, are bound to recreate the state. This helps explain, as we noted above, the processes whereby bureaucratic social democracy helped create the bureaucratic Keynesian welfare state, top-down Leninist parties helped generate top-down party-states, and nationalist parties, pursuing the 'political kingdom', enmeshed themselves in repressive postcolonial states. And, given that these states and parties were usually deeply wedded to claims to represent the 'true' interests of a class or nation, itself posited as sole authentic subject historical subject, and suppress dissent as ipso facto counter-revolutionary, scepticism about dogmatism and vanguardism makes sense.

The concomitant antipathy to conventional party politics and stress on horizontal relations and pluralism, with which this approach is associated, are profoundly important. As Neocosmos notes in his contribution, a narrow focus on capturing of power leads readily to blindness towards the value of revolutionary processes themselves. The importance of a 'particular event lies elsewhere than in the question of whether it was a "failed revolution" or not', inasmuch as practices lived and declared in struggle are themselves immanent features of a new order, and leap beyond pre-existing boundaries. The ANC's ultimate failure to create conditions for national unity or social inclusion show, he argues, the failings of a 'politics of representation'. This underlines the importance of expressions of popular self-activity like *Abahlali baseMjondolo*, which are not bounded 'within state subjectivity'.

However, the politics of 'outside-and-despite' the state is less satisfactory when it comes to issues of strategy and aims. Holloway's criticisms of past left models, largely directed at Leninist regimes, scepticism towards programmes and stated goals, and stress on process rather than outcomes leave him silent on core challenges facing any radical transition to a post-capitalist and free society. One of these issues is posed, implicitly, in the article by Byrne and Ulrich. This is the central role of ideology in transition, ideology being used here in Saksena's (2009) sense, as a set of ideas about how societies do, and should, function and change. Their account centres on the fate of the 'workers' control' tradition that characterised a key section of the independent unions in South Africa, notably the Trade Union Advisory Coordinating Committee (TUACC, formed 1973), and its successor, FOSATU. TUACC stressed building democratic structures that kept worker leaders accountable to worker members. Shop stewards, accountable to, and mandated by workers' assemblies, were the core building block of industrial unions founded upon a system of delegates and strict limitations on the powers of paid officials, with the unions linked, again through delegates, into a 'tight' federation.

In FOSATU, 'workers' control' was increasingly expanded into a vision of a society controlled by the working class, united across racial lines. This was part of the 'workerist' position that dominated FOSATU: opposed to apartheid and capitalism, it sought to keep the unions independent of the ANC and SACP, and parties, elite classes and states. 'Workerists' wanted to build the workers' movement to prefigure a new South Africa of 'workers' control', similar to the UDF's 'people's power' project – both conceptions that went well beyond traditional ANC and SACP conceptions.

However, Byrne and Ulrich note that while 'workerists' were very successful in building democratic and resilient union structures, and articulating an anti-capitalist and anti-apartheid politics, they were unable to prevent the capture of COSATU by the ANC and SACP. This was largely because of ambiguities and tensions in the 'workerist' project, including around strategy, and because they were not organised as a cohesive political force within the unions, able to challenge off rising ANC and SACP influence. The ANC and SACP captured COSATU, in large part, by winning the battle of ideas and by using the unions' own democratic apparatus.

The 'workerists' were, in essence, unable to translate their project into a sustained trajectory towards radical social change, because they were ideologically and politically limited, and lacked a strategy for transition. Back to Holloway: there is nothing to prevent sites of 'experimental communism' being captured by other forces, nothing that inherently leads alternative institutions, relations and struggles to replace capitalism with a new society, and nothing that ensures a new society will be democratic or egalitarian. If the 'asking, we walk' answer that comes back is 'Stalin' or 'Trump', then what? Ideology is an essential factor, and winning the battle of ideas requires *organising* specific political currents – winning over, democratically, pluralistic and contested popular spaces, like unions.

A second challenge to Holloway's argument relates to his invocation of an anti-identitarian mode of politics. Alexander and Helliker, examining women on FTLR sites in Zimbabwe, suggest that, in the face of the specific conditions of women's oppression, the mobilisation of gender identities can be essential to the identification of oppression, and so, to resisting and transforming. Even in a hypothetical site of 'experimental communism', and certainly in concrete struggles, there are multiple forms of inequity, not all of which are obviously reducible to the logic of capital – even if that logic plays a central role, its abolition might not suffice to remove the inequity. Thus, FOSATU, for example, specifically tackled issues of race and gender, using class identity as a unifying tool. To speak of the revolutionary subject as a 'We', as Holloway does, does not address the question of how 'We' are divided – and can be united.

Alexander and Helliker indicate such inequities create important fractures and shape the possibilities and trajectories of responses. Rural peasant women's oppressive situation has both 'specificity' and 'irreducibility', and an anti-capitalist project like Holloway's that does not specifically address, for example, the role of the sexual division of labour within capitalism, cannot adequately engage the multiple oppressions that (co-)exist with and in capitalism. They are sympathetic to Holloway's general positions, and so, seek to identify ways in which his 'overall thesis on revolutionising social relations is compatible with feminism in ways that may not be immediately apparent'. Most importantly, this requires processes of struggle that 'ultimately entail tearing asunder the link between women and social reproduction and moving towards the collectivisation of social reproduction'.

A third challenge is that Holloway's model does not clearly address the concrete obstacles facing a transition. Holloway admits that 'we have to recognize that we're not strong enough to abolish capitalism', 'referring here to building ways of living that don't depend on wage labour' (Holloway 2014). However, he also suggests that an accumulation of experiences in 'experimental communism' – identified modestly with events like meetings in squares, the re-opening of closed factories, and 'community gardens' (Bonefeld and Holloway 2014, 214–215) – can enable a transition beyond the logic of capital, by enabling a 'social network' of 'non-monetized, non-commodified social relations' that render capitalism superfluous (Holloway 2014). The general sense is that an accumulation of decentred struggles and alternative institutions in capitalism's 'cracks' will cumulatively 'crack capitalism' (Holloway 2010, 2014).

There are obvious objections that can be posed to this line of reasoning. Capitalism is created and sustained by centralised structures of exploitation and coercion run by small ruling classes, as Mikhail Bakunin and other anarchists have noted (see van der Walt's article). If so, it is unlikely ruling classes will allow a steady accumulation of struggles and relations that can pose a real threat, or tolerate any widespread exit from existing relations. Given that ruling classes *already* monopolise key resources, both economic and military, the possibility of rendering capitalism redundant through alternative sets of social relations 'strong enough' to peacefully abolish capitalism seems improbable.

But then questions of how the means of production, for example, will be placed under popular control on a meaningful scale, and how the armed might of the state will be fended off, become very serious. Holloway's model recognises that libertarian and communist relations operate by logics incompatible with the logics of capital and the state but does not address the concrete problem of how the clash between these radically different logics will be resolved – and the victory of a popular anti-capitalist, anti-statist logic will be attained, in the face of entrenched ruling class power.

It is in exactly this sense that projects like Holloway's, which stress the immediate construction of alternative social relations, and reject the state as a means of change, downplaying the obstacles posed by the state to radical change, seek to operate 'despite' the state. This is why, we suggest, they are a mode of 'politics at a distance' that operates 'outside-and-despite' the state.

'Outside-and-Against' the state

Badiou or Holloway would not deny that 'politics at a distance' must sometimes intersect with, confront, or shape, through external pressure, the state. However, both would be wary of engaging on the state's terms, emulating state hierarchies, and having 'at a distance' politics subverted by state mechanisms. The problem here is not that parliaments are 'kidnapped' by capital (Stédile) but that parliaments, like other state institutions, are centralised, disempowering and top-down elitist institutions that promote capital accumulation.

Similar points were made, van der Walt's article notes, by the historic anarchist and syndicalist tradition. This 'broad anarchist tradition' rejected state 'socialism', as well as nationalism, arguing that states were centralised institutions of class rule: they were centralised precisely in order to enable ruling class minorities to rule, by concentrating in a few hands the major means of administration and coercion; and they ensured class exploitation continued, as this served the interests of both economic and political elites; this also meant they ensured that major means of production were owned and controlled by a few, either in state or private corporations. Thus, nationalist states, social democratic governments and revolutionary Marxist regimes, alike, were class societies, even where they displaced older ruling classes or private capital.

Radical change thus required, firstly, the construction of bottom-up organs of 'counterpower' that could empower people to resist the ruling class, fight against all forms of oppression and exploitation as a means of unifying the popular classes and forging an egalitarian movement, and that would provide the nucleus of a future, self-governed socialist system. It involved, secondly, a project of promoting a revolutionary 'counterculture', or alternative world view, that would provide a critique of the existing world, embody alternative values and outline the framework of, and strategy for, a new world. This prefigurative vision, van der Walt notes, was exemplified by revolutionary and anarcho-syndicalist unions that aimed to agitate, educate and organise, building capacity to seize and self-manage the means of production.

A dialogue between traditions like autonomist Marxism, including that of Holloway, and the anarchist/syndicalist tradition has rarely taken place, despite obvious parallels (see e.g.

Pritchard and Worth 2016) and the overlapping history of anarchism and Marxism (Guérin 1989). Holloway's Marxism shares much in common with Bakunin's anarchism/syndicalism. This includes a stress on self-activity and prefiguration, pluralism and open debate in the working class movement and a rejection of the statist path (see Berthier 2015, 56–65). Both suggest a basic incompatibility between popular anti-capitalist logics and movements, and the logic and imperatives of the state and capital – which means they reject the project of 'outside-and-with' the state as impossible, since it seeks to weld together two inherently antagonistic approaches.

Like autonomist Marxism, anarchism is not homogenous. Nonetheless, there are two areas worth teasing out. The first goes to the method of analysis. Although there is a strand of anarchism and syndicalism that embraces the same narrow materialist model as mainstream Marxism, most have argued for the irreducible role of ideas, politics and the state apparatus. From this perspective, state elites are not simply subordinate to capitalist imperatives, as Holloway's analysis suggests, as they have substantial autonomous power resources. However, the interests of state elites generally converge closely with those of capitalist economic elites, the two being interdependent parts of a single ruling class. The state is therefore not an 'arena' of class struggle, as Poulantzas suggested. Besides, the centralised structure of the state, in any case, makes it impossible for the popular classes to participate or struggle within the state.

Thus, capital logic and state logic are not identical, as each has its own imperatives and resources – but they are convergent. The modern order cannot be reduced to capitalism, nor as simply arising from the logic of capital. Capitalism is a fractured and unstable system, enmeshed in a larger global system of competing states, the geopolitical order, as well as a range of other forms of inequality and domination that have their own irreducible dynamics. Nor can capitalism and capitals cannot be reduced to a monolithic entity called 'Capital'. Capitalism and the state, as class structures, help generate, entrench and benefit from, non-class forms of oppression, but those forms cannot be reduced to capitalism nor does a struggle against 'capital' intrinsically require or generate their abolition.

From an anarchist and syndicalist perspective, van der Walt argues, class-based mobilisation and identity is essential to the general emancipation of humankind, and the creation of a universal human community, since only exploited ('popular') classes – the broad working class, the peasantry – can create a system without exploitation, and have the power and interest to topple ruling classes as well as unify the oppressed. A class-based struggle against capitalism and the state is a *necessary* condition for the abolition of all inequality, but it is only an *adequate* condition when it is based on explicit and active opposition to all forms of oppression, opposition to hierarchy more generally, and a commitment to a self-governing communism – and class-based unity is only possible through precisely such opposition to specific oppressions.

Since anarchists and syndicalists argue for a class-based and anti-statist battle against all forms of oppression, the identity of any revolutionary 'We' is an (inclusive) class identity. By the same token, national liberation and the end of gender oppression are central to the anarchist project, but require, for their success, the abolition of classes and the creation of means of self-governance and autonomy free of the state. The anarchist-influenced PKK model provides glimpses of this for national liberation and women's emancipation.

This, as with Alexander and Helliker's argument, suggests that to disrupt capitalism falls short of ending class rule and social hierarchy, since capitalism is only part of a larger problem of economic and social inequality, involving domination, hierarchy and exploitation. And since capitalism can certainly be abolished by authoritarian means, a project for creating a new, bottom-up democratic and socialist order, without hierarchy, cannot be built simply on the basis of a rejection of capitalism; it requires a *moral* opposition to hierarchy in general, as well as a social theory that, while resolutely anti-capitalist, eschews economic reductionism, and specifically aims to abolish not just capitalism but the state and all hierarchies too.

This is where ideology matters greatly, and where optimism about the potential of spontaneous struggles and alternatives that can embody 'non-monetized, non-commodified social relations' (Holloway) needs to be qualified. It is perfectly possible to have such relations but for these to still include involve national, class and women's oppression e.g. feudalism. As Alexander and Helliker note, specific attention has to be paid to oppression that is 'irreducible' to, yet reinforced by, capitalism, such as gender oppression.

The other, somewhat surprising, area where anarchism/syndicalism differs with the views of figures like Holloway is regarding strategies for making and defending a revolution. The long-standing charges, by classical Marxists, that anarchists ignore the state, and fail to pay attention to the challenges of a revolutionary transition (Blackledge 2010), are false. One of the core issues in the Marx/Bakunin debate was precisely on the issue of how to make a social revolution without the state. The anarchist strategy was, essentially, to accumulate counter-power and counter-culture to a point of radical rupture, where counter-power escalated to supplant state and class power with a completely different order, libertarian communism. This option and this tradition is not registered by Holloway (e.g. 2005, 18, 156).

From this perspective, self-activity, struggle, imagination, debate and experimentation are necessary but not sufficient: the logics of popular counter-power and ruling state power are incompatible, and the victory of the former requires victory in a decisive clash. Small struggles, experiments and associations are not a revolution, but only germs of one. It is not realistic to posit alternative economies and territories on a large scale without a confrontation and a victory, precisely because most economies and territories are *already* under ruling class control.

A decisive showdown with the ruling classes does not just involve physical force, but also the moral and political victory of coordination, strategy, vision and theory. There needs to be an overarching vision of a new society, and a clear strategy to get there, which not only knits together many spaces and forms of opposition, but that also develops spaces and forms of opposition that can directly defeat and supplant the existing order. Counter-power would aim to overwhelm and supplant ruling class power, and undertake the re-organisation of the means of administration, coercion and production, establishing a new society based on common property, self-management and participatory planning. It must have revolutionary counter-culture, that is, a concrete vision, embodied in an ideology, and championed in an organised manner. What is required is a move from prefiguration to figuration, from resistance to reconstruction, a living vision similar in key respects to the current PKK project, and anticipated by FOSATU 'workerism'.

In this sense, the anarchist and syndicalist tradition represents a 'politics at a distance' that is 'outside-and-against' the state. It does not ignore the question of the state, but it also does not seek to use the state, aiming instead at supplanting the state and capital with popular bottom-up forms of governance.

19

Conclusion

In this overview, and in developing these categories, we have necessarily resorted to a degree of simplification. There is, as we have indicated, a substantial degree of variation within each category, as well as points of overlap between the categories. And, ultimately, each mode of 'at a distance politics' has its strengths and weaknesses. In terms of variation, the MST for example has been able to maintain a degree of autonomy from the PT, while COSATU has systematically ceded space to the ANC. Such variation needs further exploration, and care should therefore also be taken to avoid overgeneralisation from specific cases, either of an optimistic or a pessimistic type.

What is clear, however, is that it is possible, within radical anti-capitalist thinking and practice, to distinguish between state-centred and society-centred models of change, the one centring on the use of the state for long-term transformation, the other on society-centred transformation, consistent with anarchist, Marxist autonomist and other forms of anti-statist communism. As we have also shown, there are substantial differences within the camp of what we have called 'politics at a distance from the state', and we might add here that further complexity arises from different writers using different terms and phrases, as well as the same terms in different ways, including 'autonomy', 'the politics of the act' and 'anti-power'. The theoretical underpinnings of the criticisms of state-centred transformation also vary considerably, as becomes evident when identifying and understanding what 'at a distance' means in practical form, and when identifying how the state itself is analysed.

Secondly, we suggest that the larger tradition of 'at a distance politics' bears much closer examination as a mode of transformation that can address the challenges of the current period. In our opening points, we suggested that a widespread sense of a crisis of alternatives was closely linked to a crisis of statist projects. Non-statist anti-capitalist approaches provide actually existing alternatives, and therefore partly address the crisis of alternatives and suggest an alternative to the rising right. That means, of course, that such approaches have to gain traction with actually existing people in actually existing contexts.

And, finally, it is important to avoid imposing our hopes and fears on real-world examples or obscuring complex issues with obtuse jargon and prose. It is important to grapple instead with messier realities: experiences like the anarchists and syndicalists' Spanish Revolution from 1936, the uprising in Chiapas from 1994, and PKK activities in Rojava from 2012, require sober reflection, not a false choice between uncritical praise or purist critique (on the emergent mythology of Chiapas: Hellman 2000; on some PKK limitations: Hattingh and van der Walt 2015).

Disclosure statement

No potential conflict of interest was reported by the authors.

References

Ake, C. 1983. "Explanatory Notes on the Political Economy of Africa." *Journal of Modern African Studies* 2 (3): 1–23.

Anderson, B. 2014. "Preface." In *Anarchism and Syndicalism in the Colonial and Postcolonial World, 1870-1940: The Praxis of National Liberation, Internationalism and Social Revolution*, edited by S.J. Hirsch, and L. van der Walt, xiii–xxix. Leiden: Brill.

Ascherson, P. 1981. *The Polish August: The Self-limiting Revolution*. London: Allen Lane.

Badiou, A. 2006. *Polemics*. London: Verso.

Badiou, A., F. Del Lucchese, and J. Del Smith. 2008. "'We Need a Popular Discipline': Contemporary Politics and the Crisis of the Negative." *Critical Inquiry* 34 (4): 645–659.

Berthier, R. 2015. *Social-Democracy and Anarchism: In the International Workers' Association, 1864-1877*. London: Merlin Press.

Biney, A. 2011. *The Political and Social Thought of Kwame Nkrumah*. London: Palgrave-Macmillan.

Blackledge, P. 2010. "Marxism and Anarchism." *International Socialism* 125: 132–159.

Böhm, S., A. C. Dinerstein, and A. Spicer. 2010. "(Im)possibilities of Autonomy: Social Movements in and Beyond Capital, the State and Development." *Social Movement Studies* 9 (1): 17–32.

Bonefeld, W., and J. Holloway. 2014. "Commune, Movement, Negation: Notes from Tomorrow." *South Atlantic Quarterly* 113 (2): 213–215.

Branford, S. 2015. "Working with Governments: The MST's Experience with the Cardoso and Lula Administrations." In *Challenging Social Inequality: The Landless Rural Workers Movement and Agrarian Reform in Brazil*, edited by M. Carter, 331–350. Durham, NC: Duke University Press.

Bray, M. 2013. *Translating Anarchy: The Anarchism of Occupy Wall Street*. Winchester: Zero Books, John Hunt.

Brecher, J., T. Costello and, B. Smith. 2000. *Globalization from Below: The Power of Solidarity*. Cambridge, MA: South End Press.

Congress of South African Trade Union (COSATU)/South African Communist Party (SACP). 1999. *Building Socialism Now: Preparing for the New Millennium*. Johannesburg: COSATU/SACP.

Corke, E., and G. Nicolaides. 2015. "SASCO Calls for All SA Universities to Shut Down." *Eyewitness News*, October 20.

Dibben, P., G. Klerck, and G. Wood. 2014. "The Ending of Southern Africa's Tripartite Dream: The Cases of South Africa, Namibia and Mozambique." *Business History* 57 (3): 461–483.

Dupuis-Déri, F. 2015. *Who's Afraid of the Black Blocs? Anarchy in Action Around the World*. Toronto: Between the Lines/PM Press.

Foroohar, R. 2016. "Saving Capitalism: American Capitalism's Great Crisis." *Time*, May 12. Fukuyama, F. 1989. "The End of History?" *The National Interest* (Summer): 225–234.

Gilbert, B. 2015. "Taking Matters into their Own Hands: The MST and the Workers' Party in Brazil." *Alternautas* 2 (2): 67–80.

Guérin, D. 1989. "Marxism and Anarchism." In *For Anarchism: History, Theory and Practice*, edited by D. Goodway, 109–126. London: Routledge.

Hattingh, S., and L. van der Walt. 2015. "The Kurdish Question: Nationhood or Autonomy." *Ndivhuwo: Journal for Intellectual Engagement* 3: 70–72.

Hellman, J. A. 2000. "Real and Virtual Chiapas: Magic Realism and the Left." In *Socialist Register 2000*, edited by L. Panitch, and C. Leys, 161–186. London: Merlin Press.

Hobsbawm, E. 1992. "The Crisis of Today's Ideologies." *New Left Review* 192: 55–64.

Holloway, J. 2005. *Change the World without Taking Power: The Meaning of Revolution Today*. Revised ed. London: Pluto Press.

Holloway, J. 2010. *Crack Capitalism*. London: Pluto Press.

Holloway, J. 2012. "Crack Capitalism: 'We Want to Break'." *ROAR Magazine*, December 4.

Holloway, J. 2014. "John Holloway: Cracking Capitalism vs. the State Option." *ROAR Magazine*, September 29.

Larmer, M. 2007. *Mineworkers in Zambia: Labour and Political Change in Post-colonial Africa, 1964-1991*. London: I.B. Tauris.

Linebaugh, P., and M. Rediker. 2000. *The Many-headed Hydra: Sailors, Slaves, Commoners, and the Hidden History of the Revolutionary Atlantic*. Boston, MA: Beacon Press.

Maisiri, L. J. 2014. The New 'Workers Party' Debate on the South African Independent Left, 2012-2014. Masters thesis, Rhodes University, South Africa.

Masquelier, C., and M. Dawson. 2016. "Beyond Capitalism and Liberal Democracy: On the Relevance of GDH Cole's Sociological Critique and Alternative." *Current Sociology* 64 (1): 3–21.

Mngxitama-Diko, A. 2016. "United Front to Contest 40 Wards in Bay." *HeraldLive*, April 26.

Morobe, M. 1987. "Towards a People's Democracy: The UDF View." *Review of African Political Economy* 40: 81–88.

MST-Goiás (Landless Workers' Movement-Goiás). 2016. "MST-Goiás Statement on the Policy of Harassment against Fighters for Agrarian Reform." June 3.

MST (Landless Workers' Movement). 2016. "The True Origin of Brazil's Political Crisis." *TeleSURtv*, May 5.

Neocosmos, M. 1996. "From People's Politics to State Politics: Aspects of National Liberation in South Africa, 1984-1994." *Politeia* 15 (3): 73–119.

Ness, I., ed. 2014. *New Forms of Worker Organization: The Syndicalist and Autonomist Restoration of Class Struggle Unionism*. Oakland, CA: PM Press.

Pillay, D. 2012. "The Enduring Embrace: COSATU and the Tripartite Alliance during the Zuma Era." *Labour, Capital and Society* 44 (2): 56–79.

Poulantzas, N. 1979. "The State and the Transition to Socialism: An Interview with H. Weber." *International* 4 (1): 3–12.

Pritchard, A., and O. Worth. 2016. "Left-wing Convergence: An Introduction." *Capital and Class* 40 (1): 1–17.

SACP (South African Communist Party). 1995. "Socialism is the Future, Build it Now!" SACP Strategic Perspectives (9th Congress, April). Johannesburg.

Saksena, A. 2009. "Relevance of Ideology Today." *Economic and Political Weekly* 44 (32): 65–69.

Satgar, V. 2012. "Beyond Marikana: The Post-apartheid South African State." *Africa Spectrum* 47 (2/3): 33–62.

Satgar, V., and L. Zita, eds. 2009. *New Frontiers for Socialism in the 21st Century*. Johannesburg: Cooperative and Policy Alternative Centre (COPAC).

Satgar, V., and M. Williams, eds. 2013. *Marxism in the 21st Century: Crisis, Critique and Struggle*. Johannesburg: Wits University Press.

Shivambu, F., and J. Smith. 2014. *The Coming Revolution: Julius Malema and the Fight for Economic Freedom*. Johannesburg: Jacana.

Siebrand, Makgetla, N. 2004. "The Post-apartheid Economy." *Review of African Political Economy* 31:

Taylor, P. J. 1991. "The Crisis of the Movements: The Enabling State as Quisling." *Antipode* 23 (2): 214–228.

Wainwright, H. 2004. "Change the World by Transforming Power: Including State Power!" *Red Pepper* (November).

Van der Walt, L. 2015. "Self-managed Class-struggle Alternatives to Neo-liberalism, Nationalisation, Elections." *Global Labour Column* 213, October.

WASP (Workers and Socialist Party). 2015. "Only Socialism Means Freedom: 2014 Election Manifesto." http://workerssocialistparty.co.za/sample-page/only-socialism-means-freedom-2014-election-manifesto/.

Wilks, S. 1996. "Class Compromise and the International Economy: The Rise and Fall of Swedish Social Democracy." *Capital and Class* 20: 89–111.

Williams, M. 2008. *The Roots of Participatory Democracy: Democratic Communists in South Africa and Kerala, India*. New York: Palgrave-Macmillan.

Constructing the domain of freedom: thinking politics at a distance from the state

Michael Neocosmos

ABSTRACT

Political emancipation in the twenty-first century must be conceived and achieved through establishing a 'distance' from the state and its practices. This article argues that in order to begin to understand politics 'at a distance from the state', we need to first understand politics as a collective thought-practice. The thought of an emancipatory politics exists only when collective subjectivities exceed the limits imposed by social place, identities and interests defined and reproduced by state expressive subjectivities. In order to think a new emancipatory politics for the twenty-first century, we must therefore 'absent the state in thought', in other words, begin to understand an excessive subjectivity and how it interacts with state subjectivities which are always expressive of place. Therefore, 'distance from the state' here refers to subjective distance rather than to institutional, physical or social distance.

It is essential to tear away political practice from a fascination with power
– Alain Badiou (2011b, 20, my translation).

Politics as representation and politics as thought

In her excellent book on the May 1968 events in France, Kristin Ross argues that the importance of that particular event lies elsewhere than in the question of whether it was a 'failed revolution' or not (2002, 74). She suggests

> the narrative of a desired or failed seizure of power ... is a narrative determined by the logic of the state, the story the state tells to itself. For the state, people in the streets are people always already failing to seize state power.

Focusing on the dimension of power – and thereby restricting the idea of politics to the state – serves to efface, she argues, what was perhaps the predominant threat to power of that event: 'the subjectivation enabled by the synchronisation of two very different temporalities: the world of the worker and the world of the student'. The subjectivation produced by this transcending of the categories of the social division of labour along with the identities which accompany them 'lay in the verification of equality not as an objective of action, but as something that is part and parcel of action, something that emerges in the struggle and is lived and declared as such'.

Practices, she recounts, were developed which 'demonstrated such a synchronisation'. Because these practices demonstrated the irrelevance of the division of labour, they formed 'as direct an intervention into the logic and workings of capital as any seizure of the state – perhaps more so' (Ross 2002, 74). It should therefore be apparent that politics here are understood as thought. Despite the use of Marxist language, these practices exceeded much of what traditional Marxism could itself imagine. In fact, Ross continues, the subsequent reduction of those politics to sociological categories of 'student', 'youth' or 'generation' – in other words to a social division of labour – eventually ended up de-politicising them (2002, 207–208, emphasis in original):

> 'Students', 'youth', and 'generation' dissolve politics into sociology by positing distinct, circum-scribable social locations, a definitive residence for the movement. And yet '68 was about nothing so much as the *flight* from social location. May brought together socially hetero-geneous groups and individuals whose convergence eroded particularities including those of class and age. It realized unpredictable alliances across social sectors ... The anxiety gener-ated by the reconquest of the street by anonymous people fuels both personalization and sociological abstraction ... A movement that began by disarticulating 'sociology' and its func-tionalist version of the social was succeeded by sociology's triumphant reaffirmation. The reduction of '68 to a sociological agent, 'youth,' once again reasserts a naturalist definition of politics wholly at odds with the May movement, a determinism that produces a politics that abolishes politics.

Ross's argument illustrates, at the very least, two points concerning mass emancipatory popular movements in general. The experience of May 1968 first draws attention to the much wider phenomenon of the transcending of all existing theories and discourses of freedom by the practices of people themselves in struggle, and to the possible changes in predominant subjectivities resulting from these practices which then may take the form of 'obviousness'. It is indeed possible then for equality to become an obvious accepted reality. Remaining within the parameters of a critical analysis of these existing discourses in themselves disables an understanding of freedom, for ultimately this resides in popular practice rather than in the models proposed by intellectuals which are always developed historically after the fact. Second, Ross's discussion also shows the deep effect of de-politicisation produced by sociological and other conceptual categories which are returned to after the event in order for it to be apprehended in thought. The 'politics which abolishes politics' is in fact a politics of representation whereby people no longer speak for themselves as sociologists, historians and/or politicians speak for them. These academic categories which reduce inventive political subjectivities to the social, thereby reassert the hegemony of state modes of thought by de-politicising politics and effacing their inventiveness. Representation is simply re-imposed by the power of a *social* Science.

Similarly, the ideas of freedom and emancipation deployed by nationalism, socialism and (neo)liberalism have not been able to live up to their liberatory promise in Africa pre-cisely because they stifled and effaced an understanding of inventive popular politics and subjectivation by simply seeing it as expressive of the social (man, class, nation, etc.). While their conceptions were undoubtedly important contributions to thinking freedom at the various times they were constructed, it is apparent that they are of much less use today in the twenty-first century for they are all founded on thinking emancipation through state power; in other words on not recognising as legitimate any thought of politics which may exceed state hierarchies and practices (irrespective of which forms they may take), thereby occluding the process of subjectivation noted by Ross. Such thinking incidentally does not think politics as power relations but rather insists on ensuring 'subjectivation', the formation of a collective subject through a specific thought-practice.

It is therefore not useful today to restrict one's discussions to nationalism, socialism or neo-liberalism as such, for these amount to categories which are not central to popular thought, and consequently are frequently imposed on such thought by politicians, NGOs and academics inter alia. In all cases, these (three) categories simply reproduce a thought of politics founded on state thinking. Rather, an alternative vision of freedom must be affirmed and it is the old statist conceptions of emancipation and freedom which need to be critiqued, as well as the ideologies on which they were founded. In order to do this, we need new categories and concepts to propose as part of a new vision of freedom. Moreover, it follows that without opening up political subjectivities – including those of freedom (i.e. equality, justice, dignity, etc.) – to rigorous study, thus recognising their existence as worthy of analysis in their own terms, we will remain stuck within the parameters of these three ideologies which conceive politics simply as different versions of state politics and which are thereby proving daily to be inappropriate for our times.

Emancipation cannot be thought through these three ideologies and their categories, not so much because they are wrong but because they are redundant. The state cannot liberate anyone. All three ideologies orient their politics from within state modes of thought, in other words from within a thinking which believes political subjectivity (i.e. what used to be known as 'consciousness') to be exclusively representative of social location (e.g. class consciousness, national consciousness, etc.). Such thinking does not usually allow for the space to consider thought which is not expressive or representative of social place, as it reduces all political subjectivity to some form of identity politics.

There is therefore little space left for reason as such, for reason may at times demand an exceeding of the simply social and a fidelity to a universal humanity. Within any kind of emancipatory politics, there is always a measure of asocial thought and egalitarianism which is precisely what occurred in May 1968 as Ross shows. Politics as affirmation, as thought, an 'excess' over place which cannot be grasped as representation, yet in the concrete conditions of its unique singularity, is simultaneously related to the social in some way simply because excess is always internal to the situation of that which it exceeds. To sum up and as Alain Badiou puts it: 'In truth, the question of politics boils down to this: how to escape from representation' (2012, 87, my translation).

This argument can be briefly illustrated with reference to South Africa in the 1980s and 1990s in four ways. First, in South Africa, nationalism had leaned very much on Marxism for its thinking, much as it had done in the 1950s and 1960s in the rest of the continent. The categories which activists had at their disposal to make sense of emancipatory subjectivities proved not to be adequate for the situation. In fact, at the time, the concepts and categories available for an adequate comprehension of the new mode of politics – the politics of 'people's power' – which was developing in the 1980s did not exist. The categories of 'class analysis', 'class consciousness', 'class leadership', 'democracy' or 'national identity', for example, were not always useful or even sufficiently adequate for understanding a politics which was being forged in terms of people's daily experience of living and which involved people from all walks of life (Neocosmos 1999, 2009). Moreover, those categories which did develop at the time, such as 'people's power' or 'workers' control', were themselves not sufficiently thought out.

As a result, the novelty of what was happening was not properly understood, it was misunderstood; or rather, the consequences of the ability of people to think political agency for themselves – their subjectivation – was simply not recognised, while the universalising of the obviousness of popular capacities was soon abandoned. In fact, it was unrecognisable given the categories and logic dominant at the time. The concepts available were valid for statist politics such as guerrilla warfare, for underground parties, for attaining state power, in brief for a politics of representation. What was happening was presentation, something else completely as parties were not present, yet activists insisted on reading the unfolding situation in terms of party political categories. The debates regarding unions and politics, those concerning the class content of popular organisations, the weakness of attempts to hold leaders accountable, the deference to the African National Congress (ANC) in exile, for example, were all indicative of a politics of representation. This was similar to that which had obtained among European intellectuals in the eighteenth century, which had completely failed to recognise the capacity of slave agency in Saint Domingue/Haiti, for example. In fact, it was an example of the manner in which trusteeship fails to recognise the fact that people think.

Second, when Nelson Mandela and the ANC came to share state power after 1990, they themselves did not fully understand what had happened – that is, that people wished to 'control themselves', in the language of the time – and hence they simply talked as trustees, as representatives; they substituted their individual will or party will for that of the active people.[1] In this they were, more often than not, supported by the people themselves who implicitly assumed their leaders' thinking would be similar to theirs. Mandela was freed from his life sentence in 1990 by a mass movement of the people of South Africa but, in a very important sense, his liberation from jail symbolised a subjective change (which had begun a few years earlier) from a politics of people 'acting on the scene of history' ('we can change the system ourselves') with all its attendant practices, to one relying on their leaders to change it for them via access to power (Neocosmos 1998).[2] The freeing of leaders from jail became fused in national subjectivity with the freeing of the people from apartheid oppression. Given that the socialist model of freedom had so obviously vanished with the collapse of the state in the Union of Soviet Socialist Republics (USSR) and its satellites, leaders were now seduced by the market model of freedom to which they saw no alternative.

As contestations took place within state modes of thought, it was quite simple for nationalism to now lean on neo-liberalism for its understanding of freedom. Given that the socialist vision had been discredited, neo-liberalism won out without any opposition and also because its vision had been fully theorised, as well of course as being in a position of power to become universalised very rapidly within the state. The popular vision of freedom was not understood and had not been theorised; it was feared for what it could unleash, as was rapidly shown by the riots which followed upon the assassination of Chris Hani on 10th April 1993.[3]

The view that won out was, crudely put, that apartheid had been a state intervention in the market; therefore, all that was required for freedom to be realised was a short-term 'levelling of the playing field' such as 'affirmative action' so that a Black middle-class could develop, and the market would equalise everything in the long run through a 'trickle-down' process. South Africans have been suffering from this misunderstanding ever since. The people of the country had assumed, given their primary role in 'the struggle', that they would be taken seriously and listened to so that, as the Freedom Charter put it, they themselves 'would govern' and have access to freedom as they understood it (dignity, jobs, housing, etc.), but this did not materialise. Their attempts at agency after 1990 came to be seen, as un-procedural and illegitimate at first and much later as a real threat to both the market and to the state while their previous attempts at agency in the 1980s were rapidly turned into victimhood by the Truth and Reconciliation Commission (TRC) process; from subjects of history, people were simply turned into its victims. By 2008, a politics of fear seems to have become fully entrenched in state discourse – fear of the African poor, fear of the poor and excluded as such (Neocosmos 2008).

The third point is also germane to all experiences of national liberation politics founded on mass movements. It concerns the fact that it is when the new state is not yet in existence that the people are equated with the nation, that is, the political affirmation that the people equal the nation exists only under conditions when the new state is still absent, under the condition of an emancipatory politics (Badiou 2013a, 14). Moreover, the change in political subjectivity from a point where the nation is equated subjectively with the people, to a point where it is identified with the state, 'on the morrow of independence' as Fanon (1990, 125) put it, concerns the replacement of a politics in the true sense of the term by the hegemony of state subjectivities whereby the nation is reduced to indigeneity and political subjectivity to identity. How does this subjective shift take place? What are its conditions of possibility? Is not the idea of political representation as I have noted of central concern here? Of course, at the core of national liberation politics in the twentieth century was the idea that emancipation was to take place via the state; yet, it has eventually become apparent that the state cannot emancipate anybody, and whatever credentials it may have had on the African continent and elsewhere in the Global South through its leading a national development project in the past have now largely evaporated (De Alwis 2009). In any case, South Africa achieved its liberation during a world sequence when the state had been replaced from its role as the demiurge of freedom by the market itself; in some ways, we seem to have gone back in historical time to a period before the nineteenth-century invention of what Badiou has called the 'communist hypothesis' (2011a).

Fourth, as a result of the overwhelming dominance of a politics of representation within a post-1980s neo-liberal environment in which the national role of the state has been minimised, the 'national question' has not been resolved and is unlikely to be resolved in the near future in South Africa. Mandela and the ANC's decision to minimise the interventionist role of the state in the national interest and to take the neo-liberal route has led to the inability to unify the nation around a state-led project. The absence of a state-led project of nation-building through development in particular has meant not only the failure of reconciliation between the white middle class and the new black petty-bourgeoisie, but also, and more importantly, the exclusion of the vast majority of the poor – over half the population of the country by all accounts – from access to resources like jobs and housing. But this failure was founded directly on the politics of representation, simplified by the fact that Mandela not only represented the nation but actually embodied it. Unlike some of his successors, Mandela could not be said to have feared the people of South Africa; they absolutely adored him, yet his attitude towards people was a personal one, not a political one, as he was unfamiliar with popular politics. Arguably then, Mandela's undoubted principles were fundamentally moral rather than truly political, a not uncommon feature of charismatic leadership. The politics of representation initiated towards the end of the 1980s and systematically entrenched while simultaneously hidden by Mandela's charismatic leadership, eventually produced this fear within state thinking itself. Two simple and spectacular examples of this widespread fear are the state reaction to the rebellion in Marikana in August 2012 which was violently put down, and the building by the current president of the country (Jacob Zuma) of a bunker under his private residence.

Today, it is apparent that it is no longer possible to remain at this point and to continue thinking within a politics of representation and hence within state subjectivity, simply because the failure of previous conceptions of freedom is evident for all to see. *Abahlali baseMjondolo* (the shack-dwellers movement from Durban) has understood this as evidenced by its notion of 'unfreedom'. It has shown that it is indeed possible to be faithful to the Freedom Charter's idea that 'the people shall govern', that is, to a vision of presentation in which what people say when they think at a distance from the state is taken seriously. The political problem consists in how to sustain this vision and the practices which flow from it. That is the central question of politics according to Badiou (2011a). For this to happen, we need – at the intellectual level – to recognise and understand that political subjectivities – whether expressive or excessive of the social – exist as a specific object of inquiry. In my forthcoming book (2016), I do this by beginning with the fundamental affirmation that 'people think'; in other words, that they may add an idea to their agency and hence their practice (Badiou 2013c, my translation):

> The Idea, understood as that which orients an effective journey in the world, must always be thought as active, and not as is usually the case, as a generally static and fanciful representation. This is the reason why Marxist materialists begin from the 'primacy of practice', which must be understood as the primacy of the Idea as practice. There is no contradiction whatsoever between the ideological dimension of politics and its practical dimension; when all is said and done, they are the same thing. And already in Plato himself, the Idea is not a representation; it is explicitly destined to exist as a practice, a practice of existence, a practice of the just life.

Yet, the idea that 'people think' must be supplemented with categories which help us identify this thought in practice. Such a category is the notion of prescription. Lazarus (1996) refers to this as 'the possible under condition', in other words as the collective identifying and overcoming of what the state deems to be impossible. It is this which puts thought into practice. For example, the prescriptions of the slaves in the Saint Domingue revolution were of two different kinds: first (1791) the demand for unconditional freedom, second (1797 onwards) the struggle for parcel ownership; both of these prescriptions concerned freedom but fashioned in relation to different singularities (Neocosmos, 2016). Prescription is thus a concept which helps us to understand the purely political, in addition to the fact that it suggests that people are able to think in excess of identity. It is prescription which identifies the fact that thought is a 'relation of the real' in Lazarus' terms; in the absence of prescription, that is, of 'acting on the real' to change it, to make the impossible possible, it may not be apparent that people think. It is clear that alternatives only become possible under the condition of a new subjectivity which is maintained over time by an organised politics.

Reclaiming the right to think, a purely subjective question

When thinking emancipation, it is more often than not useful to begin from Lenin's twentieth-century formulations in order to transcend them. Lenin's main formulation regarding the state and freedom reads as follows: 'So long as the state exists there is no freedom. When there is freedom there will be no state' ([1918] 1981, 91). Following Marx, the state is thought by Lenin as 'withering away' along with the growth of communism on the horizon. Here, for Lenin, it is apparent that the state is understood objectively, institutionally and structurally,[4] and freedom is grasped as something dependent on the physical absence of the state and thus on the end of politics.

Although politics for Lenin was not immediately reducible to the social as it has been for most Marxists since (Neocosmos, 2016, ch. 7), given the fact that he did not develop a theory of practice but remained within a notion of politics as representation, his position ultimately remained that the state is politics and politics is the state. Politics ends along with the end of the state, an idea which has remained at the core of all Marxist conceptions of politics ever since. But there need be no end to politics if politics is not equated with the state, if by politics we understand a collective thought-practice. Therefore, we are now necessarily faced with the understanding that the state may disappear while politics may remain as we have detached politics from the state in thought. This was the case of course with 'acephalous' African societies and is indeed the case where the state is absent for whatever reason as it has recently been in several regions of Africa.[5]

On the other hand, for thinkers such as Badiou, Lazarus and Rancière, freedom is understood subjectively. Because we are concerned with political subjectivities we cannot think the state solely and certainly not primarily as an objective structure or structures, however complex and contradictory. Rather it must also be thought as prescribing specific subjectivities. There are two such subjectivities which are worthy of particular attention as they exist at the core of the state itself. The first is that the state prescribes divisions and hierarchies while purporting to exist above them; it is totally opposed to any egalitarian principle which while recognising difference refuses divisions. 'The idea of an egalitarian state is an oxymoron', insists Badiou (2014). The second concerns the fact that the state always prescribes what is deemed to be possible and what is said to be impossible for human agency. For example (2010, 21, my translation):

> It has been stressed profusely that the state was the real oppressor, but in a more fundamental way, the state is what distributes the idea of what is possible and what is impossible. The event on the other hand, transforms that which has been declared impossible into a possibility; the possible will be torn away from the impossible.

The problem inherent in Marx's formulation of the 'withering away' of the state, adhered to by Lenin, is that the analogy gives the impression that withering like a leaf on a tree is itself the result of something objective; not the seasons or the weather this time, but the development of the productive forces, the disappearance of classes, the end of class struggle, and so on. For example, contrary to anarchists who wanted to abolish the state overnight, Lenin argues that Marxists hold that 'the complete abolition of the state … can only be achieved after classes have been abolished by the socialist revolution' (Lenin [1918] 1981, 106–107). Lenin's position in the meantime was guided in this respect – at least until the fusion of his party with the state – by a fidelity to the Paris Commune along with a confidence in the economic benefits of the enactment of socialist state policies ([Lenin [1918] 1981, 111, emphasis in original):

> Let us learn revolutionary boldness from the Communards ... The possibility of ... [the] destruction [of bureaucracy] is guaranteed by the fact that socialism will shorten the working day, will raise the *people* to a new life, will create such conditions for the majority of the population as will enable *everybody* without exception perform 'state functions', and this will lead to the *complete withering away* of every form of state in general.

The state then finally 'withers away' after objective changes have followed the enactment of appropriate policies. But if we detach politics from the state, so that politics does not disappear with the disappearance of the state as politics are no longer reduced to the state, then it follows that the state has to be 'withered away', 'struggled away' so to speak, so that the accent is now put on agency; put simply, there is no end to political struggle as there is no end to history. It also follows that such a process of absenting the state in thought can begin in politics irrespective of whether the state exists as a set of institutions or not; this 'absenting of the state in thought' is then central to a practice of politics which wishes to think an emancipatory future today. 'What is the moment of freedom in politics? It is that when one distances oneself from the state' (Badiou 1985, 166, my translation) or again: 'Politics is about making politics exist, so that the state should no longer exist' (Badiou 2013b, 115). These formulations now alter the direction of the process of change so that politics comes first and the disappearance of the state follows. The moment of freedom can thus be understood as the absenting of the state in thought, and this means the ability to think the impossible – to maintain that what the state says is impossible (e.g. 'there is no alternative') – is indeed quite possible (Badiou 2010, 63–64, my translation):

> Ideally, politics should be organising the 'withering away of the state'; it is therefore completely related to the latter, but in such a way as to aim for its disappearance ... [for even] if politics cannot make the state disappear through the wave of a magic wand, it must nevertheless be coextensive with the idea of a gradual withering away of the state and the replacement of its management figures by figures of association and creativity.

The point then is not to forget about the state, to distance oneself from the state in an objective sense as many utopian experiments in Latin America and elsewhere have historically attempted. The position developed here is not an anarchist one; politics 'at a distance from the state' does not necessarily mean 'anti-state'.

Neither is it a liberal one which sees civil society as the domain of freedom because it is composed of 'rights-bearing citizens'. To adhere to such a position is to conflate objective and subjective distance. It should be clear that civil society, which is seen to exist at an objective distance from the state, cannot form the foundation for thinking an emancipatory politics, for that distance must be subjective and not objective; it must be political. In order to enable the thinking of an emancipatory politics, it must be insisted here that the idea of 'distance' must be understood as 'subjective distance' from state thinking and not as 'objective distance' from state institutions. In particular, state political subjectivity privileges interests, social place and political identities which the state itself has the function of managing to the benefit of the oligarchy in existing society and its given structure. It is this kind of politics which reproduces the core features of capitalism and its various ramifications. Moreover, the notion of distance employed here is a general theoretical one. One cannot simply deduce from it the specifics of any singularity; whatever political position one holds in relation to a particular state: the question of whether one opposes the state, fights it, enters it, or however one prescribes to it, is ultimately determined by specific conditions and cannot be answered at a general level.

Nevertheless, given the fact that this subjective distance is never total, is never such as to completely replace state conceptions by completely unrelated ones, it varies according to the extent to which it exhibits 'expressive' or 'excessive' qualities. The greater the excessive quality of the subjectivity in question, the greater this distance from state thinking. Of course, such excessive features vary over time, and it is precisely these that a political organisation attempts to maintain. Badiou (2011a) refers to this as the problem of sustaining the inventions of 'movement communism' over time. The difficulty in doing so accounts for what Lazarus (1996) calls the 'saturation' of the historical mode of politics, as a point is reached when excess over state thinking is no longer in evidence. This is the problem of sustaining emancipatory politics and illustrates the idea that 'distance' here must be grasped prescriptively, as sustaining a practice rather than as describing or analysing an event. This amounts to distinguishing politics from history.

I show at length elsewhere (Neocosmos, 2016) that excessive thought is never 'pure' but always 'mixed' with some expressive notions by virtue of the fact that excess always exceeds something represented in state discourses and is always formed in struggle against the expressive; for this reason, social location always exercises an effect on thought from which it is always difficult to tear away. For example, if we were to follow Chatterjee's (2004) analyses of history and note that although sovereignty through rights in civil society was demanded by the new post-independence elites in Africa, governmentality was reproduced and expanded by the idea of nation-building through a state development project, we would simply be providing a sophisticated account of subjectivities as state-induced. We need, in addition, to note that the establishment of sovereignty was accompanied by an often coercive undermining of alternatives which exhibited excessive thought over the idea that the nation equalled the state. In this manner, trusteeship was transferred from the colonial state to the postcolonial state at independence.

Without a critique of the role of the state as representative of the nation, the dichotomy empire-nation becomes difficult to transcend subjectively, for alternatives both in practice and in thought were historically closed down and continue to be closed down. However, there is ample evidence that this dichotomy had been transcended within various local struggles which posed the question of equality and popular power as people struggled for national freedom; yet, these subjectivities were then submerged by the new postcolonial state politics. The core problem with the national liberation struggle mode of politics was precisely that the struggle for freedom was a struggle against a state as well as a struggle for a new state. It is in this context of the popular struggles for national liberation that Badiou notes that (2013a, 16):

> ... [the term] 'people' here takes on a meaning which implies the disappearance of the existing state ... What is affirmed within large popular movements is always the latent necessity of what Marx considered the supreme objective of all revolutionary politics: the withering away of the state.

The contradictory political subjectivity of the national liberation struggle mode therefore could shift from a subjectivity wherein the nation was the people to one where the nation was the state, or from presentation to representation as the term 'nation' was central to thought given its 'circulating' character; the result was invariably contradictory as while freedom was conceived as the attainment of power and state construction, the people who fought for freedom insisted on equality and (relative) autonomy from the state during the process of struggle itself. One can notice this in relation to the struggles for independence in Africa as well as in the context of the anti-apartheid struggle. In Tanzania, this took the form of Ujamaa villages,[6] in Zimbabwe, it was rural egalitarianism and land redistribution and in South Africa in the 1980s, it was street committees and access to jobs and housing and so on. This process also explains the disappearance of a popular pan-Africanism – which had formed the cradle of nationalism – and its replacement by its reactive statist simulacrum of which the Organisation of African Unity (OAU) and then the African Union (AU) were outcomes. The nation as represented and conceived by the state has always been premised on forms of popular exclusion.

In Haiti, the egalitarian core of emancipatory politics was sustained over a long period. People did this successfully by thinking the 'impossible' of legal freedom followed by the 'impossible' of independent parcel-owning peasant production. The slaves tried to absent themselves totally from the state through setting up independent cultivation (Barthélémy 1990). There is a combination here of a political subjectivity combining political control outside the state with economic survival and independence. These various experiments can be read not as a way of constructing a new state form from the bottom up, but rather as an attempt to distance oneself from state power itself, which is, in a sense, what forming one's own forms of self-regulation is all about within popular subjectivity. In sum then, any struggle for freedom is a struggle against a particular form of state; yet it is bound simultaneously to contain within it elements of a struggle against power as such ('anti-power' in Holloway's 2002 formulation). It is also formed in excess of state thinking and therefore continuously shaped in relation to that thinking.

A resolution to this contradiction can only begin to be thought first through developing categories and politics from the point of people at a subjective distance from the state, and second by thinking a state which is not a state, a state which provides the conditions for its own undermining, that is, its so-called withering away. Of course, this is what Marx meant by the 'dictatorship of the proletariat', an unfortunate term because it refers to another form of state, but a term which made sense at the end of the nineteenth century. Marx and Engels saw the 1871 Paris Commune with its popular democratic features as the paradigm of the 'dictatorship of the proletariat' (Engels [1891] 1973, 259), 'the political form at last discovered under which to work out the economic emancipation of labour' (Marx [1871] 1970, 72); yet, in the twentieth century, that dictatorship took fundamentally different, much less democratic forms: the dictatorship of the party. This was precisely due to the politics of representation which maintained that the 'proletarian party' represented the class, something which was not the case during the Commune.[7] In the twentieth century, the party represented the class and spoke and acted for it within 'political society' due to its monopoly of knowledge.

Today the terms 'dictatorship' and 'democracy' have to be thought in different ways than simply as forms of state.[8] Irrespective of whether we are in the presence of an emancipatory politics or not, it is also the case that the perspective taken here opens up the study of political subjectivities that have been generally occluded by the social sciences. The social sciences have overwhelmingly understood the world we live in terms of state categories and hold that rationality is rarely present in the knowledge of the excluded

(Neocosmos 2012). This is so for the excluded are not expected to speak for themselves by definition; they are considered to be both deaf and dumb as de Tocqueville (1967, 282) noted with reference to the *Ancien Regime* before the French Revolution. Badiou himself notes that (2009a, 199, my translation):

> … ordinary history, the history of individual lives, is held within the state. The history of a life is, in itself, ordinarily bereft of decision or choice; it is a part of the history of the state of which the classical mediations are the family, work, the motherland, property, religion, customs …

Of course, Badiou is not referring here to the life of civil servants, but to the state subjectivities within which life is overwhelmingly lived. There is little in terms of excessive thought within the history of a life as habitually lived. It is for this reason among others that the social sciences, in Rancière's (2012) terms, have purported to speak for those who do not habitually speak. Therefore, speech needs to be made audible when it occurs; the theoretical and methodological space to do so must be opened up. It is this which I have attempted in my forthcoming book (Neocosmos, 2016) and which I propose to outline more formally now.

Thinking excessive politics: a diagrammatical presentation

If we assess the diagrams below, then it becomes apparent that it is the excess which is being made visible, for any social change requires a strong asocial component if change is to have any real meaning. If the excessive is inexistent or minimal, only the expressive of the social is visible and appears as reflecting the phenomena in existence such as simple identity politics. For this subjectivity which dominates in the social sciences, what exists is the only thing which can exist; real change and equality are impossible, only some form of 'evolution' – progress, development, modernisation – are possible as the habitual regularisation of social hierarchies by the state remains. With the inclusion of the excess, of the exceptional – when it exists – the extant, the expressive, the habitual become visible for what they are: only one possibility among many at the end of a continuum of possibilities which exceed it to various extents.

I have tried here to explain the distance between emancipatory politics and state politics, between a politics of excess and a politics of expressing identities and interests. I have also insisted on the fact that expressive and excessive politics mutually condition each other in a dialectical relation. To prise apart the one from the other is an intellectual struggle as well as a political struggle which every attempt to think an alternative to the present world must face. At this point, I simply wish to prise them apart more formally than hitherto in order to make an excessive politics more visible theoretically. This is undertaken in the formal schemata below in which the position on the left of the diagram represents the knowledge of social science of the habitual and the position on the right refers to the exceptional. The excess obviously refers to the part in between the two. This excess can also be referred to as a 'distance'. The distance referred to here is a distance from state subjectivities which is variable and measurable like all distance: less distance or greater distance from state thinking.

In general, the movement of thought beyond the limits imposed by the state can be represented as following a direction from the habitual where nothing really changes, as thought if represented in action is merely expressive of the existing social. The exceptional event whose consequences are more or less subjectively sustained over time is represented by a certain distance from the habitual as follows for its political subjectivities are not founded on interests but on principles; this represents an 'excessive gap' in collective political thought.

Habitual	**Exceptional**
(Politics of interest and identity)	(Disinterested political principles)

----------> Politics at a distance from the state ---------------->

The excessive gap (empirically measurable)

Subjective distance from the state, like all distance is quantitatively variable and therefore measurable. This distance can be referred to as the 'excessive gap' in other words the distance in thought between the expressive and the excessive. This gap can be said to delineate a domain of freedom (Badiou 1998, 160, my translation):

> Freedom … consists in a distancing of the state effected through a collective fixing of a measure of the excess. And if the excess is measured, it is because the collective can measure up to it.

The first case of this formalisation is thus a simple indication of a variable subjective gap whereby distance from the state or habitual thought can be measured along an axis. The socially expressive is more or less subjectively exceeded. Relatively limited forms of subjective distance such as the example of the Marikana rebellion (11–18 August 2012) can be plotted closer to the left, while major emancipatory subjectivities such as politics of the slaves in Saint Domingue/Haiti are plotted further to the right as their distance from state thought was comparatively much greater.

Expressive politics |----|----|----|----|----|----|----|----|----|----|----| **Excessive politics**

State politics	Politics at a distance from the state
(xenophobic pogroms,	(emancipatory politics of equality,
wage demands, demands for inclusion,	exceptional subjectivity beyond
gender identity, etc)	place, historical event)

Theoretically dialectical

The second case represents how expressive and excessive political subjectivities mutually oppose or effect each other so that we can even have a contradictory subjectivity as in the national liberation struggle mode of politics (beyond state and yet new state, Neocosmos 2008). The expressive/excessive dialectic of agency also points to the fact that it is through an understanding of the exceptional that we can fully understand the normal/habitual as rebellion makes oppression fully visible, for example.

Expressive politics --------------------------->|<------------------------- **Excessive politics**

Political process (politicisation, subjectivation)

The third case shows the actual movement from expressive politics to excessive politics within any singularity. This is the formal presentation of the process of subjectivation, the making of a subject. For Badiou, this process is the sustaining of the subject of fidelity and the consequent production of a truth. For the process to be sustainable and thus continuous, it requires organisation to make the innovations of 'movement communism' (apparent in the event) persist over time. This is a long process which must fundamentally focus on the correct handling/resolution of contradictions among the people in order to develop a collective position on all issues and to be sustainable. This is the fundamental meaning of democracy according to Badiou. The diagram should not be read as in any way denoting a historicism, as the question at stake is not one of social change but of delineating a political subjective 'exceeding' or 'overturning' or 'puncturing' restricted to a collective agent. Such thought is clearly reversible as in the final diagrammatic presentation.

Expressive politics --> Excessive politics

De-politicisation

The final case shows the movement from a point of excess on the continuum governed by principles back to state politics, as identity and organised interests become the main referents for politics after having been exceeded for a period. After showing evidence of a universal politics of equality and subjecthood, everyone returns to his/her place in the division of labour and acts according to his/her place; of course, sociologically such places may have changed and the subjectivities corresponding to them may have also altered somewhat but this and such effects denote a 'weak singularity' in Badiou's (2009b, 374–376) sense. For example, in South Africa, trade unionism and nationalism, although excessive in the mid-1980s, were no longer excessive from the 1990s; organised interests are now represented in civil society. This process of de-politicisation refers also to the dominance of reactive and obscure subjectivities as theorised by Badiou (2009b, 72). It is this process which helps us to identify the continuity between 'past' and 'new' forms of state politics in Africa and which accounts for the consequent political disorientation, as the reactive subjectivity of the state still utilises the names of a previous emancipatory sequence (revolution, democracy, freedom, popular power, movement, etc.) within its 'new' form of rule and as it is seen to have 'betrayed the revolution' with monotonous regularity.

Expressive politics <-- Excessive politics

Concluding remarks

Political thought – political subjectivities – can be described, analysed and explained rationally, the same as any objective phenomenon. Such subjectivities are not to be reduced to representations or expressions of the objective, but they do include them in habitual thought, within state thinking. Excessive or exceptional thought is never so reducible. Thought is fully part of the real. As political thought is part of the real, then it means that it can be studied rationally like any other aspect of the real without reducing it to psychology or any other manifestation of the necessary. In Rancière's terms (2012, 258, my translation):

> Fundamentally, the whole question is to know … whether one interprets things according to a logic of necessity or according to a logic of possibility; if one thinks a rising of an insurrectionary type according to its effects and causes, or according to something which was not predictable … To redefine a universe of possibilities is in fine to re-insert the possible into the real, to subtract from the idea of necessity.

If we are able to understand political subjectivities as the products of rational human beings, not only can we begin to overcome intellectually the tyranny of objective necessity, but we can also begin to understand with the militant activists of *Abahlali baseMjondolo (2013)* that 'real freedom will be something we feel from inside our hearts each second, each minute, each hour and each day'.

Notes

1. This point is captured in an early speech by Mandela after his release from prison:

   > Since my release, I have become more convinced than ever that the real makers of history are the ordinary men and women of our country; their participation in every decision about the future is the only guarantee of true democracy and freedom. (http://www.mandela.gov.za/mandela_speeches/1990/900225_dbn.htm, accessed August 1, 2014)

   The second sentence shows the limits of the thinking in the first: it focuses on 'participation' rather than popular independent organisational existence.

2. This contradiction is captured in a statement from a person attending Mandela's memorial service on 10 December 2013: 'The core of Mandela's life was humanity. That is why I am here today and the world is celebrating. Thanks to him, I was recognised as a human being'. Whereas the first sentence is undoubtedly correct even when Mandela was a guerrilla commander and on the 'terrorist list' of the U.S. and the U.K., the second is less so, as it was not Mandela who freed South Africa, but people's actions which freed Mandela from jail and the country from apartheid, and through their own activity that they became human subjects and hence recognised as human beings (http://www.bbc.co.uk/news/world-africa-25311513, accessed December 10, 2013).

3. Before his assassination, Chris Hani had stated in an interview that 'The perks of a new government are not really appealing to me … What is important is the continuation of the struggle, what we do for social upliftment of the working masses of our country'. Of course, the 'continuation of the struggle' was not what those in power wanted to hear (http://www.vice.com/en_uk/read/the-assassination-of-chris-hani-almost-brought-south-africa-to-civil-war, accessed December 10, 2013). Mandela writes that after Hani's murder

   > we arranged a week-long series of mass rallies and demonstrations throughout the country. This would give people a means of expressing their frustration without resorting to violence. Mr de Klerk and I spoke privately and agreed that we would not let Hani's murder derail the negotiations. (1995, 730)

   The exclusion of the people on the grounds that all they were expressing was 'frustration' is an evident marker of a politics of representation made abundantly clear.

4. This is the case with all Lenin's notions of power, including 'dual power' (e.g. Lenin 1917). This view conforms to the standard liberal conception of the state. For Weber, the state 'claims the monopoly of the legitimate use of violence within a given territory' (1970, 78). On the same

page, Weber cites Leon Trotsky approvingly that 'every state is founded on force'. Let us also recall that in the twentieth century, the term 'revolution' was used as an equivalent for emancipation. After revolution, one state form simply replaced another. Lenin's text *The State and Revolution* shows that both terms are thought together as does Gramsci's notion of 'passive revolution', for example. If we are to detach emancipation from the thought of the state, revolution must be thought differently.

5. Somalia and parts of the Democratic Republic of Congo (DRC) come readily to mind.
6. It is sometimes thought that Ujamaa was simply a top-down statist process. This is simply false. What was top-down was the policy of 'villagisation' which followed Ujamaa from 1970. Ujamaa itself was in some important cases a genuine rural social movement. For a detailed discussion of such experiments in villages of the 'Ruvuma Development Association', see Ibbott (2014).
7. It is clear, for example, that when Lenin refers to 'the tasks of the proletariat in the revolution' in the subtitle to his *The State and Revolution*, he is actually referring to the tasks of the 'proletarian party'. Moreover, for Lenin, 'socialism' was another term for the 'dictatorship of the proletariat', a transitional state which abolishes classes and hence the state itself. For both Marx and Lenin, it was absurd to see 'socialism' as a desirable end in itself for it merely referred to a form of state.
8. This does not mean that the armed people may not have to defend their political gains. Nevertheless, it should be recalled that the 2002 coup against Hugo Chávez in Venezuela was foiled by ordinary people in mass organisations, not armed force.

Disclosure statement

No potential conflict of interest was reported by the author.

References

Abahlali baseMjondolo. 2013. Unfreedom Day in Durban. http://www.abahlali.org/node/9563.
Badiou, A. 1985. *Peut-on Penser la Politique?* Paris: Seuil.
Badiou, A. 1998. *Abrégé de Métapolitique.* Paris: Seuil.
Badiou, A. 2009a. *L'Hypothèse Communiste. Circonstances 5.* Paris: Lignes.
Badiou, A. 2009b. *Logics of Worlds.* London: Continuum.
Badiou, A. 2010. *La Philosophie et L'événement.* Paris: Germina.
Badiou, A. 2011a. *Le Réveil de L'histoire. Circonstances 6.* Paris: Lignes.
Badiou, A. 2011b. "Le socialisme est-il le réel dont le communisme est l'Idée?." In *L'Idée du Communisme Volume 2, Berlin 2010,* edited by A. Badiou et S. Žižek, 9–22. Paris: Lignes.
Badiou, A. 2012. *Sarkozy; pire que prevu, les autres prevoir le pire. Circonstances 7.* Paris: Lignes.
Badiou, A. 2013a. "Vingt-quatre notes sur les usages du mot 'peuple'." In *Qu'est-ce qu'un peuple?,* edited by. A. Badiou, et al., 9–21. Paris: La fabrique.
Badiou, A. 2013b. *The Incident at Antioch/L'Incident d'Antioche.* New York: Columbia University Press.
Badiou, A. 2013c. Seminaire 2012–2013: *L'Immanence des Vérités 1, Notes de Daniel Fischer.* http://www.entretemps.asso.fr/Badiou/seminaire.htm.
Badiou, A. 2014. Seminaire 2013–2014: *L'immanence des Vérités 2.* Notes de Daniel Fischer http://www.entretemps.asso.fr/Badiou/13-14.htm.

Barthélémy, G. 1990. *L'Univers Rural Haïtien: le pays en dehors*. Paris: L'Harmattan.

Chatterjee, P. 2004. *The Politics of the Governed: Reflections on Popular Politics in Most of the World*. New York: Columbia University Press.

De Alwis, M., et al. 2009. "The Postnational Condition." *Economic and Political Weekly*, 7 March, 44:10.

Engels, F. (1891) 1973. "Introduction to the Civil War in France by Karl Marx." In *Selected Works in One Volume*, edited by K. Marx and F. Engels, 248–259. London: Lawrence and Wishart.

Fanon, F. 1990. *The Wretched of the Earth*. Harmondsworth: Penguin.

Holloway, J. 2002. *Change the World Without Taking Power*. London: Pluto.

Ibbott, R. 2014. *Ujamaa: The Hidden Story of Tanzania's Socialist Villages*. London: Crossroads Books.

Lazarus, S. 1996. *Anthropologie du Nom*. Paris: Seuil.

Lenin, V. I. 1917. *The Dual Power. Collected Works*. Vol. 24. London: Lawrence and Wishart.

Lenin, V. I. (1918) 1981. *The State and Revolution: The Marxist Theory of the State and the Tasks of the Proletariat in the Revolution*. Moscow: Progress Publishers.

Mandela, N. 1995. *Long Walk to Freedom*. London: Abacus.

Marx, K. (1871) 1970. *The Civil War in France*. Peking: Foreign Languages Press.

Neocosmos, M. 1998. "From People's Politics to State Politics: Aspects of National Liberation in South Africa." In *The Politics of Opposition in Contemporary Africa*, edited by O. Olukoshi, 195–241. Uppsala: Nordic Africa Institute.

Neocosmos, M. 1999. "Intellectual Debates and Popular Struggles in Transitional South Africa: Political Discourse and the Origins of Statism." Paper presented at Centre for African Studies, University of Cape Town, April 21.

Neocosmos, M. 2008. "The Politics of Fear and the Fear of Politics: Reflections on Xenophobia in South Africa." *Journal of Asian and African Studies* 43 (6): 586–594.

Neocosmos, M. 2009. "Civil Society, Citizenship and the Politics of the (Im)possible: Rethinking Militancy in Africa Today." *Interface* 1 (2): 263–334.

Neocosmos, M. 2012. "Are Those-Who-Do-Not-Count Capable of Reason? Thinking Political Subjectivity in the (Neo-)Colonial World and the Limits of History." *Journal of Asian and African Studies* 47 (5): 530–547.

Neocosmos, M. 2016. *Thinking Freedom in Africa: Toward a Theory of Emancipatory Politics*. Johannesburg: Wits University Press.

Rancière, J. 2012. *La Méthode de L'égalité : entretien avec L. Jeanpierre et D. Zabunyan*. Paris: Bayard.

Ross, K. 2002. *May'68 and Its Afterlives*. Chicago: University of Chicago Press.

de Tocqueville, A. 1967. *L'Ancien Régime et la Révolution*. Paris: Gallimard-Folio.

Weber, M. 1970. "Politics as a Vocation." In *From Max Weber*, edited by H. H. Gerth and C. W. Mills, 77–128. London: Routledge and Kegan Paul.

Back to the future: revival, relevance and route of an anarchist/syndicalist approach for twenty-first-century left, labour and national liberation movements

Lucien van der Walt

ABSTRACT

The failings of classical Marxism, social democracy and anti-imperialist nationalism point to the need for a radical left politics at a distance from the state. This paper examines the impact, revival and promise of the anarchist/syndicalist tradition, a rich, continuous praxis in labour, left, anti-imperialist, anti-racist and egalitarian movements, worldwide, since the 1860s. Outlining its core ideas – anti-hierarchy, anti-capitalism, anti-statism, opposition to social and economic inequality, internationalist class-based mobilisation – and critique of mainstream Marxism and nationalism, it highlights the arguments there is a basic incompatibility between state rule, and bottom-up, egalitarian, democratic, socialist relationships. The anarchist/syndicalist project cannot be reduced to an organising style, protest politics or spontaneism: for it, transition to a just, self-managed society requires organised popular capacity for a revolutionary rupture, developed through prefigurative, class-based, democratic organs of counter-power, including syndicalist unions aiming at collectivised property, and revolutionary counter-culture. Success needs formal organisation, unified strategy and anarchist / syndicalist political organisations.

Liberty without socialism is privilege, injustice; socialism without liberty is slavery and brutality

...

– Bakunin ([1867] 1971, 127)

The 1990s saws the exhaustion of the dominant progressive models of the short twentieth century: the Keynesian welfare state, associated with social democracy (in the so-called First World); centrally planned state-run economies, associated with Marxist governments (in the so-called Second World); and Import-Substitution-Industrialisation, associated with anti-imperialist nationalism (in the so-called Third World).[1] This had deep structural roots, including a global economic crisis, the globalisation of capital, popular unrest, and a changing geopolitical order (van der Walt 2015; Walton and Seddon 1994). It has proved impossible to revive the old models: while social democracy, classical Marxism and nationalism remain important political currents, neo-liberalism, in various permutations, is now the primary framework worldwide.

Since the 'enabling state' was central to the transformative projects of the 'three worlds' (Taylor 1991, 214–228), the end of the 'enabling state' meant a crisis for state-orientated radical politics, and so, a crisis for the much of the left project. This has had an enormous effect in Africa, where Marxist–Leninism and nationalism have been central to radical politics (e.g. Mayer 2016), and where neo-liberal programmes have generated immense suffering (Walton and Seddon 1994).

Yet the collapse of the old certainties (embodied in states, parties and official doctrines), and the end of the polarised cold war period (where independent alternatives were overshadowed), has also opened up space for renewed attention to modes of radical left politics that look beyond the state and statism.

Central to this process of renewal has been the growth of anarchism and syndicalism – the broad anarchist tradition – as both a diffuse influence on a range of struggles worldwide, and through the proliferation of anarchist/syndicalist organisations. Anarchism, including its trade union variant syndicalism, today exercises a considerable influence, including some unions. For example, a syndicalist summit in Paris, France, in 2007 drew 250 delegates from dozens of unions and labour groups, with Africans the largest continental presence (CNT-F 2007).

The contemporary movement draws upon – albeit in uneven ways – a rich body of theory and practice in labour, left, anti-imperialist, anti-colonial and equal rights movements that goes back to the 1860s. This includes a significant history in northern and southern Africa (e.g. Hirsch and van der Walt 2014). It is often forgotten that mass, organised anarchist and syndicalist movements, some stronger than their Marxist and nationalist rivals, were common into the 1950s. Anderson reminded us anarchism was once the 'dominant element in the self-consciously internationalist radical Left', and 'the main vehicle of global opposition to industrial capitalism, autocracy, latifundism, and imperialism' (Anderson 2006, 2, 54). It is simply not possible to adequately understand the history of, for instance, unions and rural struggles in Latin America, or peasant and anti-imperialist struggles in East Asia, or anti-colonial and anti-racist movements in southern Africa, or labour and the left in Europe, without taking anarchism and syndicalism seriously (van der Walt 2011).

This paper examines the breadth, impact and insights of anarchism/syndicalism, and its possible relevance to twenty-first-century labour, left and national liberation movements. In doing so, it unpacks the core ideas, social critique, transformative vision and strategy of anarchism/syndicalism. It pays especial attention to its views on classes, state power, equality and emancipation and its critique of statist models like Marxism and nationalism. Finally, the paper examines some important challenges anarchism/syndicalism need to address, in order to consolidate and expand.

What is anarchism? And syndicalism?

It is essential, first, to reject the 'assumption that revolutionary Socialism is ... covered by the term "Marxism-Leninism"' (Schechter 1994, 1–2), and 'recall anarchism, which Leninist Marxism suppressed', and the 'democratic ideals' for which it 'served as a repository' (Dirlik 1991, 3–4, 7–8). Here, is necessary to reject some common misunderstandings. A long tradition defines anarchism as an ideology opposed to the state (e.g. Engels 1972, 71; Shatz 1971, xiii). But this is not very helpful. Classical Marxism also insisted that the state 'wither a way' (Lenin 1975, 257, 281; Mao 1971, 372; Marx and Engels 1954, 56–57; Stalin 1942: 468–473). Liberalism too was antipathetic to the state, arguing for free markets as means of limiting state power (e.g. Friedman 1982, 23–36; Von Hayek 1944, 14–16, 52–57).

A more recent tendency to present anarchism as a 'sensibility', expressed in bottom-up decision-making and action, and/or a stress on prefiguring the future in today's struggles (e.g. Epstein 2001; also see Gordon 2007, 32–33), is also questionable. Bottom-up and democratic movements, and direct action, are not uniquely anarchist approaches. Prefiguration has no necessary link with anarchism either: Guevara, for example, insisted that, in his *foco* strategy, 'the guerrilla nucleus ... begins the construction of the future state apparatus', helping ensure the Marxist–Leninist vanguard party's 'seizure of power' (1967, 75, 83–84).

Such definitions are thus unable to distinguish anarchism from other currents. A more useful approach is to abstract the main features of anarchism from its history. The anarchist movement was born in the First International (1864–1877). A 'general awareness of an "anarchist" position did not exist until after the appearance of its representatives in the late 1870s'; anarchism 'appeared to contemporaries ... a new phenomenon' (Fleming 1979, 16). The First International, a coalition of unions, radical groups and workers' organisations, was the site of fierce struggles over the direction of the working class and socialist movement. These debates led to the International splitting in 1872 into a smaller, New York-based wing, associated with Karl Marx (1818–1883), and a far larger, St. Imier-based wing, associated with the anarchist Mikhail Bakunin (1814–1876).

The anarchist movement flows in an intellectual and organisational lineage from that time to the present, and its core ideas can reasonably be said to be expressed in the works of its great luminaries, Bakunin and Piotr Kropotkin (1842–1921). Examined this way, anarchism is a rationalist, revolutionary form of libertarian socialism, emerging from the 1860s, opposed to social and economic hierarchy and inequality, and fighting for a radically democratic, global, delegate-based federation of worker and community councils rooted in assemblies, placing commonly owned means of production, coercion and administration under popular control, so enabling self-management, democratic planning from below and production for need, not profit (van der Walt 2011, 2016a, 2016b).

Anarchism's core premise is the value of individual freedom, which it insists is only possible through cooperative, egalitarian social relations. For 'freedom', Bakunin wrote, was 'above all, eminently social, because it can only be realised in society and by the strictest equality and solidarity among men' and women (Bakunin [1871a] 1971, 238). Thus:

> A person who is dying from starvation, who is crushed by poverty, who every day is on the point of death from cold and hunger and who sees everyone he loves suffering likewise but is unable to come to their aid, is not free; that person is a slave. (Bakunin [1871a] 1985, 46)

It is on these grounds that anarchism rejects capitalism, landlordism and states (all seen as centralising wealth and power in the hands of small ruling classes), as well as the authoritarian family, and multiple forms of inequality, including gender, colonial, national and racial oppression. It aims, instead, at the revolutionary reconstruction of social relations, including interpersonal and familial ones, and the constitution of a universal human community based on voluntary cooperation. The anarchists sought, said Bakunin, 'to organise society in such a manner that every individual, man or woman, should find, upon entering life, approximately equal means for the development of his or her diverse faculties and

their utilization in his or her work' (Bakunin [1871] 1993).² This required a radically democratic and egalitarian society, constructed from below, through a strategy of revolutionary
counter-power and counter-culture (see below).

Lest it be suggested that this is an unusual or novel definition, it should be stressed that
this is the anarchism of notables like Bakunin, Kropotkin, Buenaventura Durruti, Emma
Goldman, Errico Malatesta, Juan Carlos Mechoso, Lucy Parsons, Liu Sifu, Ricardo Flores
Magón, Nestor Makhno, Kōtuku Shūsui, Shin Ch'aeho, and many others; of keystone organisations like the National Confederation of Labour (CNT) in Spain, the Korean People's
Association in Manchuria (Hanjok Chongryong Haphoi), the Revolutionary Insurgent
Army of the Ukraine, and of every significant anarchist movement; and the basis of the
syndicalism of figures like T.W. Thibedi, Fred Cetiwe and Bernard Sigamoney, and of the
entire syndicalist movement itself.

The positive content of anarchism and its location in the working class and socialist
movement are elided by any reduction of anarchism to anti-statism. Anarchism is also not
a 'sensibility' or rejection of systematic theory (cf. Feyerabend 1975). The appropriation of
the label by extreme individualist and irrationalist groups, especially in the U.S.A., should
be rejected (see Bookchin 1995). Rather, anarchism is a coherent tradition of revolutionary left thought and action, historically located in the 'popular classes' – the broad
working class and peasantry – and stressing class-based, internationalist emancipatory
struggle.

The past in the present: today's global revival of anarchism, syndicalism

At the start of twenty-first century, several accounts noted that anarchists have been key to the
'most determined and combative of the movements' fighting capitalist globalisation
(Meyer 2003, 218), with anarchism a major influence on 'today's radical young
activists' (Epstein 2001, 1, 13–14). Ironically, these accounts missed out important parts of this
resur-gence. They focused on anarchism in the 'anti-globalisation' movement of the North
Atlan-tic, and generally presented it as a 'submerged' influence and organising
'sensibility' (e.g. Epstein 2001; also see Gordon 2007, 32–33). Their framing leaves out
other, central parts of the revival, which started earlier, took place in other struggles and
other regions, and was often more consciously anarchist and syndicalist, more formally
organised, and more enduring. For example, an overtly anarchist movement, dating
back to the 1970s, is central to current rebellions in Greece, with thousands of adherents
in hundreds of groups, both urban and rural (Drakonis 2014). Similarly, many core
organisers of Occupy Wall Street in the U.S.A. were committed anarchists, consciously
using the movement to promote anarchist ideas to the larger public (Bray 2013).

While 'there are only few places left where seriously Communist parties still exist', it is
'not difficult to find very energetic … self-described anarchist (or syndicalist) groups
around the world' (Anderson 2014, xiii). Anarcho- and revolutionary syndicalist unions
remain the current's largest formations. African syndicalist initiatives since the 1980s
include Algeria, Nigeria, Sierra Leone, South Africa and Uganda, the last three linked to
the global Industrial Workers of the World (IWW). In Asia, the substantial Siberian Confederation of Labour (SKT) dates back to 1989. Spain's General Confederation of Workers
(CGT) had 70,000 members in 2004 and represented two million through works councils
(Alternative Libertaire 2004). It emerged from a split in the CNT (formed 1910), which re-

emerged in 1975 from decades underground with 200,000 members. While CNT is affiliated to the International Workers Association (IWA, formed 1922, with 14 affiliates in 2012), SKT and CGT are in an alternative syndicalist network that includes, for example, some key Italian COBAS ('committees of the base').

Anarchist and syndicalist influences appear elsewhere. Syndicalist themes are part of a current revival of 'class struggle' unionism (Ness 2014). For instance, revolutionary syndicalism is an explicit reference point for the independent Solidarity-Unity-Democracy unions (SUD, formed 1988) of France and Switzerland. Meanwhile, the Kurdistan Workers Party (PKK, originally a Marxist–Leninist national liberation movement, formed 1974), recently adopted a model of stateless 'democratic confederalism', drawing on the late anarchist-influenced revolutionary Bookchin (Ross 2015).

Also problematic is the claim in recent accounts (which identify the contemporary anarchist resurgence with diffuse influences in the Western 'anti-globalisation' movement), that 'contemporary anarchism' is distinct from 'earlier generations' (e.g. Gordon 2007, 36–37), by supposedly having a richer critique of domination and a wider struggle repertoire (e.g. Purkis and Bowen 2004, 5, 7, 15). The notion of a break with 'classical' anarchism is flawed. Anarchism did not die out in the 1930s, only to be reborn in the 1990s. Anarchism and syndicalism remained major working class and peasant currents in many contexts after 1939, including, for example, Poland into the 1940s, Bolivia and China into the 1950s, Argentina, Brazil, Chile and Cuba into the 1960s, and Mexico and Korea into the 1970s, with major revivals elsewhere from 1968; the history is continuous (Hirsch and van der Walt 2014, 402–404).

Furthermore, many new movements, like IWW in Uganda (launched 2012), are often conscious successors of older formations. IWW, probably the largest U.S.A. syndicalist formation, has existed since 1905. Spain's CGT and CNT are part of an unbroken tradition dating to the Spanish Regional Federation (FORE, formed 1870), the First International's largest affiliate. The Uruguayan Anarchist Federation (FAU, formed 1956) has been active in armed struggles, unions and student mobilisation since the 1950s (Jung and Díaz 2006). FAU is part of the Anarkismo network, formed 2005. Anarkismo linked 25 anarchist political groups worldwide, originated in developments in the 1990s, and based itself on 1920s Platformist and 1950s *especifist* texts. These argued for anarchist political groups based on theoretical and tactical unity and collective discipline – Bakunin's 1860s position.

Features presented as new – like concerns with interpersonal power relations, racism, imperialism and consumption – were actually integral to earlier anarchist and syndicalist generations, including those of Bakunin and Kropotkin (Hirsch and van der Walt 2014, 398–401). Also not new is the use of cultural struggle, the appropriation of public spaces, bottom-up organising, building transnational and cross-continental networks and broad alliances; or concern with opposing, not just economic exploitation, but all forms of oppression, and seeking emancipation, not just for the industrial proletariat, but for all the exploited (Hirsch and van der Walt 2014).

Politics beyond the politics of 'no'

The twenty-first century is marked by horror at the evils of contemporary society, like its massive inequalities in wealth and power, wars, economic instability, intolerance and discrimination – and a growing hope that a better world is possible. But these co-exist, paradoxically, with the widespread loss of a vision for such a world, and of strategy to attain it. This situation arises from precisely the current crisis wracking much of the left project. There are valiant mass struggles against neo-liberalism, state repression and injustices, from the 1980s 'IMF riots' in Africa to the 1990s Zapatista insurgency, to the 'Arab Spring', and strikes against austerity in Western Europe, East Asia and southern Africa. But these struggles are largely defined by what they are against: *anti*-globalisation, *anti*-war, *anti*-privatisation, *anti*-capitalism.

With the retreat from visions of bold change, for 'the moment at least, the agenda is one of reform rather than revolution' (Hopkins 2002, 19). But reforms are rarely linked to clear alternatives; they are repeatedly blocked or captured by elites. Struggles have toppled authoritarian regimes from the 1980s, but the space opened has been filled, not with real alternatives or new social relations, but by neo-liberals (Chiluba in Zambia), rebranded oligarchies (Obama's Democrats), right-wing capitalist demagogues (Trump; Modi in India), and populist gambles (Chávez's '21st century socialism', funded by oil price windfalls). New, left formations have emerged (like SYRIZA in Greece), but their mildly social-democratic programmes have proved unworkable.

Parliamentarism has spread dramatically, but for many it seems evident that voters have no real say in decisions, and that elected officials get co-opted into small ruling classes. As Bakunin insisted, 'the most imperfect republic is a thousand times better than the most enlightened monarchy', but parliament is not democracy ([1867] 1971, 144). Formal rights offer some protection from state officials and capitalists and are the product of popular struggles (Rocker [1938] 1989) but they are constrained and eroded by deep inequalities in power and wealth.

The above conditions form the context for a rise in the crudest forms of identity politics, of nationalist and other right-wing demagogy, and of growing religiosity, concentrated among the strictest denominations (Hooper et al. 2010). The great irony has been the dismissal of class politics and the 'ascendancy of postmodern ideas' despite a 'demographically much larger process of proletarianisation' than that of 'the West ... in all its history' and the need for rational, socialist solutions (Ahmed 2011, 14).

For anarchism/syndicalism, a progressive alternative requires an overarching vision of a new, decent society, and a clear strategy to get there, able to link a range of struggles and demands and social forces to a project of developing organisations and ideas able to challenge, then supplant, the existing order. This requires, in turn, radical organisations that can win the battle of ideas in an open, democratic manner, among large numbers of people – and action *outside*, and *against*, the state. The reasoning is that, without politics, organisation and a programme, little is achieved. This requires a conscious attention to theory (rather than its dismissal as 'dogma'), to strategy (rather than a fetishisation of immediate struggles), and to a realistic understanding of the need for, and the challenges facing, a transition to a new society (without a new order, the old problems will continue; but the old order will not fade quietly in the face of proliferating local struggles nor be destroyed by experiments with alternative institutions). Daily struggles and organising can prefigure a different, better world, but are inadequate. Only a coordinated, decisive revolutionary rupture can change society. Therefore it is not enough to focus only on immediate issues, or to praise the ways in which current initiatives can or do prefigure something better. It is essential to be clear on what order *is* desired, and so, what *should* be prefigured, and then consider *how* to move from prefiguration to figuration.

Bakunin insisted that without a revolutionary vision – the vision of an anarchist future, and of the means to reach it – the popular classes will be doomed to repeat an endless cycle: revolutions come and go, but ruler merely replaces ruler, exploiter merely replaces exploiter. He stressed, therefore, the need for a 'new social philosophy', a 'new faith' in the possibility of a new social order, and in the ability of ordinary people to create it ([1871c] 1971, 249–251). Struggles, social movements and labour unions form, from this perspective, an essential bridge to a better society, but crossing the bridge requires the accumulation of a widespread popular capacity, organised as well as ideological, to supplant the existing order with a better one. This requires, in turn, clear political perspectives, winning the battle of ideas among the majority, and bringing immense social forces – the popular classes – into play.

This is what the PKK in Rojava, Syria, has arguably shown. The 'Arab Spring' largely ended in winter: demands for parliamentary democracy ended with the election of right-wing and/ or neo-liberal forces (e.g. Egypt) or wars involving the old regime, Islamist right-wingers and imperialist forces (e.g. Libya and Syria). But the PKK, with an already strong, rooted organisation, a mass base and an emancipatory programme, was able to use the situation to implement, and militarily defend, a radical, inclusive, multi-ethnic bottom-up order.

Strategy: democratic counter-power and revolutionary counter-culture

Historically, anarchists stressed building alternative organisations *in struggle* against the ruling class, which could also form the *levers* for revolution, and the *nucleus* of new self-managed, egalitarian social order. One part of the strategy was building a popular revolutionary movement – centred on organs of counter-power. Building counter-power meant building bottom-up, democratic mass organisations that could resist, then defeat, and supplant, ruling classes. But since a revolutionary movement required a 'new social philosophy' (Bakunin) – militancy and movements were not enough – this had to accompanied by building revolutionary counter-culture (that is, a counter-hegemonic worldview). Both elements needed to exist outside of, indeed, against the state, including its elections and corporatism, since they follow a completely different logic (see below). The revolution was, effectively, the extension of counter-power across economy and society, through the abolition of the ruling class; democratic counter-power was the new, emerging within the framework of the old.

For most, this required 'mass anarchism', an approach arguing that mass movements able to change society were best built through struggles around immediate issues and reforms, for example, wages, police racism, high prices. What was crucial was that reforms were won *from below* – rather than granted from above, which undermined popular movements – and that struggles helped build democratic, independent mass organisations based on self-activity and radical consciousness (Rocker 1989). These formations would consolidate gains and advance further struggle, and provide space for fostering revolutionary counter-culture. Anarchists needed to participate in such organisations (e.g. the First International), to radicalise and transform them into levers of revolutionary rupture.

Syndicalism was always a central 'mass anarchist' strategy, and the first syndicalist unions emerged not in the 1890s (as often supposed) but dated to the First International: Spain's FORE and the General Congress of Mexican Workers (formed 1876). It argued for revolutionary unions, built through daily struggles, democratic practice and popular education, and wielding power at the point of production. Irreplaceable organs of counter-power and sites of revolutionary counter-culture, independent of the state and its parties, they built popular capacity, including union structures able to seize and self-manage the means of production (Rocker 1989). For Bakunin, such unions were 'living seeds of the new society', erecting 'upon the ruins of the old world the free federation of workers' associations' ([1871c] 1971, 255).

Syndicalism envisages bottom-up, direct-action-based, and inclusive unionism, organising across divisions and borders, and addressing a broad range of social and political issues. It rejects bureaucratic unionism and the belief that unions should engage in electing political parties. The aim is rather a revolutionary 'general strike', involving workplace take-overs and the re-orientation of production as part of creating the new society.

Anti-authoritarian class politics, non-class oppression and national liberation

While opposing all forms of oppression, anarchism/syndicalism always placed especial emphasis on class divisions, advocating class-based politics. This should not be construed as a crude 'workerism'. Anarchism/syndicalism always understood the 'working class' in very broad terms and viewed the peasantry as a revolutionary force. The working class included *all* wage workers who lacked control of their work and did not exploit, whether in agriculture, industry or services, including white collar and casual workers, workers' families and the unemployed. The peasantry included all small farmers not exploiting labour, and exploited by other classes, including tenant farmers.

But *why* class struggle? First, class is a form of oppression affecting the popular classes, the great majority of humankind. It is impossible to create a free society without abolishing classes. It is possible, in some situations to end gender, colonial, national and racial oppression within the existing order. For example, the U.S.A., a former colony, is now an imperialist – it is no longer a victim of imperialism. But class is an irremovable feature of existing society.

Class is also a unique form of oppression: *only* classes are exploited *and* dominated, and class exploitation, centred in production, is essential to funding ruling classes and states. Changing the gender, national or racial etc. composition of capitalists, judges, top officials, generals etc., does not remove class or exploitation. Only exploited classes have an interest in, and capacity to, abolish exploitation: only the popular classes can create a free society, because only they do not require exploitation to exist (Arshinov and Makhno 1989, 14–15).

Abolishing classes requires a social revolution, a great task but feasible, it is argued, because of the popular classes' numbers, ability to organise, and structural power as the producers of wealth. The popular classes cannot be emancipated unless unified, and common class interests, experiences and interests make such unity possible. Class oppression exists globally, meaning that class-based struggle is by its nature, internationalist and crosses lines like gender, nation and race. Further, Bakunin insists, 'the question of the revolution … can be solved only on the grounds of internationality' ([1869] 1985, 14) because isolated revolutions are weak, isolated and inadequate.

'Non-class' oppression by gender, nationality, race etc. affects people of all classes. But different classes have different aims in fighting non-class oppressions: elites in oppressed groups do not aim to abolish class, but to remove barriers frustrating their intrinsic class needs, as exploiters and rulers. Anarchists/syndicalists oppose all oppression on principle, and therefore fight 'non-class' as well as class oppression. However, they aim to connect all struggles into a *unified* fight to end all oppression, in a way consistent with anarchist principles and goals – including abolishing classes. Struggles against oppression are also immensely strengthened when popular class power is brought to bear by, for example, political strikes.

Capitalism, landlordism and the state play a major role in the creation and reproduction of 'non-class' oppressions: for example, racist land enclosure and repressive labour systems in apartheid South Africa were rooted, in substantial part, in the drive of agricultural and mining capital, British imperialism and the local state for cheap, unfree black labour. Not only does the complete abolition of such oppressions require removal of all the forces generating them, but it also a radical redistribution of wealth and power to uproot them and their legacy. Following this reasoning, for example, ending endemic black working suffering in today's South Africa requires revolutionary social changes, and the defeat of the ruling class – impossible without class-based revolution.

Anarchism/syndicalism proposes, rather, that all emancipatory struggles must make the popular classes' needs paramount. For Bakunin ([1867] 1971, 99):

> Every exclusively political revolution – be it in defence of national independence or for internal change … – that does not aim at the immediate and real political and economic emancipation of people will be a false revolution. Its objectives will be unattainable and its consequences reactionary.

Therefore, while anti-colonial and anti-imperialist struggles, for example, have been central to its historic praxis, the movement has fought to ensure these assumed a revolutionary, socialist character, and battled against both foreign *and* local elites (Hirsch and van der Walt 2014). Class-based organising helps prevent gender, national and other liberation struggles being hijacked by the elite class 'element' seeking to capture state power to advance its exploitative 'group … interest' (Arshinov 1987, 31). This 'element' is, unsurprisingly, extremely hostile to class struggle, and continually hides its narrow interests by stressing non-class identities (and politics) like nation (and nationalism) and race (and racism).

For anarchists/syndicalists, the popular classes have an interest in fighting all oppression, including 'non-class' oppression. The great majority of victims of these oppressions are working class and peasant people, who also experience them in their most severe forms. 'Non-class' oppressions divide the popular classes and worsen the conditions of all sectors: they divide the masses with prejudices and generate pools of cheap labour that drive all conditions down. Fighting for equality is also part of prefiguring a free future. The anarchist/syndicalist approach, in sum, does not juxtapose class struggle with the struggle against other forms of oppression, but rather sees the struggle against all forms of oppression as a core part of the class struggle to radically change society (van der Walt 2016a). Class-based unity is essential for human emancipation, but impossible unless it involves actively fighting against 'non-class' oppressions.

Open class analysis, the critique of the state, nationalism and Marxism–Leninism

Anarchists and syndicalists do not actually mean precisely the same as Marxists when defining 'class'.[3] For Bakunin, class involved inequitable 'ownership' of means of production *as well as* means of coercion and administration. Crudely, means of production are productive resources, for example, raw materials, machines; means of coercion are instruments of force, for example, weapons; means of administration are instruments of governance, for example, bureaucracies. 'Ownership' here includes various forms of legal title enabling control, as well as the *de facto* control of, such means.[4] Class inequalities are expressed in social relations of *production* and social relations of *domination* between classes, involving a majority of non-'owners' and a minority of 'owners'. Relations of production involve the exploitation of the popular classes by owners, while relations of domination involve the subjugation of the popular classes by owners.

In modern society, ownership of means of production centres on capitalists ('bourgeoisie'),[5] although landlordism remains important – and corporations constitute the primary method of organising exclusive, class ownership of these means. Ownership of means of coercion and administration centres on 'state managers', like senior officials, judges, military heads, mayors, and parliamentarians – and states are the primary method of organising exclusive, class ownership of these means. The state, as a hierarchical organisation ruling a territory, enables small elites to centralise vast resources against the majority. A strong state, Bakunin insisted, could have 'only one solid foundation: military and bureaucratic centralisation' ([1873] 1971, 337).

Together these private/'economic' and state/'political' elites constitute what can best be called a 'ruling class': capitalists are only a *part* of this class, and it is therefore misleading to call it – as some anarchists and syndicalists persist in doing – a 'capitalist' class. Rather, capitalists, landlords and state managers are class *fractions*. This understanding of class differs from, for example, both Weber and Marx, who saw class in primarily economic terms (for Weber, life chances, and 'exclusively … economic interests' (1946, 181); for Marx, ownership of means of production).

While some anarchists and syndicalists embraced an economic determinism that posited the primacy of capitalists, and so, tended towards derivative and instrumentalist theory of states, Bakunin and others developed a more open, richer class analysis. Bakunin argued, for example, that capitalists were not necessarily the dominant fraction, and that the dynamics of the ruling class need not be reduced to wealth accumulation. The logic of capital, and the logic of the state, while similar, were not identical. Corporations competed to increase the capital, living and dead, under their control, while states competed to increase the territory and populations under theirs. Capitalist competition was *paralleled* by geopolitical rivalry, arising from a competitive state system, but that system did not follow a capitalist logic: 'every state, to exist not on paper but in fact, and not at the mercy of neighbouring states, and to be independent, must inevitably strive to become an invasive, aggressive, conquering state' ([1873] 1971, 339).

For anarchists/syndicalists following this line, Marxists like Lenin were correct in claiming that the state was a 'body of armed men' that defended capitalism (Lenin [1917] 1964). However, Lenin misunderstood the relationship. The state was not a mere instrument of the capitalists but had its own irreducible imperatives – the drive for sovereignty ('to exist … in fact': Bakunin) and expanding control of territory and people ('to become an invasive … state'). These help explain both states' support for capitalists and their auton-omy from capitalists.

State managers' 'ownership' of means of coercion and administration, within a competitive interstate system, imposes distinct imperatives. Precisely because state managers' military-organisational power rests upon powerful economies, states have sought to develop powerful economies – in the modern era, this means industrial and capitalist ones. But simultaneously, their 'ownership' of major resources like guns, courts, jails, officialdom etc. means they have an independent resource base, which enables them to act autonomously. State managers *must* act, to some extent, independently, of capitalists (and landlords), and they *can* do so as well.

This model is borne out by an extensive literature on development experiences. The weaker the capitalists, argued Gerschenkron (1944), the greater the state role in economic modernisation, since the state needed capitalism. Where necessary, state managers deliberately generated the capitalists. In *Meiji* Japan, the state established the main industries and deliberately fostered a strong bourgeoisie, while in contemporary China, the state harnessed foreign direct investment (for geostrategic aims Johnson 1982; Lardy 1992).

Economic and political elites cooperate, since they have convergent interests in maintaining class exploitation and domination. Strong states need effective capitalists, since capitalist accumulation funds the military and bureaucratic resources that maintained and expanded state power. Strong capitalists need effective states, since these provide administrative and coercive resources that enable capitalist accumulation. Each requires and reinforces the other. In this sense, Kropotkin argued, the 'state ... and capitalism are inseparable concepts', 'bound together ... by the bond of cause and effect, effect and cause' ([1912] 1970, 181). Thus, the basis of contemporary society is 'the enslavement of the vast majority of the people by an insignificant minority, and ... it is precisely this purpose which is served by the state' (Arshinov and Makhno [1926] 1989, 18).

Furthermore, relations of production and domination are often deeply intertwined. States can run corporations, exploit labour and realise surplus value, while corporations routinely control extensive coercive and administrative means. Capitalists sometimes accumulate wealth in order to obtain political power, while politicians often use the state to accumulate wealth. These overlaps are not essential to either side – a state, for example, can exist without state corporations – but are common. However, the immediate agendas of capitalists and the state managers can clash (for instance, over tax rates or labour laws); and one side can act to undermine the other (for instance, inept or predatory state managers can frustrate accumulation e.g. Onimode [1986]). There are also splits and conflicts *within* both capitalist and state manager 'fractions': capitalists battle capitalists, state states, and corporations and states are internally divided by departmental rivalries, factions, party-political affiliations, sectoral differences, national and racial divides etc. Divisions also span economic and political elites, with, for example, particular capitalist groups aligning with particular state departments.

Several strategic issue points follow, once these claims are accepted. First, states, as much as capitalist corporations, are viewed as essentially incompatible with freedom and equality for the popular classes; both are reliant on the subjugation and exploitation of the popular classes. Secondly, any group taking state power – including anti-imperialist nationalists, Marxists, and social-democrats – will either replace the old ruling class or join it: the situation of the popular classes will, in essential ways, remain unchanged. Those with state power always, regardless of ideology, intent, sincerity or social origin, constitute part of an oppressive ruling class. Thus Bakunin's view that ([1873] 1971, 338):

... the people will feel no better if the stick with which they are being beaten is labelled the 'people's stick.' ... No state ... not even the reddest republic – can ever give the people what they really want ...

Any emancipatory strategy based upon the capture of state power, peacefully or otherwise, necessarily reproduces the current problem of class domination and authoritarian centralisation. Those who hold state power are, regardless of ideology, intent or social origins, a section of the ruling class, including the most radical politicians. The state can not be used for popular emancipation: it is an intrinsic part of the class system, and dependent upon exploitation for its very income. A new leadership in the state, regardless of colour, nationality or gender, is simply a personnel change for part of the ruling class. Activists do not change the state; the state changes them. Nationalist governments will be controlled by a 'new bureaucratic aristocracy', 'enemies of the people' in place of foreign elites (Bakunin [1873] 1971, 343). The Marxist–Leninist programme of nationalisation of means of production by a revolutionary state will generate 'centralised state-capitalism' (Kropotkin [1912] 1970, 186). These new elites will embrace their situation, even if they still mouth the slogans of freedom and justice: it is the 'characteristic of ... every privileged position to kill the hearts and minds of men' (Bakunin [1871a] 1971, 228). These theses seem borne out by the histories of newly independent, post-colonial states, as well as the experience of Marxist–Leninist regimes.

Divisions within the ruling class are secondary conflicts that can be resolved, as opposed to the primary conflict between classes, which are irreconcilable. While, third, a ruling class does not have a master plan, a unified vision or even a wise leadership, it does have *permanent* organisations – corporations and states – that continually maintain its rule despite its internal conflicts, and also provide a means to resolve internal conflicts and develop shared strategies. The popular classes, by contrast, are normally kept in a state of division, ignorance and division.

The aim of democratic counter-power/revolutionary counter-culture can be seen, from this angle, as redressing this asymmetry by building strong movements that unite the popular classes organisationally, strategically, ideologically – and through struggle. Such formations are the negation of corporations and states: mass-based, bottom-up, democratic, egalitarian, they build the capacity for emancipatory, revolutionary change.

Logic of self-management, counter-power vs. logic of class rule, states

If, like Weber, anarchists and syndicalists viewed the state as a centralised organisation claiming a monopoly of force within a given territory (Giddens 1971, 156), they rejected Weber's view that bureaucratic state centralisation was a *technical* necessity for large-scale administration in complex societies. Rather, they viewed state centralisation as arising from a *social* necessity in class society: a minority could rule only when coercive and administrative power was concentrated in a few hands, and decisions flowed downwards from it, in a chain of command, to the popular classes. This was necessary *only* if an undesirable social order was retained. While the state was fairly efficient as a means of ensuring minority class rule, it was profoundly *inefficient* in other ways. It crippled popular self-activity (Bakunin [1871b] 1971, 269), and was unable to deal effectively with 'all the numberless affairs of the community' (Kropotkin [1887] 1970, 50). It was an 'enormous cemetery, where all the real aspirations, all the living forces of a country' end up 'slain and buried' (Bakunin [1871b] 1971, 269).

There is a fundamental incompatibility between the logics of state power and popular self-management. As a centralised organisation for class domination, the state is antithetical to real democracy, self-management and equality. In this regard, Bakunin wrote: 'It would be obviously impossible for some hundreds of thousands or even some tens of thousands or indeed for only a few thousand men to exercise this [state] power' (Bakunin [1872] 1971, 281).

Even in its most democratic form, parliamentarism, the state reduces popular political participation to ballots every few years (with perhaps some nominal consultation between elections). A representative democracy excludes voters from any real role in governing, beyond a few minutes in poll stations, and reading the news. And no state is ever a representative democracy: it comprise a large, unelected, centralised army, police and bureaucracy, its bonded to the ruling class, and the elected representatives were simply parts of this machine. Thus, the 'day after election[s] everybody goes about his business, the people go back to toil anew, the bourgeoisie to reaping profits and political conniving' and the 'people are committed to ruinous policies, all without noticing' (Bakunin [1870] 1971, 220–222).

There was, the anarchists and syndicalists insisted, a radical *contradiction* between bottom-up self-democracy and the state apparatus, and a basic antagonism between the logic of a project of counter-power/counter-culture, and the logic of capitalism and the state. The most dramatic example of this contradiction was, perhaps, the Russian Revolution, where the Bolshevik state, taking power in the name of the working class and peasantry, soon acted against the *soviets* (peasants', workers', sailors' and soldiers' councils), factory committees, left formations, trade unions and peasant movements. When the soldiers and sailors of Kronstadt base at Petrograd rose in March 1921 in the wake of general strikes in the city, demanding a free press, open *soviet* elections, the release of left-wing political prisoners and strikers (including anarchists), and an end to forced grain requisitions, Trotsky rejected 'the workers' right to elect representatives above the Party', because the party was 'entitled to assert its dictatorship even if that dictatorship temporarily clashed with the passing moods of the workers democracy' (in Nove 1990, 181).

It is precisely this antagonism – and the deeper conflictual class relations upon which it is founded – that, for anarchism/syndicalism, requires that the popular project of counter-power/culture overwhelm and supplant states and corporations through a final, decisive show-down, that is, revolution.

Anarchism/syndicalism: democracy, pluralism and socialism without the state

While agreeing with the liberals' stress on inalienable rights and their suspicion of the state, anarchists and syndicalists rejected capitalism and free markets. Free market theory served the 'interests of the exploiters' (Kropotkin [1912] 1970, 182–183). They shared the Marxist view that capitalism was exploitative, but denied the Marxist claim that capitalism was a stage towards socialism. While adopting many elements of Marxist economics (e.g. Bakunin [1871] 1993), they insisted that capitalism was not an innovative, competitive system. Even in its most dynamic phases, it involved oligopoly, underproduction, distorted economies and wasted resources (Bekken 2009). Innovation came from artisans, scientists and workers, not the bourgeoisie (Kropotkin [1892] 1990).

The anarchist project aimed at individual freedom through socio-economic equality, requiring a new order – which Kropotkin dubbed 'anarchist-communism' – without exploitation, capitalism, markets, commodities, rents, states and corporations (or other centralised organisations enabling minority rule), and freed of oppression. Here individuals could develop to their full potential through cooperation, a 'true individuality' involving, said Kropotkin, 'the highest communist sociability' ([1902] 1970, 296–297). Individual freedom would be expressed, not through competition, but by egalitarian relations, communal duties and cooperation, democratic decision-making and social and economic equality. Society, 'far from decreasing … freedom, on the contrary creates the individual freedom of all human beings' (Bakunin [1871a] 1971, 236–237).

None of this is possible without recognising the principle that a person's 'duties to society are indissolubly linked with his rights' (Bakunin [1867] 1971, 118). The system has 'as its essential basis *equality and collective labour*' (emphasis in the original) (Bakunin [1872] 1971, 289). Without production, the society will collapse; besides, it is fair that everybody contribute to 'the common well-being to the full extent of his capacities' (Kropotkin [1887] 1970, 56, 59). Everyone benefits, and the evils of an idle few living off the labour of many others are said to be shown by capitalism and landlordism. Once labour is freed, work will become more pleasant and meaningful (CNT [1936] n.d., 4; Kropotkin [1892] 1990).

Anarchist ethics, substantive equality and meaningful democracy are the means to negate domination and exploitation, and require that productive, coercive and administrative resources move from the ruling classes', to the popular classes' control. This abolishes class division, and enables the reorientation and restructuring of these resources. If the 'whole proletariat' is in charge, then there is 'no government, no state', as there are no longer 'those who are ruled and … are slaves' (Bakunin [1873] 1971, 330). Or, as Price recently argued, 'Anarchism is democracy without the state' (2007, 172).

The abolition of the state does not mean the end of coordination, rules or decision-making, but a merger of these functions with the mass of the people through assemblies, councils and federations that enable control over all major resources. This radical redistribution of wealth and power enables the abolition of exploitation, the reconstruction of work as an empowering activity, and the end of social and economic inequality. Infused with a new ethics, the new society will consciously eradicate poverty, remove class, redress race/national, gender inequalities etc. promote a rationalist worldview and technological innovation, and create, at last, a universal human community.

Anarchism clearly did not 'reject' modern theory or modernity (cf. Pepper 1993, 202); rather it sought a *revolutionary modernity*, in which science, technology and reason were used for human emancipation, with history consciously designed by human action (Bookchin 1977, 29–30). Thus Bakunin embraces the 'absolute authority of science' in knowledge generation ([1871a] 1971, 230–233) and a universal 'general scientific education' ([1873] 1971, 327), while Kropotkin insists that anarchist social analysis must follow scientific methods ([1912] 1970, 150). Bakunin and Kropotkin devote extensive writing not just to revolutionary strategy, therefore, but also to discussions of future issues like self-management, popular participation in decision-making, crime and punishment, educational methods, the redesign of work to break down sharp mental/

manual and executive/operative distinctions, and democratic rights and political plural-ism in 'anarchist-communism' (e.g. [1866] 1971; [1871c] 1971; [1872] 1998; Kropotkin, [1899] 1974; [1892] 1990).

While promoting rationalism, the 'anarchist-communist' social order evidently had an ethical basis: effectively, it was a voluntary association premised on the value of individual freedom, created through democratic organisations with mass popular support by wide-spread acceptance of its vision. This did mean a certain amount of agreement with its basic values could be assumed at its inception. However, dissidents would have complete access to its democratic spaces. For Bakunin, anarchist society will guarantee the 'absolute and complete' freedom of speech (to 'voice all opinions' without repression) and freedom of association (including associations promoting 'the undermining (or destruction) of individ-ual and public freedom') (Bakunin [1866] 1971, 79). Not only was such freedom intrinsi-cally desirable, and a central goal of the new society, but a free society destroyed itself when it permitted only a narrow range of views, not recognising that freedom included the freedom to disagree or hold unpopular views. Thus, 'every command slaps liberty in the face' (Bakunin [1871a] 1971, 240).

Indeed, if a clear majority decided, *through the democratic process*, to (for instance) replace 'anarchist-communism' with neo-liberal capitalism under a military regime then this *must* be allowed to take place. Anarchists deemed such an occurrence exceedingly unlikely, given the advantages of the new system and a rationalist education and public culture, but recognised that a free society involves indeterminate outcomes to its demo-cratic processes. Conversely, for a minority to coerce a majority to be 'free' was completely inconsistent with anarchist positions. Freedom meant freedom for everybody, Bakunin insisting ([1871a] 1971, 236–237):

> I am truly free only when all human beings, men and women, are equally free, and the freedom of other men, far from negating or limiting my freedom, is, on the contrary, its necess-ary premise and confirmation.

However, freedom was not absolute; the basic principle was that people should be free to do as they wished so long as this did not violate the rights of others. Sabotaging the demo-cratic process, forcibly undermining the democratic system, the use of violence in dis-putes, and other crimes against persons – including exploitation – were at odds with a free society. A minority could not be permitted to coerce the majority into (to return to the example) neo-liberalism and military dictatorship but it had every right to promote its views and try *persuade* people.

Post-Marxists sometimes claim that a class-based project involves an inherently author-itarian 'Jacobin imaginary' that assumes the masses have (or ought to have) a 'perfectly unitary and homogenous collective will' (e.g. Laclau and Mouffe 1985, 2). Yet anarchism and syndicalism show that a revolutionary class politics, centred on a lively and unrest-ricted democratic process, is theoretically possible and historically real. The anarchists themselves promote the revolution, defend the new order, and participate in it, but never strive to rule as a party or an elite; on the contrary, they seek to 'give free rein' to the masses, based on 'unconditional freedom' and struggle against 'all ambition to dom-inate the revolutionary movement of the people' by 'cliques or individuals' (Bakunin [n.d.] 1980, 387).

Lessons: rise and fall and rise of anarchism/syndicalism

Anarchism and syndicalism offer, then, not just a profound critique of the current order, but a vision of a new and better world; it also suggests, as has been shown, a strategy to achieve that world that avoids the failures of social democracy, Marxism–Leninism and anti-imperialism – all of which failed to keep their own promises of sustained material improvements for the popular classes, and built class-ridden, inegalitarian and unpopular orders.

Anarchism and syndicalism also have a long record of building and influencing power-ful movements that made a real imprint on society (e.g. van der Walt 2011, 2016a, 2016b). Even a modest survey of this record goes beyond the scope of this paper (and is imposs-ible in the available space). Some data were provided in the early part of this paper, but other aspects can also be noted. For example, the movement played an important role in colonial and post-colonial countries, including in struggles against imperialism and national oppression, including in Algeria, Bulgaria, China, Czechia, Cuba, Egypt, Georgia, India, Ireland, Korea, Macedonia, Mexico, Puerto Rico, South Africa, Taiwan and Ukraine (e.g. Hirsch and van der Walt 2014). But a popular impact only took place when the move-ment was able to relate, in a realistic way, to the big issues and struggles of the time, and avoid the pitfalls of purist abstention or political liquidation into uncritical supporters of other currents.

Today, there is a worldwide revival of anarchism and syndicalism, a new wave. Its agenda and theory are heavily contested; its activities and approach differ substantially between regions; its ability to consolidate its protest power into large mass movements capable of constructive social change remains to be seen; some who identify as 'anar-chists' actually have a very tenuous, sometimes non-existent, link to the tradition.

What all anarchist history has shown is that if anarchists and syndicalists fail to organise on the basis of a clear programme and unitary organisation – with shared tactical and theoretical positions, and collective responsibility – they will lose the opportunities pre-sented to better organised rivals, many sponsored by states and capitalists. As Platformism and *especifismo* stress (Arshinov and Makhno 1989, 12):

> Anarchism is not a beautiful utopia, nor an abstract philosophical idea, it is a social movement of the labouring masses. For this reason it must gather its forces in one organisation, con-stantly agitating, as demanded by reality and the strategy of class struggle.

Anarchists are one current, for instance, in the 'anti-globalisation' movement and syndic-alists one current in the unions: without a clear programme, and concerted work, they can be displaced, their agenda defeated. A programme requires a clear strategy and a clear strategy is only possible from a thorough grounding in the history and theory of the anar-chist and syndicalist tradition. This involves clearing away the mystifications created by poor scholarship, academic fads like postmodernism, and the appropriation of the label 'anarchism' for individualist, irrationalist and rightist tendencies that have nothing in common with anarchism or syndicalism. This requires the formation of specific political groups that can fight for the leadership of the anarchist idea and an anarchist/syndicalist strategy and outcome, including within mass movements and campaigns, including within unions, and as part of fights for small reforms as well as major changes. This seems to be essential for the project of counter-power/counter-culture to succeed. And so, too, is a realistic appreciation of the need for coordinated, including military, defence of any revolution.

In conclusion: counter-power, syndicalism and prefiguration

As an alternative to the reliance of social democracy, classical Marxism and anti-imperialist nationalism on the 'enabling state', Bakunin and Kropotkin insisted that a new, better society has to be created from below, through the self-managed struggles by bottom-up, emancipatory, and politicised movements of the popular classes, that is, the broad working class and the peasantry. These movements must embody in the *present* the forms and values that they sought to achieve in the future. To use hierarchy would be to reproduce it; tomorrow, in other words, should be built today.

A 'new social philosophy' (Bakunin) had to animate popular movements of counter-power that prefigured the new society, that were built in struggle, that operated *outside and against the state* as well as capital, and that united the popular classes in a revolutionary front. Such a movement had to engage in struggles around reforms, but it must aim, ultimately, to constitute the basis of a new society within the shell of the old, an incipient new social order that would ultimately explode the old one, and supersede it.

Thus, counter-power driven by revolutionary counter-culture aimed to replace the power of the old order, creating a new society in which, through democracy, freedom, equality and socialised resources, power was held by everyone. In this schema, power was *not* abolished; it was, in fact, taken *by everyone*. In the words of Makhno, a key figure in the anarchist Ukrainian Revolution (quoted in Arshinov 1987, 58):

> ... we will not conquer in order to repeat the errors of the past years, the error of putting our fate into the hands of new masters; we will conquer in order to take our destinies into our own hands, to conduct our lives in accordance with our own will ...

Notes

1. I use these terms with caution, aware of their problems.
2. Not paginated.
3. I am expressing the core theses in a precise conceptual language, noting there is no standardised terminology for, and little academic work on, anarchist class theory, for example, Szelenyi and Martin (1988).
4. Expanding Wright's use of 'economic ownership' as 'control of the overall investment and accumulation process' (1978, 71).
5. Including *de facto* 'owners' like senior managers.

Disclosure statement

No potential conflict of interest was reported by the author.

References

Ahmed, A. 2011. "On Postmodernism." *The Marxist* 27 (1): 4–38.

Alternative Libertaire. 2004. Espagne: La CGT S'affirme Comme la Troisième Organisation Syndicale. November.

Anderson, B. 2006. *Under Three Flags: Anarchism and the Anti-Colonial Imagination*. London: Verso.

Anderson, B. 2014. "Preface." In *Anarchism and Syndicalism in the Colonial and Postcolonial World, 1870-1940: The Praxis of National Liberation, Internationalism, and Social Revolution*, edited by L. van der Walt and S. J. Hirsch, xiii–xxix. Boston: Brill.

Arshinov, P. (1923) 1987. *History of the Makhnovist Movement 1918-1921*. London: Freedom Press.

Arshinov, P., and N. Makhno. (1926) 1989. *The Organisational Platform of the Libertarian Communists*. Dublin: Workers Solidarity Movement.

Bakunin, M. (1866) 1971. "The Revolutionary Catechism." In *Bakunin on Anarchy*, edited by S. Dolgoff, 76–97. London: George Allen Unwin.

Bakunin, M. (1867) 1971. "Federalism, Socialism, Anti-Theologism." In *Bakunin on Anarchy*, edited by S. Dolgoff, 102–147. London: George Allen Unwin.

Bakunin, M. (1869) 1985. "Geneva's Double Strike." In *Mikhail Bakunin: From out of the Dustbin: Bakunin's Basic Writings, 1869-1871*, edited by R.M. Cutler, 145–151. Anne Arbor, MI: Ardis.

Bakunin, M. (1870) 1971. "Representative Government and Universal Suffrage." In *Bakunin on Anarchy*, edited by S. Dolgoff. London: George Allen Unwin.

Bakunin, M. (1871) 1985. "Three Lectures to Swiss Members of the International." In *Mikhail Bakunin: From out of the Dustbin: Bakunin's Basic Writings, 1869-1871*, edited by R. M. Cutler, 39–67. Anne Arbor, MI: Ardis.

Bakunin, M. (1871) 1993. *The Capitalist System*. Champaign, IL: Libertarian Labor Review.

Bakunin, M. (1871a) 1971. "God and the State." In *Bakunin on Anarchy*, edited by S. Dolgoff, 225–242. London: George and Allen Unwin.

Bakunin, M. (1871b) 1971. "The Paris Commune and the Idea of the State." In *Bakunin on Anarchy*, edited by S. Dolgoff, 259–273. London: George Allen Unwin.

Bakunin, M. (1871c) 1971. "The Programme of the Alliance." In *Bakunin on Anarchy*, edited by S. Dolgoff, 243–258. London: George Allen Unwin.

Bakunin, M. (1872) 1971. "Letter to *La Liberté*." In *Bakunin on Anarchy*, edited by S. Dolgoff, 274–285. London: George Allen Unwin.

Bakunin, M. (1873) 1971. "Statism and Anarchy." In *Bakunin on Anarchy*, edited by S. Dolgoff, 323–350. London: George Allen Unwin.

Bakunin, M. (n.d.) 1980. "On the Internal Conduct of the Alliance." In *Bakunin on Anarchism*, edited by S. Dolgoff, 385–387. Montréal: Black Rose.

Bekken, J. 2009. "Peter Kropotkin's Anarchist Economics for a New Society." In *Radical Economics and Labour*, edited by F. Lee and J. Bekken, 27–45. New York: Routledge.

Bookchin, M. 1977. *The Spanish Anarchists: The Heroic Years, 1868-1936*. New York: Harper Colophon.

Bookchin, M. 1995. *Social Anarchism or Lifestyle Anarchism: An Unbridgeable Chasm*. San Francisco: AK Press.

Bray, M. 2013. *Translating Anarchy: The Anarchism of Occupy Wall Street*. Winchester, UK: Zero Books/ John Hunt.

CNT. (1936) n.d. *Resolution on Libertarian Communism as Adopted by the Confederacion Nacional Del Trabajo, Zaragoza, 1 May 1936*. Durban: Zabalaza Books.

CNT-F. 2007. "Consolidate International Solidarity." Accessed November 15, 2008. http://www.cnt-f. org/spip.php/article345.

Dirlik, A. 1991. *Anarchism in the Chinese Revolution*. Berkeley, CA: University of California Press.

Drakonis, A. 2014. "Space and Society of Greek Anarchism: A Socio-Spatial Anatomy of the Greek Anarchist Movement in the 21st Century." European Social Science History Conference. Vienna. April 23–26.

Engels, F. (1872) 1972. "Letter to C. Cuno in Milan." In *Marx, Engels, Lenin: Anarchism and Anarcho-Syndicalism*, edited by N.Y. Kolpinsky, 69–71. Moscow: Progress Publishers.

Epstein, B. 2001. "Anarchism and the Anti-Globalisation Movement." *Monthly Review* 53 (4): 1–14.

Feyerbend, P. 1975. *Against Method: Outline of an Anarchistic Theory of Knowledge*. London: New Left Books.

Fleming, M. 1979. *The Anarchist Way to Socialism: Elisée Reclus and Nineteenth-Century European Anarchism*. London/ New Jersey: Croom Helm/Rowman and Littlefield.

Friedman, M. 1982. *Capitalism and Freedom*. Chicago: Chicago University Press.

Gerschenkron, A. 1944. *Economic Backwardness in Historical Perspective*. Cambridge, MA: Harvard University Press.

Giddens, A. 1971. *Capitalism and Modern Social Theory*. Cambridge: Cambridge University Press.

Gordon, U. 2007. "Anarchism Reloaded." *Journal of Political Ideologies* 12 (1): 29–48.

Guevara, C. (1963) 1967. "Guerrilla Warfare: A Method." In *Che Guevara Speaks*, 95–116. London: Pathfinder Press.

Hirsch, S. J. and L. van der Walt. 2014. *Anarchism and Syndicalism in the Colonial and Postcolonial World, 1870–1940: The Praxis of National Liberation, Internationalism, and Social Revolution*. Boston: Brill.

Hooper, J., R. Butt, R. Carroll, and X. Rice. 2010. Developing World Embraces the Rigid Faith Spurned by Secular Europe. *Mail and Guardian*, September 24–30.

Hopkins, A. G. 2002. *The History of Globalisation and the Globalisation of History?* In *Globalisation and World History*, edited by A. G. Hopkins, 12–44. New York: Random House.

Johnson, C. 1982. *MITI and the Japanese Miracle: The Growth of Industrial Policy, 1925–1975*. Stanford, CA.: Stanford University Press.

Jung, M. E., and U. R. Díaz. 2006. *Juan Carlos Mechoso: Anarquista*. Montevideo: Ediciones Trilce.

Kedward, R. 1971. "The Anarchists: The Men Who Shocked an Era." Library of the Twentieth Century.

Kropotkin, P. (1887) 1970. "Anarchist Communism: Its Basis and Principles." In *Kropotkin's Revolutionary Pamphlets*, edited by R. N. Baldwin, 44–78. New York: Dover.

Kropotkin, P. (1902) 1970. Letter to Nettlau. In *Selected Writings on Anarchism and Revolution*, edited by M. A. Miller, 292–307. Cambridge, MA: MIT Press.

Kropotkin, P. (1912) 1970. "Modern Science and Anarchism." In *Kropotkin's Revolutionary Pamphlets*, edited by R. N. Baldwin, 145–194. New York: Dover.

Kropotkin, P. (1892) 1990. *The Conquest of Bread*. London: Elephant Editions.

Kropotkin, P. (1899) 1974. *Fields, Factories and Workshops Tomorrow*. London: George Allen and Unwin.

Laclau, E., and C. Mouffe. 1985. *Hegemony and Socialist Strategy: Towards A Radical Democratic Politics*. London: Verso.

Lardy, N. 1992. *Foreign Trade and Economic Reform in China*. Cambridge: Cambridge University Press.

Lenin, V. I. (1917) 1964. "The State and Revolution." In *Collected Works*, volume 25, 381–492. Moscow: Progress Publishers.

Mao, Z. (1949) 1971. "On the People's Democratic Dictatorship." In *Selected Readings from the Works of Mao Tsetung*, 371–388. Peking: Foreign Languages Press.

Marx, K., and F. Engels. (1848) 1954. *The Communist Manifesto*. Chicago: Henry Regnery Company.

Mayer, A. 2016. *Naija Marxisms: Revolutionary Thought in Nigeria*. London: Pluto Press.

Meyer, G. 2003. "Anarchism, Marxism and the Collapse of the Soviet Union." *Science and Society* 67 (2): 226–230.

Ness, I. ed. 2014. *New Forms of Worker Organization: The Syndicalist and Autonomist Restoration of Class Struggle Unionism*. Oakland, CA: PM Press.

Nove, A. 1990. *Studies in Economics and Russia*. New York: St Martin's Press.

Onimode, B. 1986. *A Political Economy of the African Crisis*. London: Zed Books.

Pepper, D. 1993. *Eco-Socialism: From Deep Ecology to Social Justice*. London: Routledge.

Price, W. 2007. *The Abolition of the State: Anarchist and Marxist Perspectives*. Bloomington, IN: AuthorHouse.

Purkis, J., and J. Bowen. 2004. "Introduction: Why Anarchism Still Matters." In *Changing Anarchism: Anarchist Theory and Practice in a Global Age*, edited by J. Purkis, and J. Bowen, 1–19. Manchester: Manchester University Press.

Rocker, R. (1938) 1989. *Anarcho-syndicalism*. London: Pluto Press.

Ross, C. 2015. Power to the People: A Syrian Experiment in Democracy. *Financial Times*, October 23.

Schechter, D. 1994. *Radical Theories: Paths Beyond Marxism and Social Democracy*. Manchester: Manchester University Press.

Stalin, J. 1942. *Leninism: Selected Writings*. New York: International Publishers.

Shatz, M. 1971. "Introduction." In *The Essential Works of Anarchism*, edited by M. Shatz. New York: Bantam.

Szelenyi, I., and B. Martin. 1988. "The Three Waves of New Class Theories." *Theory and Society* 17 (5): 645–667.

Taylor, P. J. 1991. "The Crisis of the Movements: The Enabling State as Quisling." *Antipode* 23 (2): 214–228.

Von Hayek, F. A. 1944. *The Road to Serfdom*. London: Routledge.

van der Walt, L. 2011. The Global History of Labour Radicalisms: The Importance of Anarchism and Revolutionary Syndicalism. Keynote address. Labour beyond State, Nation, Race: Global Labour History as a New Paradigm conference, University of Kassel, Germany, 26 November.

van der Walt, L. 2015. "Self-Managed Class-Struggle Alternatives to Neo-Liberalism, Nationalisation, Elections." *Global Labour Column* 213 (October), 1–2.

van der Walt, L. 2016a. "Alternatives from the Ground Up: Globalisation School Input on Anarchism/ Syndicalism and Working Class Self-Emancipation in Post-Apartheid South Africa." *WorkingUSA: The Journal of Labor and Society* 19 (2): 251–268.

van der Walt, L. 2016b. Revolução Mundial: Para um Balanço dos Impactos, da Organização Popular, das Lutas e da Teoria Anarquista e Sindicalista em Todo o Mundo. *Pensamento e Práticas Insurgentes: Anarquismo e Autonomias nos Levantes e Resistências do Capitalismo no Século XXI*, ed. A. C. Ferreira, 81–118. Alternativa Editora, Niterói, Brazil.

Walton, J., and D. Seddon. 1994. *Free Markets and Food Riots: The Politics of Global Adjustment*. Oxford: Wiley-Blackwell.

Weber, M. 1946. "Class, Status, Party." In *From Max Weber*, edited by C. W. Mills and H. H. Gertz, 180–195. New York: Oxford University Press.

Wright, E. O. 1978. *Class, Crisis and the State*. London: Verso.

Prefiguring democratic revolution? 'Workers' control' and 'workerist' traditions of radical South African labour, 1970–1985

Sian Byrne and Nicole Ulrich

ABSTRACT
During the 1970s and early 1980s, sections of the trade union movement questioned the African National Congress (ANC) and South African Communist Party's (SACP's) narrow vision of freedom, which was based on the capture of the colonial state by a nationalist elite. Located within a distinct political current that prioritised participatory/direct-democracy and egalitarianism, workers were regarded as the locus of transformative power in society, and their organisations were viewed as prefiguring a radically democratic future. This article examines the very different kind of radical anti-colonial engagement offered by 'workers' control' in the 1970s and 'workerism' in the early 1980s that was developed by the Trade Union Advisory Coordinating Council (TUACC) and the Federation of South African Trade Unions (FOSATU), respectively. Keen to draw lessons for the trade union movement today, this article outlines the key characteristics and limits of these traditions that facilitated their decline in the post-apartheid context.

Workers obviously have political interests, but these are best catered for by workers organisations. What they should not allow is to let themselves be controlled by non-worker political parties ... or they will find their interests disregarded and their organisation and power gradually cut away. (Bonner 1979)

South Africa's anti-apartheid movement was more complex than is often acknowledged. From within its ranks emerged distinct political currents that questioned the nationalist and militarist traditions of the African National Congress (ANC) and South African Communist Party (SACP) – operating instead on the basis of mutual aid and self-reliance, bottom-up democratic practice and egalitarian structures in which 'the people', 'workers' or 'the community' were regarded as the locus of transformative power in society, and in which their organisations were viewed as prefiguring a radically democratic future.

From a historical perspective, these traditions – of 'people's power' and 'workers' control' – demonstrate the possibility of very different kinds of anti-colonial and anti-apartheid struggles, ones that embraced a broader vision of political freedom, beyond the franchise and far beyond the simple capture of a colonial or apartheid state by a nationalist party or elite. These were associated with sections of, for example, the United Democratic Front (Neocosmos 1996; Suttner 2004), and the independent trade union movement. A powerful battering ram against apartheid, this radical, democratic form of politics has proven remarkably fragile in the face of the parliamentary political settlement of 1994, quickly giving way to state and party-centred politics, a preoccupation with elections, and political machines based on patronage.

This article critically assesses aspects of this alternative democratic mobilisation, focusing on its expression in the non-racial labour movement in the 1970s and early 1980s. The specific focus is on the 'workers' control' tradition developed by the Trade Union Advisory Coordinating Council (TUACC), formed 1974, and the 'workerist' tradition associated within the Federation of South African Trade Unions (FOSATU), formed in 1979, which incorporated but transcended TUACC's 'workers' control' tradition.

TUACC's 'workers' control' stressed building strong, non-racial, independent, democratic shop-floor-based unions centred on assemblies and shop stewards. The term 'workerist' came to prominence in heated 1980s polemics between FOSATU on one side, and ANC and SACP 'populists' on the other: it was used by opponents to caricature FOSATU positions. Despite this, it *is* possible to discern a distinct 'workerist' tradition. 'Workerism' rejected narrow economism, the SACP's 'two-stage' approach ('national democracy' or majority rule first, socialism later), and the ANC's multi-class nationalism. It wanted strong, democratic, industrial, unions at the point of production, autonomous of political parties. These unions were envisaged as the centre of a larger 'working-class' movement that could challenge both apartheid and capitalism, and lay the basis for a radically democratic South Africa.

Drawing heavily from interviews with key TUACC and FOSATU activists, and primary documents, this article stresses the positive lessons to be drawn for today's oppositional movements, including the practices of accountability, democratic participation, radical workers' education, and non-racial, class-based, anti-racist politics. To serve as a useable labour history, the limitations of 'workers' control' and 'workerism' are also examined. This article will show that the radical promise of both traditions was undermined by tensions between reformist and radical strands, by weaknesses and inconsistencies in tactics, strategy and vision, nebulous long-term thinking, and by ambiguities in analyses.

Exclusion, segregation and dependence

The new unions that emerged in the 1970s and early 1980s had to contend with a legacy of institutional and legal discrimination against black workers, especially black African workers; a large, entrenched, white-dominated union movement fractured along racial lines, centred on the Trade Union Council of South Africa (TUCSA formed 1954); and a history of undemocratic and precarious workplace organisation. The 1924 Industrial Conciliation Act (ICA), the cornerstone of South Africa's modern industrial relations system, had entrenched the rightlessness of African workers (as workers) by excluding 'pass-bearing Natives' from the definition of 'employee' (Lever 1977; Davies 1978). African men were excluded from unions registered with the state under the ICA, the statutory industrial relations machinery, and denied the same rights established for Indian, Coloured and white workers. Unions for African workers were not banned, but employers were not compelled to negotiate with them. Strikes by African workers were effectively illegal.

In 1951 the ICA was brought in line with apartheid policy (Horner 1976). Racially mixed unions, consisting of Coloureds, Indians and whites – possible in terms of the 1924 ICA – were now actively discouraged. An entirely separate industrial relations system was established for African workers, all of whom (including women) were now excluded from being 'employees'. If African workers sought workplace representation, they were pressured to use statutory 'works committees'.[1]

For the most part, workers in South Africa organised along racial lines. Registered unions centred on formations like TUCSA focused on white, and to a lesser extent, Coloured and Indian workers. Some of these rights-bearing registered trade unions set up 'parallel' African unions and (as rights-bearing unions) negotiated on behalf of African workers. However, a strand of more left-wing unions sought to overcome legal and racial barriers by exploiting a legal loophole and admitted African women – who did not carry passes – as full members.

In spite of these barriers, African workers experimented with a range of union forms: these included the revolutionary syndicalist Industrial Workers of Africa in the 1910s; the syndicalist-influenced, but eclectic Industrial and Workers' Commercial Union (ICU) in the 1920s–1930s; unions linked to the Communist Party of South Africa (CPSA, reformed underground as the SACP in 1953) like the Federation of Non-European Trade Unions (FNETU) and the Council of Non-European Trade Unions (CNETU) in the 1920s and 1940s respectively; 'parallel' African unions (discussed above); and the 'political unionism' of the South African Congress of Trade Unions (SACTU) in the 1950s and early 1960s.

Forming unions was not the only way in which workers resisted. They also developed other modes of (often clandestine) organisation, autonomous from managerial control and influence, and based on established social networks and collective modes of engagement that were often profoundly democratic in nature. For instance, in his study of Durban dockworkers, Hemson (1979) noted that during a wildcat strike in 1969, workers refused to elect representatives, confronted management *en masse*, and shouted their demands in unison. This form of collective action did not point to the absence of collective organisation, but was, on the contrary, orchestrated by networks of workers that aimed to 'build up demands of the workers through discussion' and ensure leaders were not separated from other workers (Hemson 1979).

Unions would, on occasion, also draw on these traditions and modes to mobilise workers during strikes. However, these workers' democratic traditions were, at times, at odds with unions' organisational practices. Historically, unions organising African workers struggled to build durable organisational structures with transparent financial controls; many tended to be controlled in a top-down manner by charismatic leaders or bureaucrats, the ICU being a case in point; or were subjected to undue influence by political parties, with SACTU a case in point.

In all cases, African-based unions were engaged in larger struggles around civic, political and social rights. Given the country's history of colonialism, segregation and apartheid, it was difficult to separate political issues from narrower bread-and-butter demands. For instance, the ICU, which claimed over 100,000 members at its height, fought against the 'dipping' of Africans in Durban and the evictions of black tenant farmers (Bonner 1978; Bradford 1988; Van der Walt 2007). In the 1940s, many CNETU militants were committed CPSA members, and the federation sought to push the political boundaries of the time.

This political orientation continued into the 1950s. According to Cherry (1992) and Lambert (1988), SACTU unions could draw strength from their political alliance with the ANC. Yet their structures were often fairly weak, and rank-and-file members struggled to set political agendas outside the ANC (and SACP) framework, in which unions were often viewed as party auxiliaries. The CPSA was banned in 1950, and the ANC in 1960. SACTU remained legal but suffered police harassment and employer antagonism, and increasingly focused on aiding the ANC/SACP guerrilla campaign that started in 1961, rather than union work.

TUACC and FOSATU unions, emerging in the 1970s, drew inspiration from earlier, but were also critical of what they saw as their predecessors' errors. They were determined to end patterns of racial fragmentation, organisational instability, union oligarchy and party control. From the outset, the new unions aimed to establish robust, self-directed, non-racial structures based on participatory/direct-democracy rooted in the shop floor.

A new unionism

After the banning of the ANC, SACTU was at its nadir, and other efforts to organise African workers in the 1960s faltered. The revival of black trade unionism was marked by the 1973 strike-wave that started in Natal. The strikes were triggered by migrant workers who downed tools at the Coronation Brick Company in January. By the end of March, the strikes had spread to Pietermaritzburg and Port Shepstone, and an estimated 160 strikes had taken place at 146 establishments, involving over 60,000 workers (IIE 1974).

Workers struck and protested at the factories, rather than staying at home in the township ghettos, as had been SACTU's style in the 1950s (IIE 1974). Thousands marched in the streets. The collective, and mass character of the strikes – all the more remarkable given the extremely repressive era of high apartheid in which they took place – emboldened workers and gave a glimpse of their potential power. Leading unionist, Alpheus Mthethwa, remembered: 'I had never been involved in such a situation. It was like seeing the beginning of a revolution' (2003). He recalled: 'there was a wind of change ... people in the industry were beginning to say 'No!'".

In this climate, workers flocked to join the General Factory Workers Benefit Fund (GFWBF). This was formed in Durban in June 1972, drawing in SACTU activists, university-based radicals, and registered trade unions, like the Textile Workers Industrial Union (Ulrich 2007). The GFWBF had, from the outset, a commitment to broad-based and democratic participation, with regular meetings held to discuss workers' grievances, and decisions made collectively. David Hemson, who went on to play a prominent role in the workers' movement before being 'banned' from political activity in 1974, recalled:

> Initially the meetings took the form of 'hearings' at which workers told officials more about the labour process ... With time the meetings evolved into a type of executive committee of a trade union as a chairperson was elected with a committee ... the meetings were strongly democratic, with the elected leadership cautiously putting forward their views and attempting to reach consensus. (Hemson 2003)

The GFWBF was not a union, but a benefit society. Members were expected to make regular financial contributions. This meant the GFWBF also provided a source of income for a complaints service, and educational seminars (Maree 1986). Thus, unlike many community movements today, which are dependent on international donors or NGO funds, the GFWBF was able to set its own agenda through democratic meetings, and to raise its own funds from worker-members. Such financial independence was a core factor enabling an emerging practice of 'workers' control'. The GFWBF set up Metal Allied Workers Union (MAWU), the Furniture and Timber Workers Union (FTWU), the Chemical Workers Industrial Union (CWIU) and, later, the Transport and General Workers Union (TGWU). The new unions, the GFWBF and the newly established Institute of Industrial Education (IIE) were united under TUACC.

Several key principles of 'workers' control' of unions were put in place from the outset. First, TUACC was to 'evolve a common and broad based approach to the building of the unions' (TUACC 1974a). It was envisaged as a 'tight federation', which meant that unions developed joint policies and shared resources across the federation (Maree 1986; TUACC 1974a). It is this commitment to developing a common programme that would subsequently allow 'workers' control' to develop as a coherent organisational strategy by the end of the decade. Second, TUACC only accepted affiliates that were 'open' and admitted all workers regardless of race (TUACC 1974b). In so doing, the TUACC rejected apartheid laws, and redefined unionism in South Africa to prefigure a non-racial, common future. Further, TUACC was committed to establishing democratic structures that ensured that worker leaders, elected and held accountable by members on the shop floor, dominated decision-making at every level of the organisation (TUACC 1974b). In theory, democratic structures ensured that elected worker leaders controlled the organisation, and that members controlled the leaders. Un-elected paid 'officials' were deliberately given extremely limited powers, so as to remain subject to the dictates of elected and accountable worker leaders.

For TUACC, 'workers' control' was about acknowledging workers' agency, especially black workers' agency, through mass-based, bottom-up, participatory-democratic unions. It tapped into the growing confidence of workers and the self-organised character of many strikes. 'Workers' control' was about workers taking charge of their own organisations and setting the agenda for their own political and economic liberation. In a context of over three centuries of colonialism and national oppression, this approach was profoundly radical and political. It was explicitly viewed as a means of ensuring that workers had complete possession of the unions, which were not to be subjected to state controls, union oligarchies or party control. The stress on shop-floor democracy, as the centrepiece of unionism at every level, was, in this sense, seen as a key innovation.

The makers of 'workers' control'

TUACC unions were committed, from the start, to building a new type of unionism, but it is important to note that the meaning and functioning of 'workers' control' was forged through everyday struggles. Over the decade, TUACC's affiliates built unions that were both resilient and democratic, and a workers' movement that was increasingly wary of political alliances. In looking at the new unions of the 1970s, like those affiliated to TUACC, the literature has tended to focus on the influence of white, university-educated activists ('white intellectuals') and to debate the extent to which these activists promoted or limited democratic practice (Buhlungu 2006a, 2006b; Maree 2006a, 2006b). However, the literature's emphasis on this small group has, ironically, elided the central role of workers, worker leaders, and black political activists in determining union policy and practice, and in the making of the 'workers' control'.

TUACC unions mainly organised unskilled migrant men (under threat from economic restructuring) and semi-skilled urban-based women in manufacturing (a product of rapid industrialisation) (Webster 1979). Due to the lack of formal schooling among migrant members, there were few worker leaders able to administer unions and challenge management directly. Some had gained organisational experience (through participating in political parties and migrant associations), but most lacked the organisational skills needed for formal organisations and unions (including letter writing, minute taking, etc.) (Hemson, Legassick, and Ulrich 2006). They were also hampered by their inability to communicate fluently in English, the main language of business, and lacked the confidence to negotiate with management (Hemson, Legassick, and Ulrich 2006).

Strikingly, then, it was semi-skilled women who were more educated than their migrant men counterparts, who provided the fledging union movement with a crucial layer of worker leaders. According to Hemson (2003), it was women workers in textiles who spearheaded much of the industrial action and maintained the momentum of the 1973 strikes. The reach of this female leadership was not restricted to National Union of Textile Workers (NUTW), nor to the umbrella structures of TUACC, but extended into predominantly male, migrant unions such as MAWU. It is this leadership that deserves closer attention.

Bottom-up democracy and resilience

TUACC affiliates wanted to establish unions that challenged the power of employers and the state at the workplace, and that dealt directly with employers. They were overtly critical of the apartheid state and of the existing industrial relations framework. Besides the rigid racial policies that shaped society and the workplace, TUACC activists rejected the labour law, specifically designed to undermine non-racial unionisation (Maree 1986; Friedman 1987). However, sustained organisation proved difficult, and TUACC had to devise practical strategies and tactics to survive. In 1973 the NUTW secured a historic recognition agreement with the British multinational, Smith and Nephew (Maree 1986). In essence, Smith and Nephew accepted the NUTW as a legitimate representative of workers, agreeing to negotiate directly with the union at plant level and giving the union factory access to organise workers and conduct shop steward elections. This allowed NUTW to bypass the ICA's statutory industrial machinery and establish union rights directly.

A novel trade union tactic had emerged. Other TUACC affiliates quickly recognised the overwhelming benefits of such agreements, and the demand for employer recognition of unions became a key focus. It was, however, an uphill battle: most employers and managers rejected any meaningful negotiations with African workers. Some were guided by a sense of racial paternalism, even calling on experts to decipher 'Bantu' customs and provide materials and education on 'cultural distance' in the workplace (SALB Comment 1977). Such employers maintained that African workers were too unsophisticated for 'responsible' unionism. They were suspicious of independent worker initiatives and industrial action was usually attributed to outside agitators and subversives.

Victimisation of union members, lockouts, widespread dismissal and the arrest and prosecution of strikers were commonly used by employers against autonomous worker organisation (Maree 1986; Ulrich 2007). The apartheid government also disrupted the day-to-day operation of the open unions, through persistent harassment and repression: for example, pass book raids were held outside union offices to intimidate workers, and a number of unionists were 'banned' in 1974, 1975 and 1976 (Maree 1986; Ulrich 2007).

TUACC unionists feared that the new unions would not survive and decided to rationalise resources by focusing on those companies (mainly foreign-owned) that might be willing to recognise unions with African members (Maree 1986; Ulrich 2007). Building democracy on the shop floor remained central, and core responsibilities were devolved from organisers to shop stewards, who were expected to recruit, organise and collect subscriptions (MAWU 1975).

Extensive programmes of worker education became central: worker education was placed under union control and made to fit union needs (Ulrich 2007). Experienced worker leaders dismissed from employment due to union activity were sometimes absorbed into the TUACC as paid organisers: notable examples included Petrus Mashishi and Moses Mayekeso, and organisers who understood the intricacies of union work became responsible for educating and supporting shop stewards (Bonner 2003).

The focus on shop stewards deepened democracy. For instance, in 1975 the CWIU set up general Saturday forums across unions, called 'locals', to assist with the development of new worker leaders (1975). The TGWU and the NUTW started calling for 'councils' to unite shop stewards across factories (1975). While local organisation deepened, TUACC also moved into other provinces. With the assistance of the Industrial Aid Society (IAS) in Johannesburg, MAWU started to organise beyond Natal, the TUACC heartland, and in June 1978, TUACC was reconstituted as a national body (Ulrich 2007). The TUACC's commitment to national organisation was expressed in the principle 'One Union, One Industry, One Country', and its central role in driving unity talks that eventuated in FOSATU in 1979.

Pitfalls of political alliances

TUACC activists and members were motivated by broader political concerns: some supported 'Congress'; others drew from the New Left. However, they all agreed that the new union movement should avoid the kind of repression that SACTU had endured in the 1960s, when the apartheid state clamped down on the ANC. This led to a distancing from parties, less due to principles than pragmatic concerns with attracting workers regardless of political affiliation, and securing the survival of a still very vulnerable workers movement. It was only later that the TUACC became wary of political alliances with 'populist' and nationalist parties as such. A key focus was creating union structures that could operate openly, which, it was argued, facilitated clear lines of accountability and prevented decisions from being taken undemocratically by individuals or organisations not under the control of workers (Horn 2003).

TUACC distanced itself from banned organisations and sought alliances that could offer black workers some protection (Ulrich 2007). TUACC unions also decided to engage tactically with aspects of the existing industrial relations system and the state. Unionists argued that while the apartheid state was a repressive instrument, it also maintained the rule of law and could be forced to reform (Hemson 2003). Through strong, democratic organisations, they argued, unions could pressure the state to make concessions, without being co-opted. Unions should, they argued, make use of any legal advances to further their own aims. This approach differed significantly with SACTU's: now almost completely reduced to an exile body, sharing offices with the ANC and SACP, it insisted that the South African state was 'fascist' – and that therefore, armed struggle was a better option than open union activity (Hemson 2003). TUACC's 'tactical engagement' with the law included court action and the use of legally-sanctioned workplace works and liaison committees. Its pragmatism, however, also had important costs. For example, union educational courses and seminars served as one of the mechanisms through which broader political issues could be raised (Hemson 2003). Anti-capitalism and the importance of understanding class divisions within South African society emerged as a central theme in worker education (Ulrich 2007). But fear of repression led to a certain amount of political silencing within the workers' movement (Murphy 2003). Any evidence that African workers were being exposed to socialist or communist ideas could and did result in the arrest and 'banning' of unionists. This meant that political issues were not always discussed openly, and that frank debate or a clear programme for transition was hampered. In this way, the concern with survival effectively took priority over careful social analyses – for example, theorising the state – and a clear articulation between different parts of TUACC activities through a coherent approach.

One effect was that the TUACC unions did not always clearly consider the costs that certain tactics could have for a class-struggle, anti-capitalist, anti-apartheid movement. A case in point was TUACC's controversial decision to find allies among 'traditional leaders' and 'homeland' politicians: who formed an integral part of the apartheid state's apparatus. It was hoped that linkages with KwaZulu politicians would provide the fragile workers' movement with an additional layer of protection (Maree 1986; Ulrich 2007). Some within the unions were very critical of this move (Hemson 1979; Cheadle 2006). Nonetheless, the undemocratic and problematic nature of homeland structures was not discussed systematically. Instead an approach was made to KwaZulu leader, Chief Gatsha Buthelezi – at the time seen as one of 'the most outspoken of the homeland leaders in attacking the South African government': he 'warmly accepted the idea' of working with unions, and appointed his ally, Barney Dladla, a popular activist with historic links to SACTU and the Congress movement, to deal with labour (IIE 1974, 97). TUACC was not in any position to dictate the terms of this relationship, and it yielded few positive results.

TUACC was also caught off guard when Buthelezi began urging the unions to join Inkatha, a Zulu-based 'cultural' nationalist movement that was closely allied to his government and uncritical of employers (Maree 1986). As Inkatha stepped up its efforts to woo workers – specifically Zulu migrant workers, a key TUACC constituency – its differences with TUACC were brought into sharp focus. By 1978 TUACC decided not to affiliate with Inkatha, although it would not object to individual workers joining. TUACC in Natal was keen to maintain the autonomy of the new workers' movement, but also to avoid splits along party lines – as would happen if workers were to choose between Inkatha and TUACC. However, an important lesson had been learned: while the unions could enter into alliances with other formations, such relations should 'never ever exercise the slightest degree of influence on the union movement either in respect of its policies or in respect to its activities' (TUACC 1978; Maree 1986, 352).

But TUACC's updated policy effectively left the political affiliations and many of the views of workers unchallenged, and involved steering clear of controversial issues. It could be, and often was, understood to involve allowing a division of labour between unions and parties: in the absence of a clearly defined political programme, it suggested political issues could be left to nationalist organisations like the ANC and Inkatha. TUACC evolving policy on party affiliations, driven by events in Natal, was largely a *defensive* move designed to protect the unions from being swallowed up by a nationalist movement, and did not involve a coherent alternative conception in line with 'workers' control'.

From 'workers' control' to 'workerism'

TUACC unionists in the Transvaal province were meanwhile developing a more sophisticated position than in Natal. They became critical of union alliances with nationalist parties *in principle*, and sought instead to build a 'working class movement' that could fight for socialism *and* national liberation on its own terms (Ulrich 2007). This was a challenge to the notion that there could be a neat distinction between 'economic' and 'political' struggles, or division of labour between unions and parties: as shown below, this idea would become central to FOSATU 'workerism'.

After months of TUACC-led unity talks, FOSATU was inaugurated in April 1979. It was the first truly national federation of predominantly unregistered trade unions to operate openly in South Africa since the late 1960s. It was also one of the largest, growing from 45,000 members at formation to 140,000 in 1985 (Baskin 1991; Friedman 2011), which was substantially larger than SACTU at its height, and comparable to the ICU and CNETU. FOSATU was also national and had affiliates in the major industrial centres in the Natal, Transvaal and Cape provinces. But FOSATU's real significance lay not in its size, but in its innovative ideas and organisational approach. FOSATU drew on TUACC's 'workers' control', its non-racialism, its 'One Union, One Industry, One Country' policy, and its 'tight' federation model ([n.d.] 1982). But it also expanded the Transvaal TUACC's thinking about alliances. FOSATU was more explicitly socialist (even if it was sometimes vague on what this meant), overtly sceptical of nationalism and Marxism–Leninism, and more openly 'political', rejecting the 'false dichotomy drawn between politics and economics in which politics is confined to actions directed towards the state' (Bonner 1983, 35). This set of ideas came to be known as 'workerism'. Of course, not every FOSATU member was a 'workerist', and 'populists' could be found in the federation, but 'workerism' was the main current, with a decisive imprint.

FOSATU, like TUACC, emphasised strong shop-floor-based organisation and strict limits on the power of officials, partly because genuine participatory democracy could ensure FOSATU was more than a 'paper tiger' (Barrett 2010) (since new leaders could emerge from the factories in the case that existing leaders were detained). FOSATU's constitution thus stated, 'the worker member of the unions shall control and determine the objects, direction and policies of the unions' (1982b, 12), and this was achieved through a system of mandate and recall, assemblies, shop stewards and other checks and balances. FOSATU structures at all levels were majority-worker bodies, with wide powers over senior leaders. The General-Secretary was subject to ratification by the membership, via a worker-based Central Committee (CC), which could order his/her suspension. The General-Secretary, President, Vice-President and Treasurers had to 'vacate their seats during their term if they fail[ed] to be members of an affiliate' (FOSATU [n.d.] 1982, 10), which meant they had to be union members accountable to affiliates. National Office Bearers and the CC were in turn accountable to Congresses and subject to oversight by shop steward committees, themselves accountable to workers' assemblies.

This allows us to reasonably assume that FOSATU's 'workerism' was representative of its multiracial, but largely African and Coloured mass base: it was not, as critics claimed, the project of a 'tiny white bureaucratic elite [trying] to dominate the whole federation' ("Mawu and Ummawusa" 1984, 5; see also Buhlungu 2006a, 2006b). It must also be stressed that there were many influential black 'workerists': Daniel Dube, Fred Sauls, Joe Foster, John Gomomo, and Moses Mayekiso (for example). Conversely, white intellectuals, for example the SACP's Jeremy Cronin, were key figures in the 'populist' camp. 'Workerism', then, was a *mass* current in the largely black trade union movement, and the main trend in FOSATU, the biggest black-based union federation of the time (Byrne 2012, 194–207). Attempts to dismiss 'workerism' as 'white' are, at least partly, due to efforts to 'repress uncomfortable truths in order to present a seamless picture favourable to the ANC and SACTU' (Legassick 2008, 241), and the problems posed for nationalist discourse of the reality of a large, anti-nationalist, radical current like 'workerism'.

Like TUACC, FOSATU was anti-apartheid, but its aims and strategy were more consciously political. 'Workers' control' was expanded into a larger project that centred the workers' movement (rather than parties) in the national liberation struggle. Combining anti-capitalism and anti-nationalism, FOSATU was explicitly (if unevenly) critical of the 'populist' 'Congress' and SACP tradition.

Ambitious objectives

In the shorter term, FOSATU sought to build up a strong, resilient and independent labour movement that could fight for tangible improvements for members. For this, winnable demands and measurable day-to-day victories within a few targeted workplaces, conducted in ways that strengthened workplace organisation and rank-and-file participation, were paramount (Webster 1985, 79; Byrne 2012, 192, 220; FOSATU n.d.a).

In the long term, FOSATU was centrally concerned with the national liberation of the oppressed black majority, but eschewed *nationalism* as a strategy. It envisaged a key role for itself in the breakdown and ultimate defeat of the capitalist system (despite the caricatured image the 'workerist' label implies), and in the transition to a post-apartheid order. In systematically building participatory union structures, FOSATU conceived a far more ambitious project of democratising production and the economy and society more generally. It aimed for 'transformation of society as a whole' (Barrett 2010), 'a just and fair society controlled by workers' where wealth would be 'democratically produced and equally distributed' (FOSATU 1982a) and where 'no group of people are going to sit in an office and issue instructions to workers' (SALB 1980, 61). The ANC was described as 'capitalist', its venerated 1955 Freedom Charter criticised as inadequate, and the SACP's two-stage theory dismissed as a 'a waste of time, a waste of energy and a waste of people's blood' (Mayekiso, in Lambert 1985).

'Workers' control' as self-management?

Like TUACC, the term 'workers' control' for FOSATU formally had a narrow meaning, that 'shop stewards should be accountable; that they should be directly elected' (Webster

2010). But for the federation's 'workerists', the idea was expanded to signify a far larger process whereby workers would 'build up' their organisation so that they could 'control the employers' (Baskin 1982, 43), 'wrest arbitrary control from the company's management on the shop floor' (Bonner 1983, 26), and push 'back the frontiers of control' (Webster 1985, 279; FOSATU 1982c, 31; Webster 2010). Understandably, given the dangers, such positions were not always explicitly stated as those of the federation, but they were fairly common.

Further, there were ambitions to extend 'workers' control' beyond production into the 'reproductive' sphere, so that the unions' democratic practices would be 'the basis for democratic organisation both within the areas of production and of social consumption (the community)' (Erwin 1985, 55). FOSATU 'locals' drew in migrant workers (concentrated in hostels), and workers and shop stewards from different factories and FOSATU affiliates in specific areas. They fostered solidarity between workplaces, as well as engagement in black community issues like transport and housing. Locals provided a direct, 'workerist' foothold into black township neighbourhoods, and FOSATU members actively played a key role in positioning locals as linkages between workplace and township struggles, partly through their role in the formation of democratic bottom-up 'civics' (township residents' associations) and 'street committees' (Von Holdt 1987; Jochelson 1990; Dube 2009; Fanaroff 2009; Sauls 2010; Mayekiso 2010). For example, MAWU's Mayekiso was also central to the Alexandra township uprising of 1986 where the local Civic Association briefly replaced state power with 'people's power' (Jochelson 1990).

Considering this, FOSATU's approach clearly envisaged the unions' democratic structures, premised on elections, extensive mandating, recall, etc. as prefiguring a more directly democratic future society. In fact FOSATU leaders explicitly spoke of their strategy as one of 'building tomorrow today' (Erwin 1985, 55–56). An analysis of FOSATU's publications and educational material suggests that the federation's interest in these themes may have been drawn, to some extent, from historical examples of self-managed, prefigurative, popular movements. For example, the 1871 Paris Commune, the German Council Movement of the 1910s and 1920s, and the Russian *soviets* were all studied by FOSATU workers and shop stewards in its Advanced Course (FOSATU 1985a). This course also contained references to the anarchist Bakunin, the left Communist Luxemburg, and the Council Communists Gorter and Pannekoek. Another example is the 1986 *COSATU Workers Diary* (published just after the FOSATU period) that praised the early Russian *soviets* as the 'main organ of workers democracy', and featured the syndicalist Industrial Workers of the World (IWW), with its slogan 'Join the One Big Union', and the 1956 Hungarian Revolution against the Soviet Union, where 'workers councils and all sorts of revolutionary committees' were established. (It should be noted here that although discussion of these movements are mostly found in records of educational material, FOSATU's education by far outstripped that of any of the other unions of its time, both in terms of scope, scale (1982a, 17; SALB 1984) and radicalism. It is therefore probable that discussions about self-management were not restricted to officials, finding expression among workers and shop stewards too.)

According to FOSATU educator Phillip Bonner (2010), the Italian factory council movement of 1920 was also deeply formative: 'something very similar to what we were doing, and … we drew some sustenance from that and some ideas from that' (also in Motala 2010). Alongside this, inspiration and strategic guidance was drawn from the British Shop stewards Movement of the 1910s, 1920s and 1970s (FOSATU 1985b; Webster

2010).[2] Other reference points for self-management were the Spanish Revolution of 1936–1939 (Erwin 2009; Foster 2010) – in which workers and peasants, led by the anarcho-syndicalist movement, seized direct control over rural land, cities, factories, social services and transportation networks; Poland's Solidarność (Solidarity) union, as an effort by the working class to 'establish more democratic worker control over *their* socialist society' (Foster 1982, 7, emphasis original); and the Yugoslavian co-operative model of 'market socialism', which devolved substantial control over production to workers.

Examples of self-management also inspired local action, although sometimes in a more moderate form. For example, MAWU worker leaders at certain BMW satellite factories 'talked about co-determination' based on the German model, where workers would 'participate on a works council' and thus in some production decisions (Adler 2010). FOSATU also (cautiously) admired co-operative movements like Spain's Mondragon (Webster 2010; FOSATU n.d.b), and established some co-operatives of its own (FOSATU 1981) – as did the early National Union of Metalworkers of South Africa (NUMSA) (SAWCO 1987) which was interested in 'factory occupations leading to workers' taking over and running the factories' (Webster 2010).

An important aspect of 'workerism' was that it developed themes that were similar to, and drew upon the concerns of the international New Left (Plaut 1992, 103; see also Saunders 1988; TULEC 2002; Lunn 2010) – a heterogeneous movement through which comparable ideas of workers control and self-management were resuscitated globally. Indeed, many 'workerists' themselves testify to being 'product[s] of May '68 New Left' (Webster 2010). But linking 'workerism' to the eclectic New Left means appreciating that it had multiple influences, ranging from dissident forms of Marxism to existentialism, to various libertarian socialist influences and themes (Sartre, William Morris, Council Communism, early Gramsci, anarchism and syndicalism, etc.). This is in contrast to the view that views workerism narrowly as a 'form of Marxism', even if 'distinctive' (e.g. Nash 1999).

Perhaps one of the most notable links to the New Left was that many 'workerists' claimed a strong Gramscian influence, but emphasised his 'early stuff – the factory councils' (Bonner 2010). Interestingly, many of the historical examples that FOSATU invoked, like the early British Shop Stewards Movement, the German and Italian council movements, and the Spanish Revolution, had substantial anarchist and syndicalist influences (e.g. for Italy, see Levy 1999 and Williams 1975; for syndicalist influence on Council Communist theorists in Germany, Gerber 1988). The 1920 Italian council movement was essentially 'anarcho-syndicalist' (Williams 1975, 193–134), and even some of the core Marxist references for sections of the New Left, like the younger *Lukács* and Gramsci, were influenced by anarchism and syndicalism and/or expressed similar views at certain stages (e.g. Williams 1975; Tucker 1996, 212; Levy 1999; Thorpe 2011).

Therefore, at least some of the libertarian content of 'workerism' – and in the New Left more broadly – can plausibly be said to have roots in the anarchist and syndicalist tradition. This certainly does not mean that 'workerists' self-identified with the anarchist and syndicalist traditions, because they did not; nor that 'workerism' was a type of syndicalism, for it was not. Some 'workerists' did detect 'a strong sort of syndicalist strand' in FOSATU's 'deep mistrust of party politics' and the 'idea that the trade union is a political expression in itself' (interviews with Webster 2010; Horn 2010; Bonner 2010),[3] but anarchist and syndicalist influences were indirect, often unrecognised. They were certainly not the *only* influences, or even necessarily the strongest influences on 'workerism'.

Much like the New Left, 'workerism' was eclectic, and, as will be noted below, marked by unresolved tensions and ambiguities. Importantly, the range of influences discussed above should not be taken to mean that South African 'workerism' was not something unique or innovative: its novelty *was* something deeply felt by its proponents, who stressed that they 'were indigenous and developing this stuff on [their] own' (Adler 2010; Bonner 2010).

Anti-nationalist national liberation

'Workerism' operated in the very distinct context of apartheid South Africa – where the national question was a central feature of social contradictions and required an urgent answer and response – forcing FOSATU's 'workerists' to develop their own thinking on this problem. This is important to declare because of the frequent assertion that 'worker-ists" ignored race and were unconcerned with issues of national liberation (e.g. Isizwe 1986; SACP 2006; Pillay 2008),[4] or counter-posed national liberation and class struggle (e.g. Baskin 1991). This caricature usually stems from a conflation of national liberation with *nationalism*, and the inability (or refusal?) to envisage the possibility of national liber-ation without nationalism – on the basis of a working class or class-struggle programme. But national liberation via class (as opposed to nationalist) struggle was, in fact, the crux of the 'workerists' embryonic solution. 'Workerists' were sceptical of nationalism largely because it was interpreted as 'petit bourgeois politics' – 'not necessarily for worker inter-ests' (Dube 2009; Mayekiso 2010). This position was also historically grounded, given the 'failures of African nationalism in the post-colonial context' and the way unions have been 'sort of muzzled' by nationalist and 'populist' liberation leaders and regimes (Bonner 2010). The ANC was thus viewed with a considerable amount of scepticism by association (FOSATU 1982c), and the example of the suppression of independent unions by national-ists in neighbouring, post-Independence, Zimbabwe was repeatedly noted.

FOSATU rejected all structured alliances with political parties. This was an archetypal 'workerist' attitude, and it was formally enshrined in FOSATU documents (e.g. 1982). FOSATU realised that outwardly associating with banned socialist or 'worker' parties was perilous, but there were issues at play beyond this pragmatic consideration. 'Workerists' argued that multi-class parties would lead to unions being 'hijacked by elements who will have no option but to turn against their worker supporters' once in power (FOSATU 1982c). Political parties threatened to turn the union movement into a 'transmission belt' for a party agenda, while also alienating large sections of the working class (Erwin 2009; FOSATU n.d.a, 6). Based on this analysis, 'workerists' thought in terms of combining anti-nationalism and anti-capitalism as the basis of the national liberation struggle – to be fought by a united, non-racial working class (as opposed to a multi-class nationalist/ popular front) centred on autonomous unions, and infused with socialist aspirations. The building up of organs of worker power in the key industrial sectors was identified as the key to overcoming both apartheid and capitalism 'with one movement' (Erwin 2009).

Counter-culture, popular education and organic intellectuals

Linked to this, FOSATU prioritised worker education. In the short term, this equipped shop stewards and worker leaders with skills they needed to be effective. However, FOSATU provided a wider education, rooted in a broadly socialist (but anti-Soviet) perspective. This could facilitate the development of a 'working class politics' implanted in what FOSATU called a 'working class movement'[5] that went beyond the unions, influencing workers in the material, political, ideological and cultural aspects of their lives (1982c; Webster 1985).

There were three main characteristics to this, all part of the project of expanding the frontiers of control, inside and outside of the workplace (Byrne 2012). First, FOSATU built towards the formation of a counter-culture to challenge the imposed (ruling class) culture pervasive in society, often transmitted through the bourgeois media. This entailed the construction of a specifically *working class* identity – replete with its own history, newspapers, heroes, songs, choirs, cultural days, festivals, etc. Second, FOSATU conducted extensive popular education designed to counter the state schooling system, which was structured to perpetuate class and race domination and stamp out all creative and critical faculties, especially of African workers (FOSATU Worker News 1985; FOSATU n.d.c). Third, FOSATU sought to foster the development of 'organic intellectuals', a politically astute and accountable cadre of worker leaders as the fulcrum of this new worker knowledge and counter-culture. This was about 'winning the kind of ideology/consciousness battle among the shop steward leadership, in the hope, with the desire that this would spread out, and that they in turn would influence or become key players or influences in the community' (Bonner 2010).

Ambiguities and weaknesses in the 'workerist' project

By the mid-1980s, FOSATU was the strongest and most militant union movement in the country, and the leading force in the unity talks that led to the formation of the even larger Congress of South African Trade Unions (COSATU) in 1985. But 'workerism' was eventually displaced from its central position, and COSATU aligned to the ANC and SACP. By the early 1990s, many former 'workerists' were drawn into the parties, and unions once centrally identified with 'workerism', like CWIU and MAWU/NUMSA were focusing their attention on developing social democratic policies for an incoming ANC government.

This eclipse needs to be seen as partly the result of weaknesses in 'workerism' itself. The 'workerists' often did not develop a clear strategy linking current strategy and tactics to longer term 'transformation'. Future aspiration and the present mobilisation were left disconnected: if 'workers' control' was designed to anticipate 'generalised worker power' (Bonner 2010), how would the one actually become the other? What would a future of 'generalised worker power' actually involve, even schematically? It was always somewhat nebulous. 'Workerism' also suffered from problems of theoretical reflection and strategic coherence, and was weak on formulating clear alternatives and a coherent strategy and programme. Partly this related to isolation, the lack of access to theoretical materials and, to some extent, a reluctance to have open discussions, given the 'treasonable nature' (Barrett 2010) of 'workerist' aspirations. But there was also a conscious subordination of long-term thinking and strategising to short-term concerns: 'we just didn't spend a lot of our time trying to think through things that we saw being not practical at that time' (Fanaroff 2009). Serious reflection and rigorous discussion on larger issues were sometimes dismissed as 'armchair' politics (Fanaroff 2009).

Like TUACC, FOSATU tended to be very pragmatic and short-termist, downplaying theory as 'esoteric' (Fanaroff 2009; Webster 2010), leading to a 'loose and fuzzy' theoretical basis (Bonner 2010). A clear strategy and programme was exchanged for 'a bit of a blind faith that as long as you – as long as we all – sort of believed in the transformation at some point, that we would find the tools when the moment arrived' (Barrett 2010). There were ambiguities and tensions in 'workerist' thinking, which contributed to many 'workerists'' capitulation to the ANC and SACP: 'we could see no effective means of transferring factory power into seizure of state power' (Erwin interview 2009).

Between prefiguration and reformism

This ambiguity was carried into and expressed in FOSATU strategy, which vacillated between two conflicting tendencies. The first was quasi-syndicalist in character, stressing prefiguration, counter-power, counter-culture, and an ambitious project of self-management within and beyond production (Byrne 2012). This project of 'building tomorrow today' had extremely radical implications, and promoted a vision of a profoundly democratic, socialist future. But running alongside this was a second strand of thinking, more social democratic in orientation, which followed in the wake of TUACC's pragmatism, 'tactical engagement' and use of the courts. Rather than building *outside* and *against* the state in pursuit of new society, it envisaged social change occurring from *within* the institutions of the state, through *participation* and *engagement* in these structures (Byrne 2012). Its assumptions were that the state could be reformed, and that a gradual series of ongoing reforms within and through the capitalist state could cumulatively change society, without a revolution.

'Workerism' contained, in other words, two somewhat different tendencies in its strategy, a quasi-syndicalist approach (similar to the early Gramsci) and a more social democratic one (similar to the Eurocommunist reading of the later Gramsci – see Showstack Sassoon 1988). The latter approach, in the words of Fine (1982, 55), involved ideas that

the apartheid state, like any capitalist state' was 'not a monolithic entity and purely functional instrument of capital, but a force which workers can affect by their struggles and one that is itself torn by the contradictions of the labour-capital relation.

Therefore, 'dominated classes and groups may well be able' to turn concessions 'to their advantage, exploiting the contradiction in which the state is trapped', and 'transform the character of these official institutions' (Innes 1982, 62). It is difficult to see how a growing involvement of this sort could truly be reconciled with a long-run project of workers' control of unions, the economy and the larger society.

Conclusion: limitations and erosion

TUACC and FOSATU created a new type of unionism that identified workers and unions as the force to lead the challenge against apartheid and, in so doing, create an alternative, non-racial, deeply democratic, indeed socialist, future. They also managed to survive and grow in the repressive 1970s and early 1980s, no small achievement, and laid the basis for COSATU, which had an incredible 462,359 members at its launch (Macun and Frost 1994).

COSATU retained most of the core TUACC and FOSATU principles – industrial unionism, a 'tight' federation, non-racialism and workers' control of the unions – but it was initially fiercely contested between 'workerists' (centred on unions like MAWU/NUMSA) and 'populists' (centred on the National Union of Mineworkers (NUM), which were never part of FOSATU). The democratic practices and radical vision of FOSATU proved weaker than might have been expected. By the 1990s, 'workerism' as a distinct current had largely disappeared: COSATU formally allied with the ANC and SACP soon after their unbanning in 1990, and remains in this alliance, more than two decades later, despite repeatedly expressing its frustration with pro-capitalist ANC policies.

COSATU's close links to the ANC and SACP have borne out many of the 'workerists' warnings: the parties have intervened heavily in unions' affairs and many unions have become increasingly bureaucratised and distant from their worker base; the ANC has paid little heed to COSATU's policy proposals, embracing neo-liberalism, but has made use of COSATU resources at election time.

This situation has led to the fracturing of COSATU itself. NUM has suffered a series of splits, and lost majority status on the platinum mines, playing only a limited role in the mass strikes of the early 2010s. In August 2012, when police killed 44 striking miners and injured 78 at Marikana, the NUM presented the killings as a 'tragedy' rather than a 'massacre', and its leadership did not distance itself from dangerous ANC and SACP claims that rival unions were 'vigilantes' and counter-revolutionaries (e.g. Mapaila 2012). Marikana was the immediate trigger for NUMSA deciding to withdraw support from the ANC and SACP in 2013, although the massacre brought to a head the union's growing disenchantment. Following this decision, NUMSA was ousted from COSATU in 2015, costing the federation its largest manufacturing union.

We suggest that the weaknesses of workers' control and 'workerism' were due to the ambiguities and tensions in strategy and theory, exemplified by the lack of long-term perspectives and a programme. This led to key problems. For example, the tendency within FOSATU to a reformist reading of the state led to tactics that eroded genuine workers' control, a core principle. The notion, held by some, that the state was a site of class struggle led to an ongoing use of the courts, as well as (from 1979) the statutory industrial relations structures set up by the ICA. But these were institutions in which worker power and self-activity played very little role, with workers' initiative ceded to lawyers and negotiators, and the rules of engagement set by the state. The politics of using state institutions led, directly, to the politics of seeking to shape the state through the alliance with the ANC and SACP that has dominated COSATU since the 1990s. Within this context, a politics that identified ordinary workers or people as agents of change, quickly gave way to electoral and party politics after the first democratic election.

Notes

1. Works committees were extremely limited, but were the only recognised structures that included representatives selected by African workers.
2. Gramsci (1968, 30) described them as 'roughly equivalent to the shop steward committees set up in Britain during the First World War'.
3. Pat Horn remarked (retrospectively), that hearing about anarcho-syndicalism years later in Brazil 'reminded me of our syndicalism of the early days', but that it was 'regarded as a circumstantial thing', and that she 'never read any syndicalist authors' (Horn interview 2010).

4. For example, Pillay (2006, 171) suggests that 'populists' prioritised anti-apartheid struggle (ignoring capitalism), while 'workerists' prioritised anti-capitalist struggle (ignoring apartheid).

5. Joe Foster, FOSATU General-Secretary, speculated that this could comprise 'trade unions, co-ops, political parties and newspapers' (1982c, 6).

Disclosure statement

No potential conflict of interest was reported by the authors.

References

Abbreviations:
Historical Papers, University of the Witwatersrand, Johannesburg: HP.
South African Labour Bulletin: SALB.
Adler, Taffy. 2010. Interview by Sian Byrne, Johannesburg.
Barrett, Jane. 2010. Interview by Sian Byrne, Johannesburg.
Baskin, Jeremy. 1982. "Growth of a New Worker Organ – The Germiston Shop Stewards Council." *South African Labour Bulletin* 7 (8): 42–53.
Baskin, Jeremy. 1991. *Striking Back: A History of COSATU.* Johannesburg: Ravan.
Bonner, Philip. 1978. The Decline and Fall of the ICU: A Case of Self-destruction? *SALB* 1 (6&7): 38–43.
Bonner, Philip. 1979. Historical Papers (here after HP) AH1999: C1.8.2.
Bonner, Philip. 1983. Independent Trade Unions since Wiehahn? *SALB* 8 (4): 16–36.
Bonner, Chris. 2003. Interview by Nicole Ulrich, Johannesburg.
Bonner, Philip. 2010. Interview by Sian Byrne, Johannesburg.
Bradford, H. 1988. *A Taste of Freedom: The ICU in Rural South Africa, 1924–1930.* Johannesburg: Ravan.
Buhlungu, Sakhela. 2006a. "Rebels Without a Cause of Their Own? The Contradictory Class Location of White Officials in Black Unions in South Africa, 1973–1994." *Current Sociology* 54 (3): 427–451.
Buhlungu, Sakhela. 2006b. "Whose Cause and Whose History? A Response to Maree." *Current Sociology* 54 (3): 469–471.
Byrne, Sian. 2012. "'Building Tomorrow Today': A Re-examination of the Character of the Controversial 'Workerist' Tendency Associated with the Federation of South African Trade Unions (FOSATU) in South Africa, 1979–1985." Masters diss., University of the Witwatersrand.
Cheadle, Halton. 2006. Interview by Nicole Ulrich, Johannesburg.

Cherry, Janet. 1992. "The Making of an African Working Class, Port Elizabeth 1925–1963." Masters diss., University of Cape Town.

CWIU. 1975. HP: AH 1999: B4.4.

Davies, Rob. 1978. "The Class Character of South Africa's Industrial Conciliation Legislation." In *Essays in Southern African Labour History*, edited by Eddie Webster, 69–81. Johannesburg: Ravan Press.

Dube, Daniel. 2009. Interview by Sian Byrne, Port Elizabeth.

Erwin, Alec. 1985. "The Question of Unity in the Struggle." *SALB* 11 (1): 51–70.

Erwin, Alec. 2009. Interview by Sian Byrne, Cape Town.

Fanaroff, Bernie. 2009. Interview by Sian Byrne, Johannesburg.

Fine, Bob. 1982. "Trade Unions and the State Once More: A Reply to Our Critics." *SALB* 8 (1): 47–58.

FOSATU. (n.d.) 1982. HP: AH 1999: C1.8.

FOSATU. n.d.a. HP: AH 1999, C1.7.3.16.3.

FOSATU. n.d.b. HP: AH 1999. C1.7.3.16.11.

FOSATU. n.d.c. HP: AH 1999, C1.7.3.16.1.11.

FOSATU. 1981. HP: AH 1999. C1.7.1.1.3.

FOSATU. 1982a. HP: AH 2065 D4.2.

FOSATU. 1982b. HP: AH 1999, C.1.8.2.

FOSATU. 1982c. HP: AH 1999. C1.7.3.16.3.10.

FOSATU. 1985a. HP: AH 1999. C1.7.3.17.1.

FOSATU. 1985b. HP: AH 1999. C1.7.3.17.6.

FOSATU Workers News. 1985. The Making of the Working Class, Part 15: SACTU and the Congress Alliance. October. HP: AH 1999. C1.7.3.16.1.3.

Foster, Joe. 2010. Interview by Sian Byrne, Cape Town.

Foster, Joe. 1982. "The Workers' Struggle — Where Does FOSATU Stand?" *Review Of African Political Economy* 9 (24): 99–114.

Friedman, Steven. 1987. *Building Tomorrow: African Workers in Trade Unions 1970–1984*. Johannesburg: Ravan.

Friedman, Michelle. 2011. *'The Future is in the Hands of the Workers': A History of FOSATU*. Johannesburg: Mutloatse Arts Heritage Trust.

Gerber, John. 1988. "From Left Radicalism to Council Communism: Anton Pannekoek and German Revolutionary Marxism." *Journal of Contemporary History* 23: 169–189.

Gramsci, Antonio. 1968. "Soviets in Italy." *New Left Review* I (51): 28–58.

Hemson, Dave. 1979. "Class Consciousness and Migrant Workers: Dockworkers in Durban." PhD diss., University of Warwick.

Hemson, Dave. 2003. Interview by Nicole Ulrich, Durban.

Hemson, Dave, Martin Legassick, and Nicole Ulrich. 2006. "White Activists and the Revival of the Workers' Movement." In *Road to Democracy in South Africa, Volume 2, 1970–1980*, edited by Sifiso Ndlovu, 187–241. South African Democracy Education Trust (SADET). Pretoria: UNISA Press.

Horn, Pat. 2003. Interview by Nicole Ulrich, Durban.

Horn, Pat. 2010. Telephone interview by Sian Byrne, Johannesburg.

Horner, D. 1976. "African Labour Representation and the Draft Bill to Amend the Bantu Labour Relations Regulation Act (No. 48 of 1953)." *SALB* 2 (9&10): 11–39.

IIE (Institute for Industrial Education). 1974. *The Durban Strikes 1973*. Durban: Ravan.

Innes, D. 1982. "Trade Unions and the Challenge to State Power." *SALB* 8 (2): 60–71.

Isizwe. 1986. "Errors of 'Workerism'." *SALB* 12 (3): 51–63.

Jochelson, Karen. 1990. "Reform, Repression and Resistance in South Africa: A Case Study of Alexandra Township, 1979–1989." *Journal of Southern African Studies* 16 (1): 1–32.

Lambert, N. 1985. "Towards a Workers' Party: Interview with Moses Mayekiso." *Socialist Worker Review* 80: 18–20.

Lambert, Rob. 1988. "Political Unionism in South Africa: The South African Congress of Trade Unions, 1955–1965." PhD diss., University of the Witwatersrand.

Legassick, Martin. 2008. "Debating the Revival of the Workers' Movement in the 1970s: The South African Democracy Education Trust and Post-apartheid Patriotic History." *Kronos* 34: 240–266.

Lever, Jeff. 1977. "Capital and Labour in South Africa: The Passage of the Industrial Conciliation Act, 1924." *SALB* 3 (10): 5–31.

Levy, Carl. 1999. *Gramsci and the Anarchists.* Oxford, NY: Berg.

Lunn, Helen. 2010. "'Hippies, Radicals and the Sounds of Silence': Cultural Dialectics at Two South African Universities 1966–1976." PhD diss., University of KwaZulu-Natal.

Macun, Ian, and Andrew Frost. 1994. "Living Like There's No Tomorrow: Trade Union Growth in South Africa, 1979–1991." *Social Dynamics* 20 (2): 67–90.

Mapaila, Solly. 2012. "Marikana: A Story That Isn't Being Told." *PoliticsWeb*, September 6.

Maree, Johann. 1986. "An Analysis of the Independent Trade Unions in South Africa in the 1970s." PhD diss., University of Cape Town.

Maree, Johann. 2006a. "Rebels with Causes: White Officials in Black Unions in South Africa, 1973–94: A Response to Sakhela Buhlungu." *Current Sociology* 54 (3): 453–467.

Maree, Johann. 2006b. "Similarities and Differences Between Rebels with and Without a Cause." *Current Sociology* 54 (3): 473–475.

MAWU. 1975. HP: AH 1999: B4.4.

Obery, Ingrid and Mark Swilling. 1984. "Mawu and Ummawusa: Fight for the Factories." *Work in Progress* 33: 4–12.

Mayekiso, Moses. 2010. Interview by Sian Byrne, Johannesburg.

Motala, Enver. 2010. Interview by Sian Byrne, Johannesburg.

Mthethwa, Alpheus. 2003. Interview by Nicole Ulrich, Durban.

Murphy, M. 2003. Interview by Nicole Ulrich, Johannesburg.

Nash, Andrew. 1999. "The Moment of Western Marxism in South Africa." *Comparative Studies of South Asia, Africa and the Middle East* 19 (1): 66–81.

Neocosmos, Michael. 1996. "From People's Politics to State Politics: Aspects of National Liberation in South Africa, 1984–1994." *Politeia* 15: 73–119.

NUTW. 1975. HP: AH 1999: B4.4.

Pillay, Devan. 2006. "Cosatu, Alliances and Working Class Politics." In *Trade Unions and Democracy: Cosatu Workers' Political Attitudes in South Africa*, edited by Sakhela Buhlungu, 167–198. Cape Town: HSRC Press.

Pillay, Devan. 2008. "Cosatu, the SACP and the ANC in Post-Polokwane: Looking Left but Does it Feel Right?" *Labour, Capital and Society* 41 (2): 4–37.

Plaut, Martin. 1992. "Debates in a Shark Tank: The Politics of South Africa's Non-racial Trade Unions." *African Affairs* 91 (364): 389–404.

SACP (South African Communist Party). 2006. "Class, National and Gender Struggle in South Africa: The Historical Relationship between the ANC and the SACP." *Bua Komanisi* 5 (1): 3–18.

SALB (South African Labour Bulletin). 1977. "Comment. A Managerial Choice." *SALB* 3 (8): 1–5.

SALB (South African Labour Bulletin). 1980. "Interview with Freddie Sauls: Secretary of Numarwosa." *SALB* 2 (3): 53–66.

SALB (South African Labour Bulletin). 1984. "Trade Union Education and Training Programmes." *SALB* 9 (8): 27–32.

Sauls, Fred. 2010. Interview by Sian Byrne, Port Elizabeth.

Saunders, Christopher. 1988. *The Making of the South African Past: Major Historians on Race and Class.* Cape Town: David Philip.

SAWCO (Sarmcol Workers Co-Operative). 1987. "Sarmcol Strikers' Co-operative: Worker Controlled Production." *Work in Progress* 46: 13–15.

Showstack Sassoon, A. 1988. "The Gramsci Boom Continues?" *History Workshop Journal* 26 (1): 213–214.

Suttner, Raymond. 2004. "The UDF Period and Its Meaning for Contemporary South Africa." *Journal of Southern African Studies* 30 (3): 691–702.

Thorpe, Wayne. 2011. "Challenging the Cultural Legitimation of War: International Syndicalists in Europe 1914–18." *Socialist History* 37: 23–46.

TUACC. 1974a. HP: AH1999. B4.1.

TUACC. 1974b. HP: AH1999. B1.

TUACC. 1978. HP: AH 1999: B 5.1.5.

Tucker, Kenneth H. 1996. *French Revolutionary Syndicalism and the Public Sphere.* New York: Cambridge University Press.

TULEC (Trade Union Library and Education Centre). 2002. *The Formative Years of the Independent Labour Movement: 1966–1979.* Trade Union General Box, Labour History Workshop, February 18–19th.

Ulrich, Nicole. 2007. "Only the Workers Can Free the Workers: The Origins of the Workers' Control Tradition and the Trade Union Advisory Coordinating Committee, 1970–1979." MA diss., University of the Witwatersrand.

Van der Walt, Lucien. 2007. "Anarchism and Syndicalism in South Africa 1904–1921: Rethinking the History of Labour and the Left." PhD Diss., University of the Witwatersrand.

Von Holdt, Karl. 1987. *Trade Unions, Community Organisations and Politics: A Local Case Study on the East Rand.* Sociology of Work Institute Research Report 3.

Webster, Eddie. 1979. "A Profile of Unregistered Union Members in Durban." *SALB* 4 (8): 43–74.

Webster, Eddie. 1985. *Cast in a Racial Mould: Labour Process and Trade Unionism in the Foundries.* Johannesburg: Ravan Press.

Webster, Eddie. 2010. Interview by Sian Byrne, Johannesburg.

Williams, Gwyn A. 1975. *A Proletarian Order: Antonio Gramsci, the Factory Councils and the Origins of Italian Communism, 1911–1921.* London: Pluto.

Broadening conceptions of democracy and citizenship: the subaltern histories of rural resistance in Mpondoland and Marikana

Camalita Naicker and Sarah Bruchhausen

ABSTRACT

The purpose of this article is to broaden perspectives on citizenship and democracy in post-apartheid South Africa. The article focuses on two spaces within South Africa, which have specific significance for both land and labour questions in South Africa and where we have focused our research: Mpondoland in the Eastern Cape and Nkaneng Shack Settlement in Marikana. The links that can be made between the recent Marikana/Lonmin Strikes and the earlier Mpondo Revolts reveal a subaltern sphere of politics informed by older modes of political organisation that challenge dominant institutions like civil society and traditional authorities. The article demonstrates that South Africa's land and agrarian questions must, of necessity, be linked to broader struggles for justice, dignity and humanity that require structural socio-economic and political change, in line with how people practise politics.

The purpose of this article is to attempt to broaden perspectives on democracy and citizenship with reference to current and historical examples of subaltern politics in South Africa. It follows what Lefebvre called a 'regressive-progressive-method' which, as Hart (2013, 19) expressed so succinctly,

> entails starting with a description of the present and its contradictions; then moving to an explanation of the historical production of the present, and from there to a moment of opening to the future – and to the possibilities present in current contradictions.

The paper focuses on two spaces within South Africa, which have specific significance for both land and labour questions in South Africa and where we have focused our research: Mpondoland in the Eastern Cape and Nkaneng Shack Settlement in Marikana, North West Province. Both of these places are situated in the former colonial–apartheid Bantustans and are still governed under the Council of Traditional Leaders Act, No. 10 of 1997 and the Traditional Leadership and Governance Framework Amendment Act, No. 41 of 2003. This connection is not an arbitrary one either. Of the 45 people who lost their lives at Marikana, during the strikes of August 2012, 31 were from the Eastern Cape

Province in South Africa and the majority were from Mpondoland in the Transkei (Alexander et al. 2012, 196).

The Eastern Cape, and Mpondoland specifically, also has a special significance in the history of mineworkers in South Africa as a primary source of cheap labour ever since the opening of gold mines on the Witwatersrand in the late 1800s. Rock-drilling, the most dangerous and labour-intensive part of mining minerals like gold (and now platinum), has been a category of work historically occupied by men coming from Mpondoland. Moodie and Ndatshe (1994) have explored this relationship and the kinship ties between migrant labourers who came to the mines from Mpondoland in their book, *Going for Gold*. Today, however, the mining economy has moved from the urban centre of the former Witwatersrand, now Gauteng Province, into former Bantustans in the North West and Limpopo provinces.

The discovery of new minerals in these provinces has meant that mining companies have had to enter into negotiations with traditional leaders for mining rights on what is still considered traditional land under the South African constitution. In Marikana, the Bapo ba Mogale Traditional Community, also now known as Bapo ba Mogale Investments, is a multimillion rand trust which used to receive approximately R20 Million ($1,423,594) a year from Lonmin Platinum (Lonplats) in direct cash transfers (Grieve 2014). In 2014, an agreement was reached stating that the Bapo ba Mogale Traditional Authority would cease to receive these royalties in 2019 and would instead be paid a large lump sum by Lonplats in order to buy shares in the mining company, thereby fulfilling their Black Economic Empowerment (BEE) requirements (Grieve 2014). While the Bapo ba Mogale Trust is committed to enriching members of its Tswana-speaking 'community', it continues to endorse the migrant labour system linking Mpondoland to the Lonmin mines.

As the example of migrant workers and other people of the Nkaneng Shack Settlement in Marikana will illuminate, the institution of traditional authorities, as well as the narrowly conceived ethnic and racialised basis upon which it still functions, remains central to the politics of land and citizenship in South Africa. More importantly, we argue that the ways in which the striking men on the mountain who refused trade union representation, mobilised around and in many instances rejected this form of elite politics during the Marikana/Lonmin strikes, are reminiscent of older modes of political organisation and can be linked to the popular forms of resistance used during the Mpondo Revolt of 1959–1961.

When taken seriously, both these moments of resistance reveal a political sphere where, when ordinary people reject forms of top-down representation and engage in praxes of participatory democracy, the meaning of citizenship and belonging in post-apartheid South Africa is deepened. This living subaltern politics and its related histories of resistance have been almost completely excluded within contemporary attempts to rethink South Africa's land and citizenship questions. This has been particularly prevalent in discussions about the politics of land and governance in South Africa's former Bantustans. Analysing the politics of land in the former Bantustans necessarily requires a critical interrogation of the system of traditional authorities which, more than 20 years since the collapse of apartheid, continue to be a central element in geographically fixing black people in rural areas under forms of land tenure which are secured solely by customary law (Myers 2008, 99).

In his book, *Indirect Rule in South Africa: Tradition, Modernity, and the Costuming of Political Power*, Myers (2008) provides an analysis of the institution of traditional authorities and the role of chiefs in the post-apartheid era. What is most interesting about the text is that it reveals the dominant tendency in South African scholarship and policy-making circles to think about traditional authorities from within the narrow elite conceptual framework of nationalist and state histories – a tendency to which Myers (2008) himself is not entirely impartial.

In its failure to take seriously the living history of subaltern politics in South Africa, such an elite perspective is incapable of thinking beyond the silences of the Constitution in relation to this blatantly autocratic system of governance in former Bantustans, and thus is equally unable to see the potential value of alternative conceptions and practices concerning the politics of land, citizenship, democracy and belonging, which have been, and continue to be, practised by ordinary people outside of the sphere of state subjectivities.

This article argues therefore that when thinking through land-related questions in South Africa, it becomes increasingly obvious that state initiatives like land restitution programmes and traditional authorities are inadequate as a means of redistributing land in South Africa, as they are currently conceived and structured on the basis of narrow conceptions of citizenship and civil society. From this perspective, it is clear that how, when and where people gain access to land cannot be divorced from the politics and political organisation that play out in particular contexts, what we have called, following the Indian Subalternist School of thought, a 'subaltern sphere of politics'; and these alternative forms of politics and decision-making practices must be included in any conception of a 'new' and truly 'post-colonial' nation.

A note on theory

In using Subaltern Studies, we follow historian Ranajit Guha, whose focus was peasant insurgency in colonial India in the mid- to late-1800s. For Guha, there was a distinct split in the domain of politics, in which the elite politics of the official domain made invisible the 'unofficial' subaltern domain of politics, and where '[c]entral to subaltern mobilisations was "a notion of resistance to elite domination". The experience of exploitation and labour endowed this politics with many idioms, norms and values which put it in a category apart from elite politics' (Chakrabarty 2000, 8). This formulation is very useful for the South African experience as Guha's focus on rural peasant insurgency allows us to think about the elements of the rural, in both the present and the past, as outside of the domain of national government institutions – and yet still political. By illuminating this sphere of peasant activity, he opens up the debate about what counts as post-European political thought. By rejecting what both liberal and Marxist historians have often regarded as pre-political or backward forms of consciousness, Guha, as Chakrabarty (2000, 9) discusses, 'was prepared to suggest that the nature of collective action against exploitation in colonial India was such that it effectively stretched the imaginary boundaries of the category "political" far beyond the territories assigned to it in European political thought'.

We argue, as a point of departure, that understanding the history of traditional authorities, their inseparable relationship to the politics of land and citizenship, as well as popular responses to them by rural dwellers and migrant workers (both during and since the period of colonial-cum-apartheid rule) are all of critical importance for recognising how this system of governance has worked and continues to work to disadvantage and exclude some based on their 'ethnicity' and how this, in turn, functions to circumscribe citizenship and geographically fix people.

Mamdani's emphasis on space and origin as the key terms of colonial classification is also useful in understanding how 'the (colonial) state portrayed the native as the product of geography rather than history' (2013, 47). This 'tribalisation' serves to crystallise tradition and culture, in a way that 'tribesmen' are still seen and regarded as outside the 'modern'.

Land questions and ethnicity in Nkaneng, Marikana

An illustration of how traditional authorities and their associated system of land tenure function, still, to create barriers to land, citizenship and access to the nation, can be found in the Nkaneng Shack Settlement in Marikana. 'Nkaneng' is named by people who live there, and is a Sesotho word (whose equivalent in isiXhosa is 'Inkanini') described by people who live there as 'by force' or 'forceful determination'. Nkaneng symbolises the ongoing struggle for land and services; people say that they are literally there 'by force' because no one seems to care about them and everything is a struggle. In this regard, Chinguno (2013, 12) notes that it represents the intersection between ethnicity and settlement patterns. Nkaneng is home to mostly isiXhosa-speaking people from the Eastern Cape and a few other provinces in South Africa, as well as other migrant labourers from Lesotho and Mozambique. This has created tension between people who live in the shack settlement and those who are able to live in Reconstruction and Development Programme (RDP) houses and receive services based on their ethnicity, because the land here is owned by the Tswana Chief Bob Edward Bapo ba Mogale of the Batswana Traditional Authority.

Before 1994, most mineworkers lived in single-sex hostels: there were no women and children on the mines, and the mining companies did not offer a living-out allowance. From the late 1980s, when mining companies knew that apartheid was ending, they began to restructure the ethnically segregated hostels and to offer money to workers to 'live-out'. However, they did not provide any alternative housing and, as a result, there was a major growth of shack settlements around the platinum belt (Hartford 2012). In 2010, Lonmin estimated that '50% of the population who lived within a 15 km radius from its mining operations lived in informal dwellings and lacked access to basic services' (Chinguno 2013, 9).

Today, Nkaneng is home to a variety of people, directly and indirectly linked to the mining economy. Most people in Nkaneng live in shacks without access to water or electricity, and many of them have to buy water from those with access to taps. There are no roads, which makes access to transportation extremely difficult. This became a painful issue during the strikes at Marikana in 2012 as well as after the massacre when wounded and injured members of the community could not be transported easily to hospital. Furthermore, during periods of high rainfall, people are not able to leave their homes because of mud and flooding. They attribute their current living conditions to three sources: Lonmin, traditional authorities and the government. Even though many living in Nkaneng hope to one day return to their rural homes in the Eastern Cape, others have begun to make their homes around the mines. Many women and children have joined male family members on the mines, or seek to find work for themselves. Like any people who migrate to different places for work, they (as mineworkers) expect Lonmin to provide housing and, as citizens, they expect to be provided with basic services when they arrive. However, in Marikana, this is not the case, and people from the Eastern Cape are met with a differentiated system of access based on their ethnicity. For this reason, ethnicity is still a major source of tension on the mines, as has historically been the case (see Moodie and Ndatshe 1994).

The land that the residents of Nkaneng occupy is supposed to be Tswana traditional farming land. They want the government to buy the land for them because currently the municipality will not provide them with any basic services, since they are not 'from there'. In addition, there are no schools or crèches on or near the mine. It becomes clear that mine companies still function according to Wolpe's (1972) cheap labour and reserve subsidy thesis by paying the mineworker only enough money to reproduce himself, ignoring the growing poverty in rural areas as well as the very obvious new households on the mines. As such, it is due to past land arrangements which have been carried over into the present that the lives of those in Nkaneng continue to be cast in an ethnic mould. Tswana Chief Kgosi Bob Edward Mogale of the Bapo ba Mogale Royal Family will not cede the land to the residents of Nkaneng, so they cannot build formal housing. The formal housing (brick structures) that does exist belongs to Tswana people, who receive RDP housing in the area because of their ethnicity. Furthermore, since the Marikana massacre, the families of the slain mineworkers have requested a memorial be erected at the mountain where they were shot down by police. Once again, the traditional authority told people that the land is not for amaXhosa and that they should build a memorial in the Eastern Cape.

The Bapo ba Mogale family is not happy with the shack settlement on 'their' land and are demanding more money from Lonmin. Lonmin, however, has ignored the entire community there and refuses to help or to pay any more money to the Bapo ba Mogale family who, according to women in *Sikhala Sonke* (a Marikana women's group), regularly receives money from Lonmin and demands that its children and relatives receive jobs over isiXhosa people. The only time the women remember seeing the traditional leader was during the strikes when he was accompanying the other traditional leaders from the Eastern Cape who came to speak to the workers (see Naicker 2013). Another relationship between traditional leaders and the mining company has been ongoing since the massacre and they are frequently called in to settle disputes between the workers and the mine. Traditional leaders are flown in from the Eastern Cape or mining bosses fly to the Eastern Cape to meet with them there, notably the amaMpondo Kings (see *News24 2012*; Feni 2014).

Ethnicity, then, takes on a particular character in Nkaneng, which must be read through the complex structure of people's lives in that area. What should be the right of access to land and services for all citizens moving freely from one place to another in their own country now becomes a contestation of who is originally from the area, and reflects the socio-economic and political dynamics in the community. What is interesting to note is that, while the women of *Sikhala Sonke* complained about differentiated access based on ethnicity, all their community organising and initiatives, during the strikes and after the massacre, were based on broader conceptions of citizenship and democracy. For them, their activities were open to everyone regardless of where people are from, or what language they speak because they were all there 'working in the same place and trying to live well' (Naicker 2013, 96). An alternative form of political community thus will only be inclusive if it is informed by the political practice of people, which falls outside the ambit of elite civil society and state politics. Traditional authorities are an illustration of the continuation of colonial geographical fixing, in which origin is used as a justification for control, and where freedom has not meant freedom for all, particularly freedom of movement and fluidity.

Mamdani notes that, during colonialism, access by 'natives' to land, administration, representation and dispute settlement was organised through traditional authorities established for differentiated groups of 'natives' based on 'tribal ethnicity', even if there were more similarities amongst different groups of 'native' people, than there were between different races (2013, 51). This not only led to a different and specific political trajectory, which was not meant to evolve or change, but it also led to 'monoethnic governance of multi-ethnic societies, specifically when it came to "immigrants to tribal land"' (2013, 52).

This spatial differentiation is central to understanding how the 'native reserves' and later Bantustans in South Africa functioned as 'zones of exclusion' (Pithouse 2012, 7), outside of 'civil society', and how rural African people were subject to traditional authority enshrined in customary law (itself a misnomer). Today, the incorporation of traditional authorities into the South African government system has meant the perpetuation of a colonial system of customary law, where some people are, on the basis of their spatial location, subject to a different system of law which still functions to exclude them from civil society as 'natives'. This 'tribalisation' serves to crystallise tradition and culture, in a way that 'tribesmen' are still seen and regarded as outside the 'modern'. As Mamdani (2013, 51) explains, '[u]nlike race, which claimed to mark a civilizational hierarchy, tribe was said to be a marker of cultural diversity'.

Land then has not just been something expropriated through colonialism, as it has also been the tool with which to 'fix' and 'anthropologise' people. Keeping black people within reserves was not merely to ensure a cheap supply of labour to the mines and farms for white settlers, it was also a mechanism of control under tribalisation. Returning land to people may in fact become a messy process when people are required to prove their location or relationship to the land, particularly if the colonial questions are not resolved and if citizenship and democracy are not deepened through a re-scripting of the political in South Africa, especially with regard to traditional authorities. The way in which the state currently conceptualises traditional authorities, 'ethnicity' and citizenship is not inclusive, certainly in the way these institutions are actualised in everyday lived experience. If 'native' still functions as a 'political identity' as Mamdani (2013) has noted, then speaking about land questions in South Africa and land redistribution without speaking about how to create a more inclusive political community will only serve to reify colonial geography.

If then we are to better understand the politics of land and belonging in South Africa's former Bantustans, based on the notion of subaltern politics, we must, in line with Mamdani's warnings, begin from an acknowledgement of people, in terms of ontology, as historical agents and not geographically or socially fixed beings. In relation to rural dwellers and migrant workers in the former Bantustans, it leads us to the recognition of a marginalised history of rural resistance. Ntsebeza and Kepe (2011, 5) have argued that the rural sphere in South Africa's countryside has been marginalised in the history of resistance against colonialism and Apartheid in South Africa. For them (2011, 3):

The question that faces South Africans, as well as those who have an interest in South African issues, is how history features in post-Apartheid South Africa. Critical questions include, what is remembered, recorded, and by whom, and crucially the manner in which different histories contribute or do not contribute to current understandings of nationhood.

The Mpondo Revolt, which involved widespread open revolt for nine months and, in many regards, endured into the 1960s, was sustained for a longer period than most urban struggles in South Africa. As such, Ntsebeza and Kepe (2011, 21) make the important point that urban struggles culminating in the Sharpeville Massacre of 1960 should not overshadow the significance of the events in Mpondoland occurring roughly around the same time. Yet, this event, which presented an organic, organised, militant peasant rebellion, has been silenced in most nationalist historiography, and the rural sphere has been portrayed as quiescent and backward.

The Mpondo Revolt, which was a sustained resistance to colonial and apartheid policies and an affirmation of people's defence of democracy in Mpondoland, in many ways shatters modernist conceptions of the political and the way struggle should be organised, which has always been seen as an almost exclusively urban, 'progressive', project. The ways in which idioms and symbols associated with this form of militant rural resistance which were present in the Marikana/Lonmin strikes of 2012, such as traditional dress, weapons and medicine, and song, were endowed by journalists and political analysts with the characteristics of backwardness, traditionalism and violence, demonstrate the way in which the official political domain is conceptualised in South African society through the media and the academy. However, if we are able to extend our analysis beyond these narrow forms of representation to the ways in which people actually practise politics in the everyday, we are able to grasp alternative ways of imagining democracy and citizenship beyond liberal constitutionalism and state subjectivities.

Rethinking land, citizenship and belonging through the Mpondo Revolt

By the late 1800s, traditional authority in Mpondoland was a loose association of district chiefs usually recognising a paramount chief according to lineage; people chose their allegiance on the basis of the area that they occupied and people could also choose to change their allegiance by moving to another area (Myers 2008, 4; Landau 2010).[1] Size, solidarity and custom of a 'community' varied according to the extent of outside threats and the personality of the paramount (Hunter 1961, 379). While there was no standardisation in Mpondoland, chiefs were usually the commanders of their respective armies, responsible for the allocation of land, and the arbiters of district disputes (Hunter 1961, 392).

The mutual relationship between the chief and his people was measured by generosity of the chief. People were called upon to work together to build huts and cultivate land, and the chief, who was always expected to live and work amongst people, would also have to provide refreshments and hear the grievances of anyone in his district who called at his kraal (Hunter 1961, 394). Similarly, in Mpondoland, before and during the late 1800s, any taxes which were collected by the chief would be used for the benefit of his people in times of dearth; furthermore, the process of tax collection would have to be open to negotiation and the spending of any funds would have to be transparent to the community (Lodge 1983).

The significance of this is that it provides a brief sketch of the many limitations placed on the power of the chiefs in the pre-colonial political landscape as well as the way in which the institution of chieftaincy was, to an extent, controlled and conditioned by the will of the people within a given community. This also suggests that, under certain forms of pre-colonial traditional governance, people in the community had a very different understanding, and much more meaningful experience, of belonging in society than that afforded to black rural dwellers under the system of traditional authorities during the colonial/apartheid periods and the current post-apartheid era.

Emerging from within a widespread context of rurally based resistance to the implementation of the Apartheid state's Betterment and Rehabilitation schemes in the 1940s and 1950s, as well as the introduction of the institution of Bantu Authorities in 1951 (and its associated influx control, the extension of the pass system to women, and migrant labour recruitment bureaux), the Mpondo Revolt can be understood as the most important event within a historical sequence of political resistance in the rural areas of South Africa. However, in order to understand what it is that sets the Mpondo Revolt apart from other instances of resistance against the newly imposed authoritarian system of governance and land tenure during the 1940s and 1950s, it is important to understand (at least broadly) the nature of this wider context of state power and popular resistance against it in the Bantustans.

It was Proclamation 31 of 1939, which was gazetted under a provision of the 1936 Land Act, which stipulated that any area of land could be declared a 'Betterment area' by the government (Hirson 1977, 118). The essential aim of Betterment schemes was to conserve land in the reserves by limiting livestock and replacing 'unscientific' African land-use practices with 'modern', 'scientific' methods developed in the West. The processes of its implementation were largely delayed until the post-Second World War period. When the proposal for Betterment was finally introduced in the mid-1940s, it was called Rehabilitation and entailed, in addition to stock-culling, the re-division of African land into residential, grazing and cultivating areas (Chaskalson 1986, 47). It also included the setting aside of communal land for forestry schemes and thus the implementation of extremely severe restrictions on access to natural resources such as firewood.

The processes of stock-culling had drastic implications for the poorest rural dwellers as they were carried out without any consideration of the size of a person's herd or the amount of land the farmer had access to for grazing. Similarly, the forced demarcation of fallow lands, and restrictions on access to communal grazing land and natural resources, had hugely negative consequences for the majority of the rural population. Collectively, these stipulations of Rehabilitation embodied a top-down process of 'villagisation', which forced rural dwellers who were dependent upon wages to live in rural townships – at times becoming completely alienated from the land.

Chaskalson (1986, 48) argues that in the 1940s, Rehabilitation aimed to gain a monopoly over whatever resources were in the reserves and concentrate them in the hands of a minority of so-called 'good' African farmers, thus forcing the majority of rural dwellers 'to be consigned to rural dormitory villages'. However, it is crucial to note that at this stage, Rehabilitation did more than just threaten the majority of rural dwellers; it also undermined the position of chiefs (Chaskalson 1986). At first, the introduction of Betterment/Rehabilitation undermined the power of the chiefs in the reserves by taking away their control over the allocation of land. While some chiefs accepted and promoted

Rehabilitation and its new system of land use and allocation amongst their constituencies, many felt that their legitimacy and popular support would be undermined by their acceptance and thus they joined the popular resistance against it. Chaskalson argues that it was the need to 'consolidate the support of this [former] collaborationist class against the resistance which rehabilitation provoked that the state introduced the 1951 Bantu (Tribal) Authorities Act' (49). At the time of its implementation, the Bantu Authorities Act functioned to increase the powers of the chiefs who had been undermined by the Rehabilitation policy. However, this increase in power was based on the condition that chiefs accepted their new role as bureaucrats upwardly accountable to the Native Affairs Department, as opposed to their constituencies.

In *The Peasant's Revolt*, Govan Mbeki rigorously describes the 'bastardisation' of the pre-colonial system of governance by the South African colonial government and the attempt to draw the chiefs and headmen into the machinery of the state. In many ways, Mbeki's discussion of the bastardised system of traditional authorities in the former Transkei was a precursor to the theoretical insights within Mamdani's *Citizen and Subject: Contemporary Africa and the Legacy of Late Colonialism*. Of particular significance for thinking about the agrarian question in South Africa is Mamdani's historical analysis of the traditional authorities' system, in which chiefs were at once autonomous but dependent agents operating as the extended arm of the apartheid state.

However, 20 years since the publishing of *Citizen and Subject*, it is necessary to attempt to think beyond some limitations of Mamdani's thesis, in order to take cognisance of the contemporary realities of the South African political landscape. Perhaps the most significant critique of Mamdani's text is that it lacks a critical examination of bourgeois conceptions of civil society so prevalent in post-apartheid South Africa, and neglects a subaltern sphere of politics and resistance history which, when acknowledged and taken seriously, poses a significant challenge to the predominance of state subjectivities and elite forms of politics in articulating the politics of land, agriculture, citizenship and democracy in South Africa.

This article argues that though Mamdani's analytical task was to illuminate the link between politics in the Native Authority and that of civil society, as well as resistance against them, under the conditions of decentralised despotism (Mamdani 1996, 218), without providing a critique of civil society, the insights he provided remain, to a large extent, embedded within dominant elitist accounts of politics and liberal democracy. Even though Mamdani made reference to the contrived heritage of liberal thought and its anchoring in Western history, he failed to problematise the epistemological and material foundations of liberal notions of citizenship, and still clearly privileged bourgeois civil society as the ideal institution for democratisation in contemporary African states.

Subaltern Studies scholar Chatterjee (2004, 38) has claimed that in most of the world, 'civil society as an ideal continues to energise an interventionist political project, but as an actually existing form it is demographically limited'. Chatterjee (2004) argues that the practical functioning of civil society in 'most of the world' (problematically termed the 'developing' or 'third' world) is such that it is an exclusively bourgeois sphere whose membership has been almost entirely reduced to NGOs, bourgeois technocrats and bureaucrats. In this narrow space that is the reality of civil society, all members ultimately share in the same anti-democratic and elitist ontology that believes that ordinary people are fundamentally irrational and apolitical, incapable of collective decision-making, and therefore need to be managed as if they were subjects requiring guidance from enlightened political experts.

The consequence of this has been the reduction of the majority of *citizens* (political agents participating in the sovereignty of the state) to mere *populations* (apolitical subjects represented by numerical proportions) in most of the world, which, in turn, has given rise to the ironic situation in which the NGOs and agents of civil society – who claim to be the 'trustees' of the people – actually propagate the inequalities and injustices in society that they claim to be working against, and systematically silence the genuine voice of the people – deemed as illegitimate and even criminal (Neocosmos 2011, 2). This understanding of the distinction between the inclusive *ideal* of civil society and the exclusive *reality* of civil society is a fundamental insight, which seems to have been downplayed in Mamdani's work.

In a self-created zone of political autonomy which is situated *outside* of bourgeois civil society – a domain which Neocosmos (2011, 13) terms *un-civil society* and Chatterjee (2004, 50) calls *political society* – one can witness an 'emancipatory and inclusive process of collective self-determination' (Hallward, quoted in Pithouse 2011, 227), as well as the operation of the 'will of the people', which has been met with hostility and violent repression by the state and NGO-based civil society at large. Chatterjee therefore warns that theoretical practice must recognise the politics of the people or risk 'governmental techniques that will continue to proliferate and serve, much as they did in the colonial era … as instruments of class rule in a global capitalist order' (2004, 41). By applying Chatterjee's (2004) nuanced problematic of civil society to *Citizen and Subject,* it seems that an understanding of the politics of land and agriculture in contemporary South Africa, which is anchored solely in nationalist, state, NGO or other elitist perspectives, is incapable of thinking beyond state subjectivities and making sense of subaltern forms of popular politics and democratic praxes both past and present. However, in his most recent work, *Define and Rule: Native as Political Identity*, Mamdani (2013, 106) highlights the need for alternative historiography and broadening conceptions of citizenship and democracy, and he argues that 'the formulation of an alternative historiography would not be enough to overcome the colonial political legacy; it also required an alternative political practice, one that would create a form of citizenship adequate to building an inclusive political community'.

Mamdani (2013) goes on to describe how British colonial indirect rule created two differentiated systems of law: 'civil' law and 'customary' law, which he referred to in *Citizen and Subject* (1996) as the *bi-furcated* state. In the colonial occupation of Africa, it was not merely that people were divided and ruled, but rather that the project became to 'define and rule' – a process whereby the colonised were divided into two different categories, which would have two different trajectories of growth (49). This categorisation saw the colonised split between 'races' and 'tribes' in which 'non-natives' (i.e. migrants or those not indigenous to sub-Saharan Africa, like Asians, Europeans, Arabs, etc.) were defined as separate races and the 'native' populations (indigenous to Africa) were separated into tribes (47). This separation meant two different legal systems: all *races* were governed under a single law, namely civil law, and thus formed part of civil society. However, *tribes*, which were far more differentiated by colonial authority, were governed by different sets of customary law. Mamdani (48) describes this technology of the colonial state as having very specific ends:

With *races*, the cultural difference was not translated into separate legal systems. Instead, it was contained, even negotiated, within a single legal system and was enforced by a single administrative authority. But with *tribes*, the case was the opposite: cultural difference was reinforced, exaggerated, and built up into different legal systems, each enforced by a separate administrative and political authority. In a nutshell, different races were meant to have a common future; different tribes were not. The colonial legal project – civil and customary – was an integral part of the colonial political project. (emphasis in original)

Similarly, applying the insights of Subaltern Studies scholars to theorisations of citizenship in postcolonial African states requires us not only to provide a critique of the institution of traditional authorities in the rural areas, but also of certain kinds of liberal institutions and elite forms of politics, such as civil society and modern nationalism, which claim to represent the full extent of democratic practices and possibilities in South Africa.

What made the Bantu Authorities system so unpopular with rural dwellers at the time of its introduction was, firstly, the fact that they now had to pay a host of addition taxes in order to finance the, at times lavish, lifestyles of the tribal authorities; and secondly, they directly bore the burden of the rising institutionalised corruption amongst chiefs who were compliant with the state. Therefore, Chaskalson (1986, 50) explains, 'the total drain on the reserve population increased substantially at the same time as the rehabilitation measures (which were now enforced by the Tribal Authorities) undermined their material position'. In addition to these, tribal authorities became closely associated during the 1950s with the deepening policies and practices of 'influx control', which included the extension of the pass system to women as well as the forced removal of 'illegals' from urban areas to the reserves. All of these processes were carried out and enforced by tribal authorities in the reserves during the 1950s and 1960s, resembling Mamdani's description of chiefs embodying a great fusion of powers.

A comparative analysis of the various instances of resistance documented in the literature reveals that the popular politics in the reserves during the 1940s and 1950s cannot be simply dismissed as 'reactionary', 'parochial' or evidence of some 'innate peasant conservatism' (Chaskalson 1986, 50). However, it must be noted that, of all the instances of popular political organisation which comprised this broad moment of rural resistance, it is the Mpondo Revolt which stands out as the most politically important event within the sequence. It was in eastern Mpondoland, during the nine months of sustained open resistance during 1959–1961 where tens of thousands of rural dwellers and migrant workers gathered on mountains, in forests and (for women) in villages to organise a campaign of resistance in which they rejected the institution of tribal authorities as well as the idea of chieftaincy *entirely*.

The significance of this point cannot be overstated. In many of the other instances of resistance during this period, people in the rural areas fought against what was understood as a bastardised version of the chieftaincy, usually against one particular chief seen as 'illegitimately' placed in power by the apartheid state, and called for a reinstatement of a system of 'legitimate' traditional governance under a chief who is horizontally accountable to his constituency. As Mbeki argued, 'when a people have developed to a stage that discards chieftainship, when their social development contradicts the need for such an institution, then to force it on them is not liberation but enslavement' (1964, 47). In the case of the Mpondo Revolt, no such call for a return to some idea of a benevolent or legitimate chieftaincy took place. The call made by the members of the *Intaba* movement in eastern Mpondoland was instead a call for self-governance, equality and democracy, which amounted to a complete rejection of their allotted social location as subjects and not citizens under the system of Bantu Authorities.

Lodge (1983, 282) argues that, unlike in other rural areas, in eastern Mpondoland, 'the traditional political structure was completely discredited and consequently dissatisfaction was unlikely to cohere around any representative of the old order'. As a consequence of this rejection, Lodge (1983) claims that the people in eastern Mpondoland 'were compelled to create *new* leadership structures' (emphasis added). This insight highlights that the Mpondo Revolts represented a moment in which people were creating something new, an alternative form of politics and political community which was not based on the traditional political structure or modern nationalism, civil society and party politics. It is this element of 'the new', as discussed above, which makes the Mpondo Revolt such a significant historical moment for scholars to draw upon in their attempts to think afresh about the politics of land, citizenship and governance in the former Bantustans 20 years since the fall of apartheid.

A defining feature of the Mpondo Revolt was the featuring of mountains as sites of subaltern politics and spaces for the organisation of resistance by ordinary male rural dwellers and migrant workers (Bruchhausen 2014, 7). It is important to note that women's politics, although rarely acknowledged by historians, were taking place and being organised in the villages and in the fields (see Naicker 2013, 56–60). While women were not expected to attend mountain meetings directly, they held a fundamental role in facilitating the presence of men in the mountain's gatherings by providing them with food, water and intelligence reports throughout the duration of the Revolt. An important aspect of the mountain meetings concerned the issue of egalitarianism, the distribution of power, and, specifically, the issue of power being overly concentrated in the hands of chiefs who were widely considered to be illegitimate, autocratic, and incapable of acting on behalf of the will of the people (Bruchhausen 2014, 12).

Another important feature of the mountain movement during the nine-month period of open revolt was in relation to land. By May 1960, the *Intaba* movement had a constituency of over 180,000 members and was 'establishing itself as an alternative political authority to the prevalent order, assuming, for instance, the functions of the chief's courts in settling land allocation matters' (Lodge 1983, 279). What is significant about the way in which the mountain movement dealt with the issue of access to land is that it represented a new type of politics that did not inaugurate private ownership of land (which is seen as the most progressive and modern form of land tenure by liberal scholars); nor did the movement members simply replicate the so-called traditional politics of land by choosing for themselves a new chief to establish a court and take up the responsibility of land allocation. Instead, the men on the mountain adopted aspects of the communal land tenure system and reinvented it to fit with a process of collective decision-making in the context of a participatory democratic movement. By taking the authority to allocate land out of the hands of autocratic traditional authorities and placing the responsibility upon themselves, the members of the Mpondo Revolt engendered a moment in South African history from which we today can draw insights from in order to think the possibility of alternative and new means of land allocation.

The practice of meeting on mountains which characterised the Mpondo Revolts can be traced back to the earliest years of the 1900s in the former Transkei and was carried over by migrant workers all over the country but, most significantly, to the mines on the East Rand throughout the twentieth and twenty-first centuries. In the space of the mountain, poor and working-class people who are usually considered and treated as lesser beings (both materially and intellectually) by dominant social groups in society demand that their full humanity and political agency be recognised and that they are treated with equality, dignity and respect. Moodie and Ndatshe (1994) have demonstrated that, during the period between 1946 and 1982 on the gold mines in South Africa, amaMpondo migrant workers often organised themselves and other workers on the mines in ways very similar to those seen during the Mpondo Revolts.

In these instances of resistance on the mines, just as in the case of the Mpondo Revolts, emphasis was placed on meeting attendance and on democratic forms of participation in decision-making processes which used consensus as the means by which to elect spokes-people as well as collectively decide upon which forms of action were to be taken. These instances of organised resistance on the mines presented organic forms of democracy which amaMpondo miners were already accustomed to from their experiences and histories at home in the Transkei. This more organic and horizontal praxis of democracy occurs in a subaltern sphere of politics which takes place in different forms and spaces compared to what Guha (1997, xvi) describes as the 'official domain' of politics.

Recalling our earlier discussion of the politics of land and belonging in the Nkaneng shack settlement, it is important to note that the parallels that can be drawn between the Marikana/Lonmin strike of August 2012 and the political praxes of the Mpondo Revolt are in many cases stark. Like the Mpondo Revolt, the space of the mountain was critical to worker organising during Marikana. Thus, in both instances, people chose to occupy a mountain and, via means of democratic consensus, in fact elected a mountain committee to act as spokesmen and maintain peace and order. In both instances, people demanded to be treated as equals in the space of the mountain and, furthermore, demanded that they were not represented by anyone and instead spoke directly for themselves. In both instances, the praxis of a subaltern form of politics consists of a much deeper conception and practice of democracy and notion of citizenship than that offered to us by political parties, NGOs or other elite forms of politics in the 'official domain', which tend to categorise the majority of black South African citizens (particularly those with direct ties to the rural areas) as 'the unthinking masses' in need of guidance by some kind of 'enlightened' vanguard.

It is also important to recall that no less than 31 of the 45 people who died on and since the 16th of August 2012 held their regular homesteads in the Eastern Cape Province. Breckenridge (2012) and Hartford (2012) were the only scholars who wrote early accounts of the massacre at Marikana which identified the importance of the fact that the initial driving force behind the strike was not just rock-drill operators (RDOs) but in main specifically migrant workers from Mpondoland. Hartford (2012, 3) identified that the RDOs who hold their rural bases in Mpondoland and were a significant force in the Marikana/Lonmin strikes were generally between the ages of 45 and 55 years. This means that they would possibly have already been born at the time of the Mpondo Revolt, or at the very least and even for those who had not yet been born, it is extremely likely that many of the people would have grown up hearing stories of their parents' involvement in the rural resistance politics of the late 1950s and early 1960s in the former Transkei. Furthermore, many songs that were sung by mineworkers as well as other cultural features of the Marikana strikes refer to rural struggles like the Mpondo Revolts.[2]

Although this is not the space to go into elaborate detail about these parallels between the Mpondo Revolt and the Marikana/Lonmin strikes, what is most significant for the purpose of this article is to highlight that the connections between the two events represent a *living* subaltern history of politics in South Africa which, when taken seriously, offers us insights into existing practices and conceptions of democracy and citizenship which challenge the limitations of representative democracy and the sustained existence of the system of traditional authorities 20 years since the fall of apartheid. While 'ethnic politics' is regularly viewed as 'backward' or 'pre-modern', there must be an attempt to understand how ethnicity functions in South African society and how people, who are the subject of traditional and customary law, themselves feel discriminated against and are struggling for a kind of citizenship that is more inclusive and a democracy that embraces their political desires and organisation. Furthermore, by taking seriously the forms of politics employed by ordinary black South Africans during the Mpondo Revolt and Marikana/Lonmin strikes, we are presented with a stunning challenge to many dominant assumptions underpinning mainstream understandings of South African resistance history. In many ways, both the Mpondo Revolt and the Marikana/Lonmin strikes create the conditions for, to borrow a phrase from Trouillot, 'thinking the hitherto unthinkable', that ordinary rural Africans are political, rational and complex agents who are not tied to a static notion of 'tradition' in the sense that they are ontologically fixed within the realm of the pre-modern and a-political.

Some conclusions

The political insight that can be gained by considering South Africa's history of subaltern politics is of fundamental importance for our attempts to rethink South Africa's land, governance, and citizenship questions in relation to the former Bantustans today. This rethinking has allowed us to understand how colonial-cum-apartheid governance mechanisms are being reified in the post-apartheid state, and how land has been used to geographically fix and control people. This article aims to broaden conceptions of democracy and the political, and to stress that we cannot afford to ignore the way ordinary people practise politics in the everyday. The usefulness of this insight is that it encourages us to begin our deliberations by starting from the simple assertion that 'people can think' and it equips us with the understanding that the politics which has taken place and continues to take place outside of the 'official domain', and which are conceived outside of the sphere of state subjectivities and forms of elite politics (Guha 1997, xvi), in certain instances, presents examples of practices of democracy, citizenship, dignity and belonging within a subaltern sphere.

It also serves to illustrate that when we think about South Africa's land and agrarian questions, these cannot be narrowly defined simply through land restitution claims or land redistribution measures, as they must of necessity be linked to broader struggles for justice, dignity and humanity that require structural socio-economic and political change, in line with how people practise politics. In *Disabling Globalisation* (2002), Hart thus stresses that 're-articulating the land question could potentially link together diverse demands and thus help to unite a broader opposition to the brutal neoliberal economic policies that were ravaging livelihoods'.

What the examples of the Mpondo Revolt and the Marikana/Lonmin strikes reveal to us is that, in certain moments, ordinary people organise themselves collectively and engage in political acts of resistance, which defy their social location. In the case of the Mpondo Revolt, rural dwellers who in line with the state's narrow ethnic and racial conception of 'identity politics' were collectively perceived as ontologically beholden to obeying a hereditary system of chieftainship, defied their allotted social location as subjects and created new forms of political leadership. This was based on popular participation in democratic decision-making processes and notions of egalitarianism that stood in opposition to the institution of chieftaincy and the apartheid state. In the case of the Marikana/Lonmin strikes, migrant workers totally confounded the basic assumptions held by traditional labour historians by rejecting trade union representation and bringing to the fore the politics of human dignity, access to land and resources, as well as the meaning of democracy in post-apartheid South Africa, in conjunction with the call for a living wage of R12,500.

Notes

1. For a detailed discussion of popular politics in South Africa before the 1800s, see Landau (2010).
2. For a detailed discussion, see Bruchhausen (2014).

Disclosure statement

No potential conflict of interest was reported by the authors.

References

Alexander, P., T. Lekgowa, B. Mmope, L. Sinwell, and B. Xezwi. 2012. *Marikana: A View from the Mountain and a Case to Answer*. Johannesburg: Jacana.

Breckenridge, K. 2012. "Revenge of the Commons: The Crisis in the South African Mining Industry." In *Histories of the Present*. Accessed February 22, 2013. http://www.historyworkshop.org.uk/revenge-of-the-commons-the-crisis-in-the-south-african-mining-industry.

Bruchhausen, S. 2014. "Understanding Marikana Through the Mpondo Revolts." *Journal of Asian and African Studies* 50: 412–426.

Chakrabarty, D. 2000. "Subaltern Studies and Postcolonial Historiography." *Nepantla: Views from the South* 1 (1): 9–32.

Chaskalson, M. 1986. "Rural resistance in the 1940s and 1950s." *Africa Perspective* 1 (5–6): 47–59.

Chatterjee, P. 2004. *The Politics of the Governed*. Delhi: Permanent Black.

Chinguno, C. 2013. "Marikana and the Post-Apartheid Workplace Order." *Working Paper 1: Society, Work and Development Institute*, University of the Witwatersrand.

Feni, L. 2014. "Mines Ask Kings to End Strike." *Dispatch Live*. http://www.dispatchlive.co.za/news/mines-ask-kings-to-end-strike/.

Grieve, N. 2014. Lonmin Inks Landmark BEE deals with Traditional community. *Creamer Medias: Mining Weekly*. http://www.miningweekly.com/article/lonmin-inks-landmark-bee-deals-with-traditional-community-2014-07-30.

Guha, R. 1997. "Introduction." In *A Subaltern Studies Reader*, edited by R. Guha, ix–xxii. Oxford University Press.

Hart, G. 2002. *Disabling Globalisation: Places of Power in Post-Apartheid South Africa*. Berkley: University of California Press.

Hart, G. 2013. *Rethinking the South African Crisis: Nationalism, Populism, Hegemony*. Durban: University of KwaZulu-Natal Press.

Hartford, G., 2012. "The Mining Industry Strike Wave: What Are the Causes and What Are the Solutions?" *Ground Up*. Accessed February 22, 2013. http://groundup.org.za/content/mining-industry-strike-wave-what-are-causes-and-what-are-solutions.

Hirson, B. 1977. "Rural Revolt in South Africa, 1937–1951." *Collected Seminar Papers. Institute of Commonwealth Studies* 21: 115–132.

Hunter, M. 1961. *Reaction to Conquest*. London: Oxford University Press.

Landau, P. S. 2010. *Popular Politics in the History of South Africa*. Cambridge Press: New York.

Lodge, T. 1983. *Black Politics in South Africa Since 1945*. Johannesberg: Ravan Press.

Mamdani, M. 1996. *Citizen and Subject: Contemporary Africa and the Legacy of Late Colonialism*. Princeton, NJ: Princeton University Press.

Mamdani, M. 2013. *Define and Rule: Native as Political Identity*. Johannesberg: Wits University Press.

Mbeki, G. 1964. *South Africa: The Peasants' Revolt*. Harmondsworth: Penguin.

Moodie, T. D., and V. Ndatshe. 1994. *Going for Gold*. London: University of California Press.

Myers, J. C. 2008. *Indirect Rule in South Africa: Tradition, Modernity, and the Costuming of Political Power*. Rochester: University of Rochester Press.

Naicker, C. 2013. "Marikana: Taking a Subaltern Sphere of Politics Seriously." MA Thesis., Rhodes University.

Neocosmos, M. 2011. "Transition, Human Rights and Violence: Rethinking a Liberal Political Relationship in the African Neo-Colony." Unpublished Manuscript.

News24. 2012. "Traditional Leaders Head to Marikana". *News24*. http://www.news24.com/SouthAfrica/News/Traditional-leaders-head-to-Marikana-20120820.

Ntsebeza, L., and T. Kepe, eds. 2011. *Rural Resistance in South Africa: The Mpondo Revolts after Fifty Years*. Cape Town: UCT Press.

Pithouse, R. 2011. "Fidelity to Fanon." In *Living Fanon: Global Perspectives*, edited by N. C. Gibson, 225–234. Palgrave.

Pithouse, R. 2012. "Thought Amidst Waste, Conjunctural Notes on the Democratic Project in South Africa." Paper at Wits Interdisciplinary Seminar in the Humanities, WISER, University of the Witwatersrand, 28 May.

Wolpe, H. 1972. "Capitalism and Cheap Labour-Power in South Africa: From Segregation to Apartheid." *Economy and Society* 1 (4): 425–456.

A feminist perspective on autonomism and commoning, with reference to Zimbabwe

Tarryn Alexander and Kirk Helliker

ABSTRACT

This article engages with the autonomist Marxism of John Holloway from a feminist standpoint. The positions developed by this feminist critique are used to shed new light on the land occupations in contemporary Zimbabwe. Though sympathetic to his work, we argue that Holloway does not sufficiently address gender identity with specific reference to social reproduction and women. The notions of the commons and the process of commoning are consistent with Holloway's autonomist framework and its complementarities to Silvia Federici's Marxist feminist lens on the commons is highlighted. Against a tendency within autonomist and commoning theories, we argue for a pronounced identitarian politics as grounded in localised struggles undertaken by women as women. We privilege the significance of women asserting and revaluing their identities as part of a possible project of transformation. For us, struggling against and beyond what exists is invariably rooted in struggles within what exists (including identities).

Towards an autonomist feminism

Autonomist Marxism is heterogeneous and difficult to circumscribe (Eden 2008; Weeks 2011; Marks 2012). Broadly speaking, however, autonomist theory problematises the pursuit of centralised control as a basis for constructing a post-capitalist society and therefore tends to question power-centric and state-focused socialist strategies. Practices of social struggle are articulated as those which take place at the level of the everyday via the self-activity of ordinary people. Holloway (2002, 2010) is one of the foremost contemporary autonomist thinkers. He espouses a particular brand of autonomism, what he labels as 'negative autonomism' in seeking to differentiate his work from the supposed 'positive autonomism' of Negri. Holloway's Marxism is an optimistic treatise on the power of ordinary people – through pre-figurative politics – to transform the conditions of society away from capitalism and towards a new horizon of dignity and egalitarianism. As a result, he speaks of small-scale everyday acts of revolt opening up the cracks in capitalism as the most likely pathway in the direction of anti-capitalism. Drawing significantly on his understanding of the Zapatista movement in Chiapas, Mexico, Holloway prompts images for revolution based on the construction of (and experimentation with) social relations which stand asymmetrical to the *status quo* in the immediate spaces of everyday social life. This can be considered as part of the current broader emancipatory moment of anti-power politics or anti-politics (Binford 2005; Katsiaficas 2006; Franks 2008; Cuninghame 2010; Newman 2010).

But the position of gender and women poses a significant challenge to Holloway's perspective. In spite of his contributions, he seems to have left an often struggling theme within Marxist theory underrepresented, namely how sexual oppression in society is entwined with the development of modern capitalism. He tends to shove the sex-gender question (as if it were a discrete and movable agenda) to the corner of his theory. As Cockburn (2012) notes, Holloway fails to take into consideration substantially or sufficiently the issues of women in his sweeping and universalistic call for a politics of anti-power.

Nevertheless, we believe that his overall thesis on revolutionising social relations is compatible with feminism in ways that may not be immediately apparent. To demonstrate this, we make two separate but connected points which show that part of thinking today necessitates a greater inclusion of feminist thought and gender politics in contemporary critical Marxism. The two issues which we believe mark the juncture of (particularly socialist) feminism and autonomist Marxism are: (i) the contradictory relationship between anti-identitarian thought and the feminist agenda and (ii) the possibilities which exist for a stronger inclusion of theories of social reproduction within the autonomist paradigm.

Anti-identitarian thinking and feminism

First of all, Holloway offers a resounding critique of politics based on social identities, as identities are said to stabilise existing situations. In this regard, we claim that his anti-identitarian thinking tends to lead to the dismissal of any kind of politics of identity and ends up putting the future of feminist thought within Marxism in a troubling spot as a result. Indeed, from the perspective of women's liberation, how do we mobilise against specifically patriarchal nodes of oppression using a regime of anti-identitarian emancipatory thought? In particular, in speaking rightfully of the need to work against and beyond existing social categorisation (or identities), we believe Holloway wrongly dismisses the importance of working politically within such categorisations.

Socialist feminists have historically argued that, when we ignore the divisions wrought into society by the relationship between patriarchy with capitalism, or at least fail to understand the specificity or irreducibility of patriarchy as a system, we not only preclude the successful achievement of horizontal social arrangements but we also distance ourselves conceptually from a *sine qua non* of capitalism's total existence, that is, pronounced gender inequality (Ollenburger and Moore 1997). For example, Federici (2004, 2012), Mies (1998) and Dalla Costa (2008) have made critical contributions to the history of capitalism by illustrating the 'civilising' processes which women were subjected to at the rise of capitalist modernisation for the purpose of naturalising the preconditions for capital's everyday survival. They also illustrate the ways in which this continues today.

Holloway's work becomes problematic in this context. Holloway (2002) does not include a sustained analysis of the sexual division of labour when discussing his distinction between 'doing' (or becoming) and 'done' (or being, including fixed identities), a split which he makes crucial to his understanding of revolution. More precisely, he not only excludes women as a political entity from his theory of revolution but in effect rejects 'woman' as a category as he rejects all categories as inherently regressive politically. For Holloway, 'woman' is sweepingly equated with other 'external identities' (such as black, Jew and gay) as merely an identitarian mask reaffirming relations of domination and inhibiting emancipation. He thus argues that '[i]t is the fracturing of doing that creates the idea that people *are* something [or being] – whatever, doctors, professors, Jews, blacks, women' (2002, 63; our emphasis) such that '[i]dentity is the antithesis of mutual recognition, of community, friendship and love' (68), with the antithesis raising the importance of an autonomist-type commoning as a political project. In his most recent book, he reiterates this by saying that '[t]o name is to identify and what concerns us here is that which goes against identity' (2010, 217).

According to Holloway, then, processes of identification which lead to the formulation of objective categories and formed identities in society – be they race, gender or nationality – have in turn led to divisiveness and consolidated the prominence of 'is-ness' and being (contra movement, becoming and change) in revolutionary thought, social relations and political practice. Identity for him is represented by the dramaturgical notion of 'the character mask'.

What is needed, he argues, is not the counter-power offered via identitarian thought (including seemingly feminist-based thinking) but rather visions of anti-power to create that which is 'not-yet' (or becoming) instead of perpetuating a struggle for 'is-ness', for identity. But, again, where does an anti-capitalist politics which privileges anti-power as well as anti-identity leave women and progressive feminist impulses and their fight against male supremacy and patriarchy? While one can most certainly empathise with Holloway's cautionary analysis against identitarian modes of thought and practices which have prompted so often the de-radicalisation and regression of social movements, his portrayal of identity as a 'character mask' is far too limiting particularly, we argue, in the case of women.

All politics need concrete, fixed and localised points of reference – including identities – around which to galvanise. Women as a unique historical category need space to mobilise using the identity of 'woman' in a way separate to (and from) men, albeit not in a way which acquiesces to closed classifications or normalises the existing order. Ultimately, then, in the need to elicit autonomist conceptions of revolutionary radicalism, we cannot simply understate the significance of social identities. Our identities do not inevitably and always result in us doing divisive work for capital and state as Holloway (2002) apparently suggests. In fact, identities such as queer, black and woman have helped to provide stability, consistency and communicability around sites and subjects of oppression in the quest to oppose hierarchy, capital and domination. Aspirations of identity can provide points of departure for reflections on power and change.

The starting point for feminist politics must centre on the question, 'what is woman?' And this certainly does not promote a frozen conception of gender in the manner suggested of identitarian thought by Holloway. Feminism in reality is an identitarian framework quite unrecognisable alongside Holloway's depiction of identitarianism. Feminism as an emancipatory force can only be properly described and understood by its tensions and contradictions, and with a perpetual awareness of the diversity and complexity of the category 'woman'. This has meant that the feminist movement as a whole revolves around contesting the notion of woman, not enclosing, stabilising and suturing it.

Holloway argues that ordinary people exist simultaneously within and against an identity (or a multiplicity of identities) because 'if capitalism were characterised by the total objectification of the subject, then there is no way that we as ordinary people, could criticise [it]' (2002, 89). He speaks of an excess of thoughts, experiences and practices (a becoming) which rises above categories of being (or identities). But, for us, he overemphasises the rigidifying and regressive effects of identitarian principles on politics, and overplays the existence and possibilities of a politics which somehow moves beyond and transcends identity. As Cockburn (2012, 216) writes: '[W]e should never assume, *pace* Holloway that the self is a free floating, formless, nameless actor free to jump on "our" political bus, born to be "we"'. This is not an argument against anti-identitarian praxis, but a recognition that politics invariably begins from where and who we are – our identities.

Thus a politics based on identities, including the identity of 'woman', potentially takes on a transformative (or an 'against and beyond') character. As Castells (1997, 8) rightly argues, 'no identity has, *per se*, progressive or regressive value outside its historical context'. Despite this, Nancy Fraser (like Holloway) is generally critical of pursuing identitarian politics because this form of politics regularly displaces redistributive politics, and tends to 'enhance social group differentiation' (1995, 82) and 'reify group identities' (2000, 108). Gender-based identity politics, she claims, leads to 'valorising femininity' without 'overcoming subordination' (Fraser 2007, 31) and therefore it affirms and stabilises identities rather than challenging and undermining them. Against this, and more consistent with Castell's argument, she at times recognises historical variation and emancipatory potential in identity politics (Fraser 2004, 377):

> Claimants may need to affirm devalued aspects of their identity; in other cases they may need to unburden themselves of excessive 'difference' that others have foisted on them and to emphasise their common humanity; and in still other cases they may need to deconstruct the very terms in which common sense differences are typically elaborated.

All of these options, we argue, by necessity begin with identity and do not emerge from above and beyond it. More importantly, they all provide specific springboards for transformative politics which, of course, may or may not be realised (Alcoff 2007). The key point is that their transformative potential cannot be ruled out *a priori*. The challenge then is to simultaneously make vivid and valorise oppressed identities in the pursuance of transformative projects which ultimately transcend identities, while stigmatising the essentialisms to which they have historically been bound.

To put more fully into perspective Holloway's view that identitarian thought is part of a system of ideas which fits into desiccated forms of politics and to understand how his insistence on this radically short-changes feminist politics, we must interrogate the question of social reproduction and women. In this regard, the inattention by Holloway to women's reproductive labour is seen as a conceptual gap.

Labour, social reproduction and women

Thus, another supposition by Holloway, apart from the dismantling of 'identity', which strikes a less than pleasing chord with regard to the status of gender in contemporary Marxism is the problematic manner in which Holloway foregrounds the characteristics of 'work'. The overall conception of labour that Holloway recovers from Marx's work is based on the commodity-form and the double character of labour, namely the dual existence of work as abstract labour and concrete labour under capitalism and the dominance of the former over the latter (which he also describes as involving the separation of doing from done, the antagonism between them, and the privileging of done over doing). Concrete labour is said to be complex and un-commodified life activity, whereas abstract labour is impersonal, simple, alienating and socially necessary work. In the end, dignified life-affirming human activity is enclosed within abstract labour as liberating anti-identitarian practices are trapped within categories of identity.

Holloway (2010) argues that the two-fold character of labour has been downplayed in Marxist accounts of revolution. However, he argues that this character should be the focus of emancipatory politics because, as indicated, human oppression is characterised by the dominance of abstract over concrete labour, the 'rupture of doing' and the 'rupture of doer from done'. As a consequence, he claims that the possibility for a freer society resides in elevating the primacy of concrete 'doing', that is, forms of human activity which are uncaptured by the fetishising forces of the capitalist system. He describes the core realisation of this as 'the struggle *against* the labour [abstract labour] that produces capital' (Holloway 2010, 199, our emphasis).

Holloway talks about the importance of exposing and engaging in (often hidden) forms of concrete 'doing' as the pinnacle of new revolutionary praxes. For Holloway, this exposition of 'doing' extends beyond production and exchange because 'the separation of doing from done permeates our whole relation to the world and to those around us' (2002, 49). And therefore, to rage, to reclaim dignity, to glimpse into a better society, is to pose concrete doing against the here-and-now of constituted, hackneyed and abstracted 'done' (including identity). Again, though, these claims downplay the significance of women as a category and, in this case, with specific relation to the work of social reproduction.

In fact, we argue that his dual labour-based revolutionary theory finds an antecedent in socialist feminist theories on social reproductive work. Because of this, a more critical and specifically feminist conception of 'social reproductive work' and of 'woman' would give insights into material strategies for Holloway's philosophic conceptions of interstitial change. Thus, from the lens of women's liberation, what is at once striking about Holloway's theory of labour is that he negates any meaningful discussion of reproductive labour which under capitalism is naturalised as women's work. As Laslett and Brenner (1989, 382) argue, social reproductive work is:

> Directly involved in maintaining life on a daily basis and inter-generationally. Social reproduction involves various kinds of socially necessary work … .Among other things, social reproduction includes how food, clothing and shelter are made available for immediate consumption, how the maintenance and socialization of children is accomplished … and how sexuality is constructed.

Holloway's depiction of labour manages to downplay the work most fundamental to the power division between men and women in society, namely the assignment of social reproductive and care-work as a naturalised activity of women. This, we suggest, must be explored as a shortcoming, not of Holloway's work alone, but as a deeper malaise within Marxist theory, where the construction of women in a way particular to patriarchal capitalism is often under-theorised.

In its current formulation, Holloway's conception of labour does not address reproductive labour sufficiently. But, from a socialist feminist position, it is easy to imagine where the largely unpaid and invisible reproductive activity performed by women would fit into Holloway's understanding of labour. The often atomistic character of social reproduction, and its direct involvement in reproducing labour-power, gives it an abstract form. But its deeply personal and caring dimension gives it a very pronounced concrete and life-affirming form which is not easily commodified. Like all labour, reproductive labour has a fascinating dual existence as both abstract and concrete labour (Fortunati 1995, 105). But, given the specifically patriarchal character of this form of labour, social reproduction becomes a necessary and central site for working against the privileging of all the forms of existence Holloway condemns under capitalism, namely abstract labour, being, identities and 'done'.

In the end, Holloway underestimates what cannot be underestimated – that women have a very particular and special historical place in the story of the capitalist transformation of work. Indeed, socialist feminists have repeatedly shown how the system of wage 'labour' was developed on the back of its invisible counterpart – the unwaged condition of women's social reproductive labour. The historical facts about social reproduction (particularly its gendered character) must however be underestimated by Holloway in his work if he seeks to retain his suggestion that in order to alter our lives, we need to relinquish our identity masks, including what he unfortunately sees as the character mask of 'women'.

Undoubtedly, in order to understand a politics that begins in the everyday, we need to understand the potential of the everyday. But this *potentia* which Holloway repeatedly highlights cannot be understood in the absence of understanding the 'she' who does most of capitalism's most ignored 'doing', the most invisible 'labours of creation', the most devalued 'productivity', she who performs much of the 'concrete labour' that is essentially swallowed by the dominance of 'abstract labour' – she who is 'woman'.

In briefly concluding this section, it seems clear that combining questions about patriarchy and the significance of women's reproductive labour with Holloway's desire for anti-hierarchical class politics can potentially offer practical and constructive content to 'cracking capitalism' in an autonomist way. Additionally, while we agree with Holloway that autonomist practices necessitate acting against (and ultimately moving beyond) identity and 'done', we claim that acting within identities (at least the identity of woman) and even asserting such identities in new ways is critical for advancing feminist struggles.

A feminist commoning

Holloway's autonomist theory is undoubtedly consistent with the type of commoning perspective we discuss, as both, for instance, challenge state-centred change. But, in examining commoning, we need to highlight the significance of women as we did in discussing autonomism. After all, central to processes of enclosure historically under capitalism has been the enclosure of women under conditions of patriarchy, and specifically the almost natural connection drawn between women and social reproduction.

There is now a considerable volume of literature on 'the commons' and commoning from an autonomist and other related anti-statist perspectives. In seeking to delineate the importance of 'the commons', a clear distinction is regularly made between 'the commons' on the one hand and the public and private spheres under capitalism on the other, which are 'two sides of the same capitalist coin' (Roggero 2010, 366). As Thorburn argues (2012, 254), 'a politics of the common' is 'not mediated by the State or capital'. For instance, the public space, which is not to be confused with the commons, is a space 'given from a certain authority to the public under specific conditions that ultimately affirm the authority's legitimacy' (Stavrides 2012, 587). To simply reclaim the public, though important under pronounced conditions of privatisation, then is merely to claim the legitimacy of the state and thereby assert or reassert its authority.

Central then to the commons (and Holloway would agree with this) is a radically different understanding of sociality, an understanding that recognises the commons as emergent and becoming, and not designed and implemented. In this regard, Linebaugh (2010, 2) refers to 'the actuality of communing' and 'communing practices', and Federici (2011a, 2) as the 'movement for the commons'. Commoning involves communities in processes of becoming such that 'the community is developed through communing, through acts of organisation oriented towards the production of the common' (Stavrides 2012, 587). What these commoning practices entail are open to differing interpretations, but they would include 'self-established rules, self-determination, self-organisation and self-regulating practices particularly vis-à-vis the state and capitalist social, economic and cultural relations' (Bohm et al. 2008, 6). This does not mean though that the commons-as-process exists outside the clutches of state and capital as it entails practices within, against and potentially beyond capitalism. As Stavrides (2012, 594) notes, for example, 'the realm of the common emerges in a constant confrontation with state-controlled "authorised" public space'. Likewise, Bohm et al. (2008, 10) highlight that autonomous practices around the commons are in a 'permanent and ongoing struggle' with existing structures, practices and discourses of hegemonic power. Indeed, 'the commons' can be (and often is) domesticated and incorporated by hegemonic regimes.

Hence, it is not a question of romanticising 'the commons'. Again Stavrides (2012, 591) argues astutely in stating that 'discrepancies, ambiguities, and contradictions are necessary ingredients of a potential community in action'. Jeffrey, McFarlane, and Vasudevan (2012, 1254) make a similar point in arguing that 'the struggle for the commons has never been without its own politics of separation and division', as commoning movements 'often actively deploy walling as a means of protecting the commons'. There is often a tension between openness and inclusiveness on the one hand, and regulating the space by democratic and just means on the other – but possibly thereby protecting it and excluding others (an apparent enclosure moment of its own). Intriguingly, in this context, De Angelis (2014, 304) speaks of a 'patriarchal form of commons' which simply reproduces prevailing patriarchal structures and practices. But we suggest in this section that the assertion of the identity of 'woman' (or women's identities) in commoning struggles, and the revaluing of women in all their diversity, should not be seen as inherently regressive insofar as this may entail a basis for challenging patriarchal tendencies.

Reference is often made in the commoning literature to the commons of social reproduction/social reproduction commons. Because of this, and in trying to disentangle 'itself' from the rhythms of state and capital, the commons must entail 'autonomous spaces from which to reclaim control over the conditions of our reproduction' (Caffentzis and Federici 2014, i101). Women and patriarchy become critical in this regard, due to the historical centrality of women in social reproduction at household level, in which women's work has been appropriated as unpaid labour just as – under capitalism – nature has been expropriated for purposes of corporate gain. In a sense, then, both women and nature have been subject to processes of enclosure. As Mies and Bennholdt-Thomsen (1999, 156) put it, 'women are treated like commons and commons are treated as women'. Unless animated by feminist practices, a commons is not a commons as it continues to subject women to enclosure. Thus, moving beyond the naturalised connection between women and social reproduction and finding new ways of undertaking the concrete labour of social reproduction become central to commoning.

In thinking about the commons, the category of woman is not an identity which can be dislocated. Instead, sociologically, what is needed is to complicate and revalorise the category of woman. We need to historicise it in all of its differences and show its material and social significance to the continuation of the separation of doing from done. Marxist feminist Federici, who writes from an autonomist and commoning perspective, makes this clear in her work (2004, 2012). Capitalist accumulation, proletarianisation and the wage-relation which organises society today all depend on the centrality of women and social reproduction. For Federici (2004, 14):

> [Th]e debates that have taken place among postmodern feminists concerning the need to dispose of 'women' as a category of analysis, and define feminism purely in oppositional terms, have been misguided. … [I]f 'femininity' has been constituted in capitalist society as a work-function masking the production of the work-force under the cover of a biological destiny, then 'women's history' is 'class history', and the question that has to be asked is whether the sexual division of labour that has produced that particular concept has been transcended. If the answer is a negative one (as it must be when we consider the present organisation of reproductive labour), then 'women' is a legitimate category of analysis, and the activities associated with 'reproduction' remains a crucial ground of struggle for women.

Federici (2011b) puts forward an argument for the 'doing' of social reproduction, including the re-collectivisation of social reproduction as an ongoing goal for a commoning society. The 'feminist commons' which she discusses are experiments in collective possibilities steeped in the radical redress of who performs subsistence tasks within communities and society at large. This would also be crucial to Holloway's arguments for 'everyday revolutions'.

However, what is important in Federici's take on the commons and critical to her understanding is the notion that capitalism quietly recreates itself in the present as it did in the past, with the help of men, on the backs of women, through primitive accumulation at the 'point (zero)' of work, namely, the point at which social reproductive labour takes place. Any successful revolutionisation of social relations, she argues, must therefore target and bring into clarity the ways in which the construction of 'women' through the rendering of social reproduction as invisible is used to keep primitive accumulation not as a stage in the annals of modernity, but rather as an ongoing process where capital periodically reacts to social revolts by its establishment of ever new enclosures on communal life.

The new enclosures of the twenty-first century create systems of economic domination and dependence which are extremely intricate by locking people internationally into a system of capitalist oppression more impersonal and indistinguishable than any system of domination before. For Federici (2012, 12), reimagining society can be bolstered through revisiting the notion of ongoing primitive accumulation through a feminist lens. The progress of capitalism has historically relied on a sexual division of labour which places social reproduction and reproduction of the labour-force as secondary to waged-work. This is a patriarchal form unique to capitalism which must be undermined through struggle.

This connection between women's work and ongoing primitive accumulation has special significance today as we find ourselves in a system of global capitalism renowned both for exacting the largest enclosures in world history (Midnight Nights Collective 2009) as well as having social reproduction more intruded upon by capitalist relations than ever before (Dalla Costa 2008, 87). This contemporaneous development is no coincidence; instead it is a present indication of the fundamentally gendered infrastructure of capitalism.

Women have played a pivotal role in struggles through defending existing commons and creating new ones. And this is regularly pursued by women as women in seeking at least as a first step to restore their dignity and agency, rather than arising through some un-mediated leap into anti-identitarian struggle. In this respect, Federici derives her belief in the possibility of the feminist commons from the observation of female subsistence farmers in Africa, Asia and Latin America and their struggles to defend land from ongoing enclosures. She sees a double reality for women in the realm of social reproduction – women are subjugated to capitalist patriarchy but they may also use their presence and reach in the domain of reproductive activity to plant the seeds of a reconstructed society. Despite a lack of theoretical representations of the feminist commons, pragmatic examples in the real world, while few, have been inspiring.

There is hope in the idea of the feminist commons. But the commons is also contested terrain. It is in this sense that we consider the notion of feminist commoning as more apt than feminist commons, as the former highlights that the defence of existing commons or the creation of new ones is a process subject to continual tension and conflict. The most apparent challenge to the creation of the commons in Africa is possibly the existence of dual systems of land ownership which incorporate both customary land systems and neo-liberal systems of commercialisation, which, acting together, can destroy the chances of women in their struggle to attain land in spite of the fact that women make up the bulk of farmers on the continent. In this context, women do organise as women around their own social reproduction activities (including seeking to de-naturalise the relationship between women and social reproduction) and they at times open up cracks within local systems of patriarchy to better themselves and their often female-headed households. This acting 'within' identity should not be dismissed outright, as implicitly it often entails the potential for far-reaching change.

In summary, we cannot think about Holloway's interstitial change without thinking about the sex-gender impediments to revolution in the same way that we cannot think of commoning without thinking about social reproductive tasks and those who perform them. The alteration of social values and the possibility for the re-socialisation of people rests so strongly on the power of those who perform social reproduction (women) that a sustainable commoning process will have to privilege deep social co-operation based on the empowering of women. We therefore agree with Federici that it is not yet a commons if it does not involve the existence of a community openly cognisant of the need to collectivise reproductive work. But, from our perspective, this collectivisation (or moving beyond) is invariably rooted in everyday practices in the here-in-now and in concrete local situations in which women often foreground their gendered identity as a basis for expressing agency and reshaping society.

Fast track land occupations in Zimbabwe

In light of our discussions about autonomism and commoning, we now turn briefly to Zimbabwe and specifically the land occupation movement from the year 2000 and less so to the state's subsequent Fast Track Land Reform (FTLR) programme. There is a vast literature on the FTLR programme in Zimbabwe but significantly less on the occupations themselves. Only a few scholars (Moyo and Yeros 2005, 2007; Masuko 2011; Sadomba 2011) have offered a reasonably nuanced account of the land occupations, but none of these studies have focused specifically on gender. There is admittedly a growing body of literature on the FTLR programme and gender (for example, Goebel 2005a, 2005b; Chingarande 2010; Mutopo 2011), but the gendered perspectives adopted fall completely outside the realm of any kind of autonomist feminist and commoning theoretical framing.

The character of the land occupation movement and FTLR is open to considerable contestation within the Zimbabwean literature. The dominant argument (for example, Hammar, Raftopoulos, and Jensen 2003) is that the occupations, which began in early 2000, were regressive politically as they were simply an electoral ploy by an authoritarian ruling party Zimbabwe African National Union-Patriotic Front (ZANU-PF) to garner rural support for the upcoming national elections in June 2000, where ZANU-PF faced a substantial opposition.

The alternative argument (Moyo and Yeros 2007), and the argument to which we largely subscribe, is that the occupations were in large part decentralised (all the way down to district and indeed farm level), at least initially. Social groupings of a diverse range occupied farms to varying degrees and for different reasons, and these included communal farmers, urban workers, war veterans, agricultural labourers, civil servants and party elites. The main war veterans' association played a significant role at the local level. As well, local ruling party structures slowly but surely became involved in the movement (or at least in specific occupations) even before the FTLR programme was announced by the state in mid-2000. This argument also claims that, with FTLR, the state sought not only to legitimise the occupations (and therefore protect them) but to also subdue and co-opt them. Thus, the state's intervention was a contradictory two-edged sword – legitimation as progressive and co-option as regressive. This implies though that the occupations themselves were inherently progressive, which, we argue, is highly dubious particularly from a feminist perspective.

It is clear that the occupations entailed, often explicitly, a rejection of market-led land reform (which in the main prevailed until the year 2000) and, additionally, an undermining of the racially-based private property regime dominating the agrarian landscape in Zimbabwe. This seems, at first sight, to involve a commoning tendency. Because of this, at least before the state became involved in the occupations more directly, the situation on the ground (on the occupied farms) has been described by Moyo and Yeros (2007) as a revolutionary-type moment. However, the occupation movement, as a people-driven land redistribution programme, simply sought to restructure the agrarian space on a strictly racial basis. It was in no sense an anti-patriarchal movement.

It is questionable then to what extent, or if at all, the occupation movement was in any real sense a proto-revolutionary moment, at least from a feminist commoning perspective. Admittedly, more broadly (and without referring specifically to gender) there were some commoning impulses, for instance in cases where the occupiers sought to defend their base camps or settlements on occupied farms not only against the white commercial farmers but also against state and ruling party intrusion.

Certainly, any regressive character embedded in the land events in the year 2000 cannot be reduced to the state subduing the movement, for the movement itself was not as progressive as Moyo and Yeros constantly claim. At the broader level, there were always pronounced exclusions, notably of the tens of thousands of farm labourers who worked and lived at the time on the occupied commercial farms.

It was also a movement which in many ways simply reproduced the pronounced gendered relations existing in the colonially constructed communal areas of Zimbabwe – from which many occupiers came – in relation for instance to women's restricted access to land (mediated invariably through husbands or male relatives). In this regard, there should be no confusion between communal lands and the commons. As Mies and Bennholdt-Thomsen (1999, 157) argue more generally, a clear distinction needs to be made between 'a community based on reciprocity that is, relying on the commoners, and so called communal regimes imposed from above'. Undoubtedly, the communal areas are imposed from above with, for example, the chieftainship system in Zimbabwe's communal areas effectively being part of the local state system. Likewise, the occupied farms now under Fast Track are state-regulated.

Though the occupation of privately-held (enclosed) land might appear as some sort of commoning process, entailing the re-establishment of a commons once existing and then undermined through colonial dispossession, the land occupation movement (and later the Fast Track programme) entailed the inscribing of local patriarchies on the occupied farms in a manner similar to communal areas.

Coordination of occupations took place at farm level and across farms within districts, with war veterans (mostly men) being particularly important in this respect. Women normally played a subordinate role in the occupations. Though the occupations were marked by substantial district-level and local farm-level variations, informal arrangements existed and formal structures were generally put in place to coordinate the activities of occupiers once farms were occupied (Chaumba, Scoones, and Wolmer 2003; Sadomba 2011), including the formation of a Committee of Seven on each farm. These tended to have a distinct patriarchal form. The committees, which emerged as a form of local authority on the occupied farms, included a women's representative though the critical position of chief of security on farms was rarely a woman.

The continuation of gendered relations during the occupations, including with respect to social reproduction, was very pronounced, as women were in large part confined to the domestic sphere. In relation to Masvingo province, Scoones et al. (2010, 55) for example note that women 'often took on highly gendered roles in the base camps [on the occupied farms] (including cooking, collecting firewood and water), and were rarely in top leadership positions'. Women were also directly affected by water shortages that regularly existed on occupied and then FTLR farms, as it is their duty in rural communities to collect water. The problems experienced by women are vividly portrayed in the following comment from a woman at Dunstan Farm in Goromonzi district (in Chakona 2011, 101):

> As women we always bear the burden of walking long distances in search of water ... We don't have rest. If we are to wash clothes then we have to dedicate the whole day to that particular activity since the [distance to the] place is long ... This also takes part of our productive time when we should be in the fields.

Social reproduction responsibilities also inhibited women's active involvement in the occupations. Thus, in her study of Merrivale Farm in Mwenezi district in Masvingo province, Mutopo (2011) makes the point that women were not able to engage fully in occupying Merrivale because of family responsibilities in the nearby customary (or communal) areas from which they came.

But, in certain instances, women led the occupations or in fact occupied farms on their own in the absence of men. The study by Chingarande (2010) of 'ordinary' women now living in Nyambamba in Chimanimani district is a good illustration of this, though their leadership role in large part arose because most men in the nearby customary areas were employed elsewhere at the time of the nation-wide occupation movement. At times, women as war veterans or with important political party affiliations spurred on the occupations, such as in Mazowe district (Chiweshe 2011; Sadomba 2011).

Further, married women on A1 farms (a FTLR farm model replicating communal area land tenure arrangements) often had their presence formalised by the state in and through their husband and this arrangement thereby simply reproduced the conditions prevailing in customary areas. On certain occasions, married women whose name originally appeared along with their husbands on the offer letter under FTLR were pressurised by their husbands to have their name removed from the letter and they bowed to this in order to maintain cordial relations in their marriage. One woman named Chenai, who had land registered in her name, claimed that 'there was no peace in the home and my husband complained all the time about me having land in my own name and even threatened to divorce me' (Mazhawidza and Manjengwa 2011, 30). Even in the case of Merrivale farm (which was occupied by women and cleared of wattle by women), the names of the husbands of the female occupiers appeared on the state's Fast Track offer letters as plotholders because 'their husbands processed all the paper work' (Chingarande 2010, 4).

Despite these challenges, there is considerable evidence that certain groupings of women used the openings provided by the occupations to manoeuvre, *as women*, for purposes of advancing their social security. As Mazhawidza and Manjengwa (2011, 7) argue about gender in relation to the land occupations and FTLR, 'old and new actors are negotiating the path, producing trade-offs, as the process unfolds'. The position of unmarried women – divorced, widowed or single – is particularly important. Many unmarried women from customary areas took advantage of the movements onto commercial farms during the year 2000 to gain access to land which was not available to them (or which they had lost) in communal areas because of their unmarried status; and, in certain cases, their status as occupiers was formalised by the state under the Fast Track programme. In this respect, it is quite common for widows and divorcees in customary areas to be accused by in-laws of witchcraft and causing the death of husbands (particularly in HIV and AIDS cases), and they are frequently even chased away by their in-laws (Chaumba,

Scoones, and Wolmer 2003). Hence, for some women, embedded in the occupations were the 'emancipatory potentials of joining a new community' (Scoones et al. 2010, 52).

Overall, the occupations had a commoning moment and potential though, from a specifically autonomist feminist perspective, this claim becomes particularly problematic. Patriarchal relations and practices were maintained during the occupations and under FTLR, which is specifically evident in the sphere of social reproduction as the naturalised link between women and social reproduction was never challenged. There are, however, instances of women, as women, seeking to go beyond their naturally assigned roles, such as through occupying land in their own right (whether married or not) and thus claiming primary and not simply secondary rights and access to land. Additionally, married women on occupied farms were able to start pursuing livelihood strategies which facilitated some degree of economic independence from their husbands and this sometimes enhanced their decision-making powers within households (Chakona 2011). These strategies often involved specifically women-related activities such as vegetable gardening and petty commodity trading focusing on 'feminine' products (such as woven baskets and mats), such that they used their identity as women in some small way to change their lives.

Conclusion

Like Holloway, we believe that meaningful transformation requires moving against and beyond identity in the form of anti-identitarian struggles. And, like Federici, we believe that processes of commoning ultimately entail tearing asunder the link between women and social reproduction and moving toward the collectivisation of social reproduc-tion. However, advancing along these political roads necessitates recognising the salience of identities and specifically the identity of woman. All struggles are rooted in social experiences under local and concrete circumstances and these experiences (as structured by identities) cannot be simply wished away or transcended automatically. In moving against and beyond gendered identities, women need to assert, revalue and re-signify the identities through which they (as women) experience the world.

Disclosure statement

No potential conflict of interest was reported by the authors.

References

Alcoff, Linda. 2007. "Fraser on Redistribution, Recognition, and Identity." *European Journal of Political Theory* 6 (3): 255–265.
Binford, Leigh. 2005. "Holloway's Marxism." *Historical Materialism* 13 (3): 251–263.

Bohm, Steffen, Ana Dinerstein, and Andre Spicer. 2008. *(Im)possibilities of Autonomy: Social Movements in and Beyond Capital, the State and Development*. School of Accounting, Finance and Management, University of Essex. Working Paper No. WP 08/1, November.

Caffentzis, George, and Silvia Federici. 2014. "Commons against and Beyond Capitalism." *Community Development Journal* 49 (s1): i92–i105.

Castells, Manuel. 1997. *The Power of Identity*. West Sussex: Wiley-Blackwell.

Chakona, Loveness. 2011. "Fast Track Land Reform Programme and Women in Goromonzi District." Zimbabwe. MA thesis, Rhodes University.

Chaumba, J., I. Scoones, and W. Wolmer. 2003. "From Jambanja to Planning: The Reassertion of Technocracy in Land Reform in South-Eastern Zimbabwe?" *The Journal of Modern African Studies* 41 (4): 533–554.

Chingarande, S. D. 2010. "Gender and Livelihoods in Nyabamba A1 Resettlement Area, Chimanimani District of Manicaland Province in Zimbabwe." In *Livelihoods after Land Reform in Zimbabwe Working Paper 5*. South Africa: PLAAS.

Chiweshe, Manase. 2011. "Farm Level Institutions in Emergent Communities in Post-Fast Track Zimbabwe: Case of Mazowe District." PhD thesis, Rhodes University.

Cockburn, Cynthia. 2012. "Who are 'we'? Asks one of us." *Journal of Classical Sociology* 12 (2): 205–219.

Cuninghame, Patrick. 2010. "Autonomism as Global Social Movement." *WorkingUSA: The Journal of Labor and Society* 13 (4): 451–464.

Dalla Costa, Giovanna. 2008. *The Work of Love: Unpaid Housework, Poverty and Sexual Violence at the Dawn of the 21st Century*. New York: Autonomedia.

De Angelis, Massimo. 2014. "Social Revolution and the Commons." *The South Atlantic Quarterly* 113 (2): 299–311.

Eden, David. 2008. "Against, Outside & Beyond: The Perspective of Autonomy in the 21st Century." PhD thesis, Australian National University.

Federici, Silvia. 2004. Caliban and the Witch: Women, the Body and Primitive Accumulation. New York: Autonomedia.

Federici, Silvia. 2011a. *Feminism, Finance and the Future of #occupy* (Interview with Max Haiven). Communications. www.libcom.org/library/feminism-finance-future-occupy-interview-silvia-federici .

Federici, Silvia. 2011b. "Feminism and the Politics of the Commons." *Commoner*, January 24 www.commoner.org.uk/?p=ii3 .

Federici, Silvia. 2012. *Revolution at Point Zero: Housework, Reproduction and Feminist Struggle*. Oakland, CA: PM Press.

Fortunati, Leopoldina. 1995. *The Arcane of Reproduction: Housework, Prostitution, Labor and Capital*. New York: Autonomedia.

Franks, Benjamin. 2008. "Postanarchism and Meta-Ethics." *Anarchist Studies* 16 (2): 135–153. Fraser, Nancy. 1995. "From Redistribution to Recognition? Dilemmas of Justice in a 'Post-Socialist' age." *New Left Review* 212: 68–93.

Fraser, Nancy. 2000. "Rethinking Recognition." *New Left Review* 3: 107–120.

Fraser, Nancy. 2004. "Recognition, Redistribution and Representation in Capitalist Global Society: An Interview with Nancy Fraser." *Acta Sociologica* 47 (4): 374–382.

Fraser, Nancy. 2007. "Feminist Politics in the age of Recognition: A two-Dimensional Approach to Gender Justice." *Studies in Social Justice* 1 (1): 23–35.

Goebel, Allison. 2005a. "Zimbabwe's 'Fast Track' Land Reform: What about Women?" *Gender, Place and Culture* 12 (2): 145–172.

Goebel, Allison. 2005b. *Gender and Land Reform: The Zimbabwe Experience*. Montreal: McGill-Queen's University Press.

Hammar, Amanda, Brian Raftopoulos, and Stig Jensen, eds. 2003. *Zimbabwe's Unfinished Business: Rethinking Land, State and Nation in the Context of Crisis*. Harare: Weaver Press.

Holloway, John. 2002. *Change the World Without Taking Power*. New York: Pluto.

Holloway, John. 2010. *Crack Capitalism*. New York: Pluto.

Jeffrey, Alex, Colin McFarlane, and Alex Vasudevan. 2012. "Rethinking Enclosure: Space, Subjectivity and the Commons." *Antipode* 44 (4): 1247–1267.

Katsiaficas, George. 2006. *Subversion of Politics: European Autonomous Social Movements and the Decolonization of Everyday Life*. Oakland: AK Press.

Laslett, Barbara, and Johanna Brenner. 1989. "Gender and Social Reproduction: Historical Perspectives." *Annual Review of Sociology* 15: 381–404.

Linebaugh, Peter. 2010. "Meandering on the Semantical-Historical Paths of Communism and Commons." *The Commoner*, 1–17. http://www.commoner.org.uk/wp-content/ uploads/2010/12/ meandering-linebaugh.pdf.

Marks, Brian. 2012. "Autonomist Marxist Theory and Practice in the Current Crisis." *ACME: An International Journal of Critical Geographies* 11 (3): 467–491.

Masuko, Louis. 2011. "Nyabira-Mazowe War Veterans" Association: A Microcosm of the National Land Occupation Movement." In *Land and Agrarian Reform in Zimbabwe: Beyond White-Settler Capitalism*, edited by Sam Moyo, and Walter Chambati, 123–156. Dakar: CODESRIA/AIAS.

Mazhawidza, Phides, and Jeanette Manjengwa. 2011. The Social, Political and Economic Transformative Impact of the Fast Track Land Reform Programme on the Lives of Women Farmers in Goromonzi and Vungu-Gweru Districts of Zimbabwe. Women Farmers Land and Agriculture Trust/Centre for Applied Social Sciences, University of Zimbabwe.

Midnight Notes Collective. 2009. "Promissory Notes: From Crisis to Commons." Accessed February 2015, www.midnightnotes.org/Promissory%20Notes.pdf.

Mies, Maria. 1998. *Patriarchy and Accumulation on a World Scale: Women in the International Division of Labour*. London: Zed Books.

Mies, Maria, and Bennholdt-Thomsen, Veronika. 1999. *The Subsistence Perspective: Beyond the Globalised Economy*. London: Zed Books.

Moyo, Sam, and Paris Yeros. 2005. "Land Occupations and Land Reform in Zimbabwe: Towards the National Democratic Revolution." In *Reclaiming the Land: The Resurgence of Rural Movements in Africa, Asia and Latin America*, edited by Sam Moyo, and Paris Yeros, 165–208. London: ZED Books.

Moyo, Sam, and Paris Yeros. 2007. "The Radicalised State: Zimbabwe's Interrupted Revolution." *Review of African Political Economy* 34 (111): 103–121.

Mutopo, Patience. 2011. "Women's Struggles to Access and Control Land and Livelihoods after Fast Track Land Reform in Mwenezi District, Zimbabwe." *Journal of Peasant Studies* 38 (5): 1021–1046.

Newman, S. 2010. *The Politics of Postanarchism*. Edinburgh: Edinburgh University Press.

Ollenburger, Jane and Moore, Helen. 1997. *A Sociology of Women: Intersection of Patriarchy, Capitalism and Colonization*. Upper Saddle River, NJ: Pearson Press.

Roggero, Gigi. 2010. "Five Theses on the Common." *Rethinking Marxism* 22 (3): 357–373.

Sadomba, Z. W. 2011. *War Veteran's in Zimbabwe's Revolution. Harare: Challenging Neo-Colonialism and Settler and International Capital*. Rochester: Boydell and Brewer.

Scoones, I., N. Marongwe, B. Mavedzenge, J. Mahenehene, F. Murimbarimba, and C. Sukume. 2010. *Zimbabwe's Land Reform*. Harare: Weaver Press.

Stavrides, Stavros. 2012. "Squares in Movement." *The South Atlantic Quarterly* 111 (3): 585–596.

Thorburn, Elise. 2012. "A Common Assembly: Multitude, Assemblies, and a new Politics of the Common." *Interface: A Journal for and about Social Movements* 4 (2): 254–279.

Weeks, Kathi. 2011. *The Problem with Work: Feminism, Marxism, Antiwork Politics, and Postwork Imaginaries*. Durham: Duke University Press.

From below: an overview of South African politics at a distance from the state, 1917–2015, with dossier of texts

Compiled and edited, with introduction, by Lucien van der Walt[1]

Introduction

This dossier outlines three modes of types "politics at a distance from the state," and discusses examples of these different modes in modern South African politics.

"Politics at a distance from the state" refers, here, to a break with the "subordination" of politics to the question of state power and political parties (Badiou, Del Lucchese and Del Smith, 2008: 649–650), "a rupture with the representative form of politics" and the "spectre of the party-state" (Badiou 2006: 289, 292). This is a "descriptive, negative, characterisation" (Badiou *et al*, 2008: 649–650), and covers a range of positions that stress society-centred, rather than state-centred, change. These share a politics of anti-capitalist transformation, but reject strategies – such as those of traditional social democracy, or Marxism-Leninism, or anti-imperialist nationalism – that emphasise the capture and the use of the state apparatus for social transformation. It is anti-capitalism and popular self-emancipation that most obviously distinguish "politics at a distance" from neo-liberal modes of anti-statism, which present competitive markets and strong states as essential cornerstones of individual freedom.

The dossier arises from a larger process of reflection and engagement. A key moment took place in September 2012, when a conference of radical academics and activists was held at Rhodes University, Grahamstown, in the Eastern Cape Province, South Africa. This event brought together a diverse range of people and formations interested in exploring, debating and understanding "politics at a distance from the state," as theory and practice.[2]

One published outcome of the event was a collection of academic papers: the current volume. This dossier complements those papers, but provides a historical overview, and a collection of primary sources. Its focus is on documenting the scope, and demonstrating the value, of radical South African popular traditions of "politics at a distance from the state."

Groups involved in the 2012 conference included the Church Land Programme (formed 1996) in Pietermaritzburg; the Mandela Park Backyarders from Cape Town; various farmworkers committees, linked to the Eastern Cape Agricultural Research Project (ECARP, formed 1993); the Landless People's Movement (LPM, formed 2001), from Soweto; the Unemployed People's Movement (formed 2009); members of *Abahlali baseMjondolo*; the anarchist-influenced hip-hop collective Soundz of the South (founded 2010), from Cape Town; and the Zabalaza Anarchist Communist Front (ZACF, formed 2003), from Johannesburg, Khutsong, Sebokeng and Soweto in Gauteng.

This dossier brings together a selection of movement texts and interviews and discussions that were circulated that conference, or undertaken at that conference, or referenced at that conference. These texts represent a small slice of an alternative political praxis, a tradition often elided and ignored, which rejects centring radical politics on the capture of state power. The texts in this dossier are:

- International Socialist League, December 1917, "Industrial Unionism in South Africa";
- Industrial and Commercial Workers Union of Africa, 1925, "Revised Constitution of the ICU" (Preamble);
- Alan Lipman, "Two Conceptions of Democracy" (2007, extracts);
- "The Worker in the Community," undated paper by panel of Federation of South African Trade Unions (FOSATU) shopstewards in Springs (extracts);
- Murphy Morobe, May 1987, "Towards a People's Democracy: The UDF View" (extracts);
- The Unemployed People's Movement (UPM), 2011, "Ten Theses on Democracy," Grahamstown (extracts);
- Lekhetho Mtetwa, 29–30 September 2013, "The Landless People's Movement Fights for the People's Rights";
- Soundz of the South (SOS), 29–30 September 2013, Anti-Capitalist, Anti-Authoritarian African Hip-hop and Poetry;
- Zabalaza Anarchist Communist Front, 16 December 2014, "Interview With Warren McGregor: Anarchist-Communism, Building Black Working Class Counter Power against State, Capital and National Oppression";
- Abahlali baseMjondolo, 18 December 2015, "Occupy, Resist, Develop."

"Politics at a distance from the state"?

The vision of the enabling state was central to the left and anti-imperialist projects of the "short twentieth century" of 1917–1991, and its adherents included social-democrats, mainstream Marxists and anti-imperialist nationalists (Taylor, 1991: 216). The logic of these projects was neatly captured in the pithy phrase of Ghanaian anti-colonial leader and Pan-Africanist, Kwame Nkrumah (1909–1972): "Seek ye first the political kingdom and all things shall be added unto you" (quoted in Biney, 2011: 2). For example, both social democrats and Marxist-Leninists saw the central issue as "a political battle against capitalism waged through . . . centrally organised workers' parties aimed at seizing and utilising State power" (Thorpe, 1989: 3).

In reality, all of these projects foundered by the 1970s. They ran aground the rocks of economic crisis: Keynesian demand-management, central planning, and import-substitution-industrialisation all proved incapable of restoring economic growth, or maintaining earlier welfare and employment levels and commitments by the start of the 1980s. Their legitimacy leaked away, as promises of equality and freedom broke in the face of large-scale, ongoing inequalities in power and wealth. Badiou comments, for example, of Marxism-Leninism, that it led, not to emancipation, but "a new form of power that was nothing less than the power of the party itself," exemplified by regimes like the Union of Soviet Socialist Republics (USSR).

Nkrumah's own government, which emerged from the first successful post-war struggle for decolonisation in sub-Saharan Africa, with the independence of the one-time Gold Coast (renamed Ghana) in 1957 under the Convention People's Party (CPP), is another example. In 1958, the CPP-led state placed the unions under government control; in 1961 it cracked down on a mass strike centred on the Sekondi-Takoradi working class districts; in 1964 the CPP became the sole legal party, with Nkrumah the centre of a personality cult; in 1965, there was a military coup, which was met with widespread approval by the disenchanted popular classes (Fitch and Oppenheimer, 1968; Mbah and Igariwey, 1997).

All of these statist currents remain very influential, as the influence of the Coalition of the Radical Left (SYRIZA) in Greece, the ongoing strength of the Workers Party (PT) in Brazil, the African National Congress (ANC) and the South African Communist Party (SACP) in South Africa, and the Communist Party of India (Marxist) (CPI-M), all demonstrate. But attempts to revive these older models have consistently failed over the last four decades, with the ignoble capitulation of SYRIZA to neo-liberal austerity within weeks of being elected on an anti-austerity ticket in 2015 only the latest example. The old approaches are not self-evidently desirable, and they are not really feasible in the current political economy and balance of class forces (Helliker and van der Walt, 2016; Wilks, 1996).

With neo-liberal policies now standard, it has been the radical right that has ridden the wave of popular dissatisfaction with the economic and political establishments, a trend that ranges from the rise of the Bharatiya Janata Party (BJP) in India to Donald Trump's movement in the United States to the rise of violent, politicised, religious fundamentalisms.

One ray of hope, however, has been the revival of society-centred approaches on the left (Helliker and van der Walt, 2016). These range from the neo-Zapatista movement in Chiapas, Mexico, which from the 1990s explicitly rejected vanguardist conceptions of armed struggle and politics; developments in, or from, Marxist theory that have sought to rethink revolution, including strands of autonomist Marxism; and the revival of anarchism and syndicalism, expressed in, for example, Occupy Wall Street (Bray, 2013), radical labour organising (Ness, 2014) and revolutionary developments in the Rojava region of Syria, where the Kurdistan Workers Party (PKK, formed 1974) has redefined its aim as a "democratic system of a people without a State" (Hattingh and van der Walt, 2015: 72).

In such movements, the "organisation of the masses is still the fundamental issue," but the "politics of emancipation" is envisaged as taking place at a "distance from the state" (Badiou et al, 2008: 647, 649–650). This is to be distinguished from neo-liberal anti-statism, which does not seek the abolition of capitalism, and its replacement by a new, bottom-up, socialist order, but rather, aims to deepen the commodification of social relations, while retaining the state as guardian of a market-based society centred on wage labour.

Modes of "at a distance politics": a short outline

Within the heterogeneous category of "politics at a distance from the state," it is possible to think of three main variants. This is not to deny a substantial degree of variation within each category, as well as points of overlap between the categories. Nor is it to suggest that these modes necessarily take the form of carefully articulated ideologies. Rather, they express types of praxis, more or less identifiable, which are associated with particular lines of argument and which are influential in particular moments and movements.

Kirk Helliker and I suggest a distinction between three modes of "at a distance" politics: "outside-but-with" the state; "outside-and-despite" the state; and "outside-and-against" the state (Helliker and van der Walt, 2016).

1. The **"outside-but-with"** approach argues that popular initiatives, movements, and autonomy should be combined with transforming and democratising the state (e.g. Wainwright, 2004). From this perspective, popular mobilisation complements radical changes in, and through, the state. It does not reduce politics to the state, but it is also not anti-statist. This approach has a long history. An early variant was Guild Socialism. This argued that the means of production should be owned by the state, but run by self-managed workers' "guilds" (Schechter, 1994; for a recent appreciation: Masquelier and Dawson, 2016). Recent iterations have stressed a combination of popular self-activity with parliamentary democracy, taking inspiration from, for example, the so-called participatory budgeting process in the Porto Alegre, Brazil.

2. The **"outside-and-despite"** approach, by contrast, explicitly rejects the state apparatus, and argues for the creation of new social relations within the interstices – the cracks and gaps – of the existing order, arguing that that these can somehow cumulatively develop the capacity to supplant capitalist and statist relations with "experimental communism" (e.g. Bonefeld and Holloway 2014; Holloway, 2005). There is a stress on open-ended and indeterminate processes, and scepticism towards grand programmes and revolutionary schemas. A key expression of this approach is the strand of autonomist Marxism identified with John Holloway.

3. The **"outside-and-against"** approach rejects the use of the state apparatus in principle, stressing the prefigurative construction of new social relations, outside of and against the state and capital, which can underpin a new social order (e.g. van der Walt, 2016). Anarchism and syndicalism are a key expression of this approach, which stresses the necessity of a decisive showdown with the ruling classes, based on coordination, strategy, vision and theory, and developing mass, bottom-up organisations, able to both defeat and supplant the existing order. This entails the construction of bottom-up organs of "counter-power" that empower and unite ordinary people, enable resistance, and provide the nucleus of a future, self-governed socialist system, and the promotion of a revolutionary "counter-culture," that is, a counter-hegemonic, world view. Rather than focus on constituting experimental forms in the interstices of the existing order, it aims at mass-based, confrontational movements with a unified strategy, that draw the widest possible layers into the struggle for a new world, and a revolutionary rupture based on a final confrontation that forcibly overthrows the ruling class and state.

A historical outline of "at a distance" politics in South Africa

A critical discussion of these different modes of "at a distance" politics falls outside the scope of this dossier and can be found elsewhere (see Helliker and van der Walt, 2016). The remainder of this discussion will focus, instead, on examples of these different modes in modern South African politics, and on locating the primary texts in the dossier in their context.

From below

As we have argued elsewhere – and this is worth reiterating here – an examination of popular struggles should not involve romanticisation, nor forcing them to fit into pre-existing categories. Thus (Helliker and van der Walt, 2016: 328).

> ... it is important to avoid imposing our hopes and fears on real-world examples, or obscuring complex issues with obtuse jargon and prose. It is important to grapple instead with messier realities: experiences like the anarchists and syndicalists' Spanish Revolution from 1936, the uprising in Chiapas from 1994, and PKK activities in Rojava from 2012, require sober reflection, not a false choice between uncritical praise or purist critique ...

The discussion and the dossier are not, therefore, intended as exercise in uncritical celebration or sectarian critique. Instead, I proceed from the premise that it is always important to draw lessons from past experiences, to engage in serious political discussions and education, and to ensure political pluralism and respectful dialogue within popular movements, including unions (van der Walt, 2014: 22–23).

Anarchists, syndicalists and radicals, 1900–1940s

Is it possible to speak of a tradition of "politics at a distance from the state" in South Africa? Certainly. It began in the early socialist and labour movements as an alternative to statist approaches.

Trade unions emerged from 1881 in South Africa, amongst immigrant white workers. Various attempts to form a Labour Party, modelled on the Labour Parties of Britain and Australia, culminated in the formation in October 1909 of a South African Labour Party. This party combined social democratic reformism with racist segregation policies, made substantial gains in the 1910s at municipal and provincial levels, and helped form a national coalition government from 1924 to 1933, championing race-based welfare, collective bargaining and pension reforms. After this initial growth, it declined rapidly, withering away in the 1950s.

Various nationalist parties emerged in the nineteenth century, but South Africa-wide nationalist parties only emerged after the final British conquests ended in 1902. Before then, "South Africa" did not exist, except as a region with a patchwork of African polities, Afrikaner republics, and British colonies. The unified South African state was created by an Act in the British parliament in September 1909, effective on 31 May 1910. The black nationalist ANC was formed in 1912 as the South African Native National Congress, the Afrikaner nationalist National Party (NP) was founded in 1914, and *Inkatha yakwa Zulu* was formed in 1928, a Zulu nationalist formation that was revived in 1975 as *Inkatha yeNkululeko yeSizwe* (later: the Inkatha Freedom Party).

Like the Labour Party, and the Communist Party of South Africa (CPSA, formed 1921, reformed as the South African Communist Party, SACP, in 1953), these parties stressed the capture of state power as the central means for introducing their programmes. The same statism was shared by various breakaways from the big parties, including the non-racial Democratic Labour Party (from the Labour Party, formed 1915), the Pan-Africanist Congress (PAC, from the ANC, formed 1959), the white Conservative Party (KP, from the NP, formed 1982), and the Economic Freedom Fighters (EFF, from the ANC, formed 2013).

But running alongside this powerful statist tradition were a series of groups and initiatives that implicitly or explicitly advocated more democratic, bottom-up and radical models of transformation and political organization than the statism of the nationalists and the Marxist-Leninists. While hidden by state-centric struggles and politics and historiographies, this alternative tradition points to a form of politics at odds with the top-down logic of state hierarchies and governance.

The Social Democratic Federation in Cape Town (SDF, formed in 1904), started out as an orthodox Marxist group, claiming affiliation to the SDF in Britain (Erasmus, 1905). It developed into a looser group, in which anarchist-communists played a central, often leading, role (van der Walt, 2011). It also included representatives of South Africa's small (and short-lived) Guild Socialist tradition, alongside more orthodox Marxists and social democrats (Johns, 1995: 31). The SDF is notable for forming non-racial trade unions and for promoting socialist ideas in central Cape Town as well as in the District Six ghetto (van der Walt, 2011).

A significant revolutionary syndicalist tradition emerged from 1910, which exemplified a politics of "outside-and-against," and soon centred on the International Socialist League (formed 1915), the Indian Workers Industrial Union (formed 1917), the Industrial Workers of Africa (formed 1917), the Industrial Socialist League (formed 1918, not to be confused with the International Socialist League), the Sweet and Jam Workers Industrial Union (formed 1918), the Clothing Workers Industrial Union (formed 1919) and the Horse Drivers Union (formed 1919).

The movement wanted to be "founded on the rock of the meanest proletarian who toils for a master," and "as wide as humanity" (*The International*, 1915). It's ultimate aim was to create One Big Union that would unite the working class, break down racial oppression, and institute workers' self-management as "an integral part of the International Industrial Republic" (*The International*, 1918). Its prefigurative approach to struggle – building a new South Africa, from below, through daily mass resistance and democratic organising – anticipated the radical "worker's control" and "people's power" threads of the 1980s anti-apartheid struggle (see below). A sample of the International Socialist League approach is included in this dossier (see **INTERNATIONAL SOCIALIST LEAGUE, 1917, "MANIFESTO OF THE SOLIDARITY COMMITTEE"**).

The local syndicalist current, which dominated the revolutionary left in 1910s South Africa, also had an influence on sectors of the early ANC in the Cape and Transvaal provinces, the African Political Organisation (formed 1902, renamed the African People's Organisation in 1919), a layer of white workers (notably in the Council of Action group on the mines), and the Industrial and Commercial Workers' Union of Africa (ICU, formed 1919) (van der Walt, 2007).

The ICU, into which a large part of the Industrial Workers of Africa would eventually merge, was the largest black and Coloured protest movement in 1920s South Africa: with at least 100,000 members at its height, it eclipsed the ANC and CPSA, which rarely reached 5,000 each. The ICU did not just operate in South Africa; it spread into in neighbouring colonies: South West Africa (now Namibia) from 1920, Southern Rhodesia (now Zimbabwe) from 1927, and Northern Rhodesia (now Zambia) from 1931 (van der Walt, 2007, 2016).

Like the South African syndicalists of the 1910s, the ICU drew on the ideas of the Industrial Workers of the World (IWW), a revolutionary syndicalist movement that started in the United States of America in 1905, which also spread worldwide. It considered forming cooperatives as well as occupying white-owned farms. At the same time, it flirted with political parties, including both the ANC and NP, and besides syndicalism, it was influenced by Christianity, liberalism, social democracy, and pan-Africanist racial nationalism in the form of Garveyism (van der Walt, 2007). A number of ICU statements clearly indicated a conception of "at a distance politics," notably its 1925 Constitution, which was modelled on that of the IWW (see **INDUSTRIAL AND COMMERCIAL WORKERS UNION OF AFRICA, 1925, "REVISED CONSTITUTION OF THE ICU,"** in this dossier).

The SDF, the International Socialist League, the Industrial Socialist League and other socialist groups all played a central role in forming the CPSA in 1921, with the International Socialist League's paper, *The International*, becoming the CPSA organ (it has been renamed and revived several times over the years; it is today incarnated as the SACP's *Umsebenzi*). The CPSA adopted the Leninist principles of the Communist International (Comintern), to which it was affiliated in 1921.

In its early years, however, the CPSA remained, nonetheless, a relatively loose group, of little interest to the Comintern. Its ranks included activists linked to the emerging "Council Communist" current, some of who wrote for, and sold locally, the British councilist paper *The Workers Dreadnought* (van der Walt, 2007, 2011; on these links, also see Béliard, 2016). As Also, as noted in the official party history, "syndicalist concepts remained within the Communist Party for many years after its foundation; echoes of their approach and phraseology appear in many documents and journals" ("Lerumo," 1971: 40).

From the late 1920s, the libertarian socialist threads began to be broken. As elsewhere, Guild Socialism was fading fast (its main British organisation collapsed in 1925). The ICU in South Africa disintegrated in the late 1920s, and was a shadow of its former self in the early 1930s (Wickens, 1973). The Comintern insisted that the CPSA "Bolshevise" itself, leading to processes and purges that dramatically changed the party's political culture and composition (Drew, 2002).

The CPSA (and its underground successor, the SACP) became marked by "intolerance, intellectual pettiness and political dissembling," and "support for every violation of freedom perpetrated by the Soviet leadership, both before and after the death of Stalin" (Jordan, 1990: 88; also see Maloka, 2013). This included disrupting the activities of rival left-wing groups, with Trotskyists (see below) viewed as especially counter-revolutionary (see e.g. Lipman, 2009: 92). The party also embraced a two-stage (and statist) conception of revolution from the late 1920s: first, national liberation, through a nation-state; later, socialism, modelled on the USSR. In the 1950s, the SACP decided that stage one was to be led by the ANC, and effectively subordinated itself to that party, a situation that continues today (see e.g. Everatt, 1991). The socialist stage was placed on indefinite hold, awaiting completion of a "national-democratic" revolution, despite the party's many achievements.

A Trotskyist movement emerged in South Africa in the 1930s. It has provided important criticisms of the CPSA/ SACP, Communist Parties more generally and of the USSR itself (Drew, 2002; Hirson, 1993). It has supported workers' councils and workers' control of production, giving it some common ground with anarchists and syndicalists; it has had many heroic figures, and an important role in labour and left politics; it has generally rejected the CPSA/ SACP postponement of socialism.

However, its radical commitments to emancipatory change co-exist, uneasily, with a strong statist thrust. In presenting the pre-Stalin USSR as a model for socialism, and (in most cases) identifying the USSR and similar states as "workers' states" (following Trotsky's defence of the USSR: e.g. Trotsky, [1936] 2006), local Trotskyism has identified itself with authoritarian regimes. These have routinely crushed unions, strikes and the left, and oppressed the popular classes, despite some welfare reforms. Repression against the working class started in the Lenin period, whose leaders insisted that the "dictatorship of the proletariat" could not be exercised by the whole working class, "only by a vanguard" (Lenin, [1920] 1962: 21), and that the "road to socialism lies through a period of the highest possible intensification of the principle of the state," including the "militarisation" of labour, top-down management and unequal wages (Trotsky, 1920: 132, 138, 150, 157). The "suffo-cation of even the most basic let alone liberal human rights" was common in the Marxist-led states (Ndamase, 2011: 20).

Nonetheless, a number of individuals who identified with anarchism continued to operate in South Africa in the 1920s and 1940s, swimming against the powerful tides of statism. Rather than form distinct groups, they tended to join the existing parties and unions.

Leonard Motler (1888–1967), an English anarchist and pioneering critic of the USSR, came to South Africa in 1921 (Heath, 2011). A prolific writer, he had contributed to *Workers Dreadnought* and the anarchist *Freedom* in Britain, and found that both were sold in South Africa. Living in Johannesburg, he wrote in the *Communist Review* published by the Communist Party of Great Britain (e.g. Motler, 1923), and for the CPSA press, and joined the (moderate, craft-based) South African Typographical Union, writing the introduction to its official history in 1952 (Heath, 2011). He was in contact with a few other local anarchists, but seems to have worked largely in the union and CPSA milieu.

Sarah Neppe, an elderly Jewish anarchist from Russia who knew the American anarchists Emma Goldman and Alexander Berkman (both strident critics of the USSR), was a member of the CPSA in the 1930s (Sachs, 1973: 105, 123–5). Sholem Schwarzbard, the anarchist who assassinated the Ukrainian nationalist leader Symon Petliura in Paris in 1926 for his role in pogroms against the Jews, lived out his final years near Cape Town (Johnson, 2012: 253–254). He had ties to key anarchists, like Nestor Makhno, and, during the anarchist Ukrainian revolution of 1918–1921, had fought in Red Guard militias and in "two independent, mostly Anarchist brigades" (Johnson, 2012: 10 n 27, 18–19, 101–118, 155–156, 204–209). Most of his activism was outside South Africa: he came to Cape Town in 1937 or 1938, and was buried at Maitland in 1938 (Johnson, 2012: 245–254).

Libertarian and left, 1940–1960s

The largest and most diverse radical scene at this time seems to have been in Cape Town and Johannesburg. Réshard Gool's *Cape Town Coolie* (1990), a semi-fictional account of Cape Town on the eve of apartheid, provides some glimpses into the political debates of the time, and the activities of the CPSA and the Trotskyists. It also has interestingly, several anarchists in its account, including the narrator (1990: 80–82, 84, 90–94, 154, (156–157, 179–180).

A trickle of anarchist materials continued to be available in South Africa through Vanguard Booksellers. This Johannesburg shop was founded by Frank Glass: initially a syndicalist in the Industrial Socialist League, he was subsequently a founder of the CPSA, then a champion of local Trotskyism (Hirson, 1988: 35–37). When he left South Africa in 1930 for China, control passed to Fanny Klennerman, who ran literacy classes for the ICU, and was expelled from the CPSA in 1931 (Hirson, 1988: 32–35).

Klennerman turned the shop into a hub of the 1930s and 1940s left scene in Johannesburg. Here, "in cramped premises," "Marxists rubbed shoulders with trade unionists; students with activists; radicals rubbed shoulders with liberals; rationalists confronted scientists": "It was more than a shop – it was forum for informed political ideas, and also for the latest currents in philosophy, literature and art" (Hirson, 1988: 37). Among the materials available were anarchist classics by Mikhail Bakunin, Berkman and Goldman, including Goldman's first-hand account of Lenin and Trotsky "crushing … the Russian Revolution."[3]

Another libertarian socialist current emerged in the 1950s, the Movement for a Democracy of Content. Its roots were in an unlikely milieu: the Workers International League (WIL), a Trotskyist group centred on Johannesburg. Formed around 1944, the WIL was active in the CPSA-led Council of Non-European Trade Unions (CNETU, formed 1941). The WIL closed in 1946, when the majority turned their backs on unions, in favour of "study and a retreat to community organisation" (Hirson, 1993: 95).

Vincent Swart, a key figure in the WIL and a champion of this shift away from unions, was a prominent poet and lecturer at the University of the Witwatersrand (see Leveson, 1981). Swart and his partner and comrade, Lillian Swart, another activist-intellectual, had come into contact with Josef Weber in New York in the 1940s. Josef Weber argued for a global movement for a "democracy of content," based upon "purposeful struggle against every internal bureaucratisation," an "anti-party" aiming at a "concrete democratic alternative," based on self-management, and opposing capitalism and the state (van der Linden, 2001: 132–133). Himself a former Trotskyist, Weber insisted that the USSR system and German and Italian fascism were essentially the same, and that unions and parties were unable to overthrow capitalism. In 1948, Weber helped launch the Movement for a Democracy of Content (MDC) as an international tendency, an example of "outside-and-against" politics.

In 1951 the Swarts, along with another former WIL member, Issy Pinchuck, launched the MDC in Johannesburg; it was joined by key figures like Dan Mokonyanae and Simon Noge. Mokonyane had previously been involved in another Trotskyist group, the Non-European Unity Movement (NEUM). Perhaps because of these origins, the MDC has been (inaccurately) described in South African studies as having "Trotskyite leanings" (e.g. Bonner and Nieftagodien, 2001: 145).

The local MDC was involved in fighting against the forced removal of Sophiatown in Johannesburg and rural "betterment" schemes in the black rural Natal, and it played a key role in the 1957 Alexandra bus boycotts (van der Linden, 2001: 134–7, 143 note 59; also Bonner and Nieftagodien, 2001: 9, 143–146). It lasted into the early 1960s, hammered by the massive state repression that started in 1960. Mokonyane and Swart were jailed during the 1960 State of Emergency, while the international MDC journal, *Contemporary Issues*, was banned in South Africa (Leveson, 1981: 21–22). After his release, Mokonyane left for Britain, where he later wrote several works on South Africa, passing away in 2010 (Mokonyane [1979] 1994a, 1994b). Swart remained in South Africa: officially restricted from political activities, he passed away in 1962.

After this period, there are no signs of organised left-libertarian currents in South Africa before the 1990s, when an organized anarchist/ syndicalist current re-emerged, and when the influence of autonomist Marxism also expanded. However, elements of "at a distance" politics continued to exist in this period.

For example, Alan Lipman, Durban editor of the SACP's *Guardian* in the 1950s, also involved in the development of the 1955 Freedom Charter, a key ANC and SACP text, was one of a very small number who quit the then-underground party over the USSR's 1956 invasion of Hungary (Lipman, 2009: 123–125). He subsequently joined the National Liberation Committee / African Resistance Movement (formed 1960, a mixture of leftists and radical liberals), and was involved in its brief armed struggle. He fled to Britain in 1963, where he moved towards an anarchist position and became a leading figure in the Campaign for Nuclear Disarmament (CND) (Fisher, 2003; Lipman, 2009). Returning to South Africa in 1990 at the request of ANC leader Walter Sisulu, he self-identified as an anarchist, passing away in 2013 (see **ALAN LIPMAN, "TWO CONCEPTIONS OF DEMOCRACY,"** in this dossier).

New left, old left, students, workers, 1970–1990s

There were others who, through their own experiences, moved towards libertarian socialist positions. Selby Semela, a key figure in the 1976 uprisings in South Africa, was influenced for a time by Situationism. Situationism, an anti-statist, anti-Leninist socialist tradition, emerged in the 1960s: drawing heavily on Marxism, it stressed self-activity and an end to alienation in daily life, including in revolutionary struggles.

Semela had been centrally involved in the Soweto Student Representative Council (SSRC), and was one of the organisers of the tragic Soweto march of June 16, 1976. He was, at that time, influenced by Black Consciousness Movement (BCM) nationalism, which had emerged following the suppression of the ANC, PAC and SACP in 1960. In August 1976, he fled South Africa, ending up in exile in Berkeley, California, the United States. In 1979, Semela co-authored a Situationist-influenced critique of the ANC, BCM, SACP and Marxism-Leninism, entitled *Reflections on the Black Consciousness Movement and the South African Revolution*.

This text was written with Sam Thompson (reportedly the pseudonym of an American, Chris Shutes, author of several pro-Situationist works: 1974, 1979, 1983) and Norman Abraham (another South African) (Semela, Thompson and Abraham, 1979). At its core was a sharp critique of political parties – ANC, BCM, PAC, SACP – for operating in a top-down way that rendered ordinary people spectators in their own struggles, passive followers of supposed vanguards, which acted as alienating mediators between people and their demands and emancipation. Thompson and Abraham also wrote, in a similar vein, *South Africa 1985: The Organisation of Power in Black and White* (Thompson and Abraham, 1985).

Like the CND, Situationism was part of a larger milieu that has come to be called the "New Left." The New Left emerged from the 1950s. Its main impact, internationally, was from the late 1960s – in repressive South Africa, its impact was delayed into the early 1970s (see e.g. Lunn, 2009). Some roots of the New Left lay in growing disillusionment with Soviet-type Communist Parties, but the New Left included Leninists, notably Maoists and Trotskyists, along with anarchist, syndicalist, libertarian Marxist, feminist, nationalist, liberal and existentialist influences and currents. Some on the New Left rejected class struggles; others stressed the need to mobilise workers and peasants.

Rick Turner, an influential South African intellectual, was a key conduit of New Left ideas. He studied at the Sorbonne, University of Paris, in the 1960s, and published the remarkable *The Eye of the Needle: Towards Participatory Democracy in South Africa* in 1972. This text argued for socialism, based upon self-management, and a democratic state, and outlined arguments against reducing politics to parties and the state (see McQueen, 2011; Morphet, 1980). Turner was banned from political activity in 1973, and assassinated in 1978 (Morphet 1980).

Turner's libertarian conception is difficult to fit into the three categories of "at a distance" politics outlined above, because he did not outline much in the way of a clear strategy (Turner was extremely pragmatic), nor did he analyse the state itself in much detail (Turner, 1972). It is, however, a bit misleading to present Turner as a "Western Marxist" (e.g. Nash, 1999), as his key intellectual reference points were Christianity and existentialism. Although he was involved in workers' education initiatives in the early 1970s, his role in the unions was limited and relatively brief. He was not therefore, as sometimes claimed (e.g. Nash, 1999), a key theorist of the 1970s and 1980s wave of independent unionism (see below).

Turner was, rather, a central figure in a new radical milieu in South Africa in which New Left and counter-cultural ideas exercised substantial influence (see e.g. Lunn, 2009; McQueen, 2011). It is in this context that his stress upon self-management and self-activity needs to be understood. As Sian Byrne's work (2012, 2013) has shown, the New Left provided a repository of radical ideas, including of elements of Marxism and revolutionary syndicalism, that influenced activists involved in the new South African unions that emerged in the 1970s and 1980s. The early Gramsci, with his stress on factory councils, was a notable reference point.

Meanwhile, as Nicole Ulrich (2007) has argued, the "workers' control" tradition – workers' assemblies, shopstewards' committees, mandates and careful work – that marked new union bodies like the Trade Union Advisory Coordinating Council (TUACC, formed 1974), provided a glimpse of the power of autonomous workers' movements, and their ability to prefigure a new South Africa. "Workers' control" and New Left ideas provided some of the foundation for the radical "workerist" current associated with the TUACC's immediate successor, the Federation of South African Trade Unions (FOSATU, formed 1979) (see Byrne and Ulrich, 2016; Byrne, Ulrich and van der Walt, 2017).

FOSATU's "workerism" eschewed alliances with political parties, leading it to be carica-tured by opponents – notably in the ANC and SACP – as advocating an "economistic" and a-political unionism (Byrne, Ulrich and van der Walt, 2017). However, FOSATU workerism was far more nuanced and radical: criticising ANC nationalism and SACP Marxist-Leninism as authoritarian, it advocated "workers' control" over not just the unions, but an expansion of "workers' control" in the workplace, the community and in the larger economy and society as well; it engaged in a range of struggles beyond wages and working conditions, both within and beyond the workplace, and embraced a prefigurative approach to social change (Byrne 2012, 2013; Byrne and Ulrich, 2016).

FOSATU jealously guarded its autonomy. It participated in the statutory industrial rela-tions system once that system was deracialised, but it insisted that union negotiators be held accountable to workers' assemblies and union structures, and operate under strict mandates (Byrne 2012, 2013). The same concern with autonomy helps explains FOSATU's distance from the ANC and SACP, and its decision not to affiliate to the United Democratic Front (UDF, formed 1983), a broad anti-apartheid coalition of church, community-based, sports, youth and other organisations.

FOSATU also rejected the two-stage theory of the SACP, was critical of the USSR, and argued that nationalist parties, like the ANC, tended to turn against workers' movements and the working class after taking power. Instead, it favoured included a class-based approach to fighting oppression by race and gender, and an anti-capitalist approach to anti-apartheid struggle (Byrne, Ulrich and van der Walt, 2017).

Rather than ignore issues outside the workplace, FOSATU therefore sought to engage with them through autonomous unions based on "workers' control," being skeptical of political parties (Byrne, Ulrich and van der Walt, 2017). It cooperated with a number of community-based struggles, and the UDF at times, and there were FOSATU initiatives to extend "workers' control" and bottom-up organising on the FOSATU model into the townships and into township organisations (see e.g. **FOSATU SHOPSTEWARDS' PRESENTATION: "THE WORKER IN THE COMMUNITY,"** in this dossier). Militants from the FOSATU tradition played an important role in a number of township struggles, including in Alexandra (see e.g. Mayekiso, 1996).

FOSATU's "workerist" project certainly had elements of "at a distance" politics, but it was also fractured by unresolved tensions over tactics and strategy, and between more social democratic and quasi-syndicalist strands (see Byrne, 2012, 2013). Some of its ideas were carried into the early Congress of South African Trade Unions (COSATU), formed in 1985 from a merger of "workerist" FOSATU unions, and "populist" (ANC/ SACP-aligned) unions. Jay Naidoo, COSATU's first general-secretary argued, for example (Naidoo, 1986):

> ... power in working class terms is the ability to assist and defend our class interests against those of opposing classes. This involves control over every aspect of our lives – at work, school, where we live, over structures of local and national government, the media, church and the economy as a whole.... when the workers can share the wealth they create, when there is democratic control of society and the need for cheap labour is done away with ... The key element in the building of the labour movement was, and still remains, the democratic principles of workers' control ...

FOSATU did not adequately spell out its vision of the future South Africa, nor did it articulate a clear medium-term strategy linking its current activities to such a vision. By contrast, COSATU soon moved to a close alignment with the ANC and SACP, and the two-stage approach.

For its part, the UDF had a complex system of regional and national structures, but these had limited control over its grassroots, especially during waves of mass struggle (Seekings, 1992). Although the UDF aligned itself with the ANC tradition, it was far from ideologically homogenous. In the early-to-mid-1980s, a growing number of UDF affiliates were involved in insurgent attempts to render apartheid municipal government unworkable, and replace it with "organs of people's power." As government and police officials fled the townships, representative community elements took control of important aspects of township life (Suttner, 2004). "People's power" initiatives ranged from crèches, to efforts to create "people's parks," to anti-crime patrols and "people's courts," to administration by street committees and other residents' associations (e.g. Lodge, 1991).

The UDF notion of "people's power" had obvious parallels with FOSATU's "workers' control" project, upon which it partly drew (e.g. Mayekiso, 1996). It was an example of "at a distance" politics that was "outside-but-with" the state: "people's power" was envisaged by UDF leaders as involving "active, mass-based democratic organisations and democratic practices within these organisations", that could fight the apartheid state in the present, but that would work alongside a future democratic state (see **MURPHY MOROBE, 1987, "TOWARDS A PEOPLE'S DEMOCRACY: THE UDF VIEW,"** in this dossier).

There was an important element of prefiguration involved in "people's power," as with "workers' control": structures of "people's power" were to be the emergent core of "a future, democratic South Africa," with "all South Africans, and in particular the working class, having control over all areas of daily existence" on a daily basis (**MOROBE**, in this dossier). Structures of participatory "people's power" would, in this conception, complement more traditional forms of representative democracy in the state.

Like those of FOSATU and COSATU (and unlike the BCM or PAC), UDF structures were non-racial. This did not mean they were race-blind but, rather, that they drew in people, across the colour line who were committed to the struggle against apartheid-era oppression. Part of the rationale for this approach, too, was prefiguration. The "enemy," said the UDF's Mosiuoa Lekota, was not a race or an ethnic group, but a social system (quoted in Neocosmos, 1996: 88):

> In political struggle . . . the means must always be the same as the ends . . . How can one expect a racialistic movement to imbue our society with a nonracial character on the dawn of our freedom day? A political movement cannot bequeath to society a characteristic it does not itself possess. To do so is like asking a heathen to convert a person to Christianity. The principles of that religion are unknown to the heathen let alone the practice.

Statist politics and its shadows, 1990–2010

The 1990s saw a marked shift towards statist politics in South Africa. Within COSATU, FOSATU's "workerism" was defeated by the ANC/SACP tradition. COSATU then became formally allied to the ANC and SACP (these were unbanned in 1990, along with the PAC) in a Tripartite Alliance that persists to this day. From the 1990s, COSATU and the SACP adopted positions 1990s that were unmistakeably social-democratic in character (e.g. COSATU and SACP, 1999), even if this was obscured by the use of Marxist-Leninist rhetoric. Some elements of the older project of "workers' control" and "people's power" remained, in the form of proposals for cooperatives and workplace co-determination, but it was the enabling state, above all, and the political parties, the ANC and SACP, that were seen as indispensable and central engines of change.

The scale of popular struggle and organisation in South Africa in the 1980s had differed from the struggles elsewhere in the continent in the 1950s and 1960s in important ways. It had involved an unparalleled and urban-centred "involvement of large numbers of ordinary people in a mosaic of political organisations of an enormous variety and in independent and coherent nationwide political activity, which transformed people's lives" (Neocosmos, 1996: 77). But the outcome was, in the end, roughly the same as that of most other African countries: a nationalist elite took over the old state, which it envisaged as the instrument of emancipation, and made various accommodations with the capitalist system. Popular structures were subordinated to the state, or expected to partner with it, popular politics was replaced by state politics, and the "centre of gravity of 'national politics' was more or less gradually, more or less rapidly, moved from the people to the state" (Neocosmos, 1996: 77).

The move from "workers' control" and "people's power" to state power and party politics involved important shifts in the political landscape. From 1990–1991, the UDF was disbanded, its constituents either dissolved into the ANC movement as wings of that party or as closely allied organisations, or closed or marginalised. For example, the South African Youth Congress (SAYCO), a major UDF affiliate, became the basis of the relaunched ANC Youth League, while UDF-aligned township residents' associations (widely known as "civics") formed the ANC-aligned South African National Civic Organisation (SANCO) in 1992.

The two largest university and technical college ("technikon") student formations, the National Union of South African Students (NUSAS), and the South African National Students Congress (SANSCO), had been aligned to the UDF. In the 1980s, NUSAS and SANSCO called for "people's education for people's power," developing "people's power" into the "people's university" project, rejecting any "Africanisation" of exploitation (Badat, 1999: 228–229, 238–240, 345–347). In 1991, they merged to form the South African Students Congress (SASCO), which was launched in 1992. But a major aim of the new body was win post-apartheid battles for "progressive social policy" by engaging in the formulation of state policy (e.g. SASCO, 1996, not paginated), and SASCO was closely aligned with the ANC. It has declared itself Marxist-Leninist, but along the lines of the SACP (e.g. Kunene, 2011).

These shifts have had major implications for popular formations. COSATU has been deeply affected by process of bureaucratisation, and penetration by the machinery of the ANC and SACP, with an attendant decline of workers' control of the unions and the integration of a substantial layer of its leadership into ANC-and state-linked networks of patronage (see Buhlungu, 2010). Battles between ANC factions have spilled over into the federation, leading to purges in 2007–2008, with frustrations with the ANC and SACP also leading to a major split in the federation in 2013–2015. SANCO has struggled to manage the contradiction between supporting ANC-led local governments and defending township residents against the user-fees and rising rates that these very same municipalities impose on the townships (see e.g. Phadu, 1997). SASCO's links to the state have made it vulnerable to challenges from student groups linked to other parties, as well as from those opposed to party politics.

These shifts did not, and could not, lead to a complete eclipse of struggles, including by ANC- and SACP-aligned movements like COSATU, SANCO and SASCO. The 1994 transition was a major breakthrough, but was an incomplete transition that failed to resolve the country's pressing economic, national and social problems. COSATU remains central to strike action and union organising; it is by no means simply a wing of the ANC, nor is it on its deathbed. No union[4] can survive unless it continues to represent, to a significant extent, the class interests of its membership – and these interests can never be fully realised under capitalism. This means that – contrary to the claims of a section of anarchists, Marxists and Situationists – unions can never be fully incorporated into capitalism, since capitalism cannot incorporate the working class.

SASCO played an important role in the massive university protests of 2015 and 2016, and continues to control a majority of elected Student Representative Councils (SRCs) at universities and technikons. SANCO still operates, although it is far weaker than it was in the 1990s. From the late 1990s, it has faced challenges in the form of the so-called "new social movements," a term that refers, in the South African context, to new residents' protest movements outside the ANC camp and SANCO. Many of these movements were linked through umbrella bodies like the Anti-Privatisation Forum (APF), formed in 2000 in Gauteng province, the Western Cape Anti Eviction Campaign, formed in 2000, and the Concerned Citizens' Forum (CCF), formed 1999 and centred on Durban.

These umbrella bodies emerged from a wave of struggles against the local state, centred on battles against neo-liberal cost recovery measures, like the installation of prepaid water meters, demands for the redress of the apartheid legacy in urban services and housing, and anger at political corruption. The APF, for example, brought together groups fighting outsourcing and marketisation at the University of the Witwatersrand (Wits) and a coalition opposing the ANC-led City of Johannesburg's neo-liberal "Igoli 2002" project. As a result, its initial affiliates included two COSATU unions, a section of SASCO, the Johannesburg SACP, and a range of township groups, none of them with close ANC ties.

But since APF struggles continually brought it into direct confrontation with the ANC, ANC- and SACP-aligned groups soon dropped out, with COSATU keeping a marked distance (McKinley, 2012). Small left groups, including anarchists, affiliated to the APF at an early stage, as did individual radicals, some influenced by autonomist Marxist politics. Affiliated political groups included the Democratic Socialist Movement (DSM), rooted in the Trotskyist tradition, and the Bikisha Media Collective, which helped launch the Zabalaza Anarchist Communist Federation (ZACF, later the Zabalaza Anarchist Communist Front) in 2003.

Meanwhile, the LPM was launched in Durban in 2001. Despite its name, origins and international affiliations, the LPM did not engage in farm occupations or in organising alternative agrarian production systems. It was affiliated to *Via Campesina*, and built links to the Landless Workers Movement (MST) in Brazil, but much of its activity has centred on the struggles of urban squatter communities for housing and public services.

Its politics was complex and contradictory. Much of the initial impetus came from a left NGO body, the National Land Committee (NLC). The LPM's first major public demonstration was as part of the civil march on the World Conference against Racism (WCAR) in Durban in 2001. Many LPM marchers carried placards defending the Robert Mugabe regime in neighbouring Zimbabwe – seen as supportive of land reform, despite its authoritarian political regime, including severe crackdowns at the time of the WCAR. Yet in 2004, LPM supporters protested the national elections declaring "No Land! No Vote!"

Four years later, the *Abahlali baseMjondolo* ("shack residents'") movement was formed in Durban. This, like the LPM, was a unitary body, rather than a coalition like the APF. It gained attention for its use of direct action tactics like road blockades and election boycotts, stress on democratic organising, history of repression at the hands of local party political machines and libertarian affinities.

There were several efforts to form a countrywide coalition of the various post-apartheid social movements. The APF initiated a Coalition against Water Privatisation (CAWP) that engaged in a range of activities, including legal action against the City of Johannesburg around water cut-offs, pursuing the case up to the Constitutional Court (Concourt) (McKinley 2012). The APF also raised donor funding, which became a source of conflict.

The Social Movement Indaba (SMI) was a forum launched in 2002 by the APF, the LPM, Jubilee South Africa and the Western Cape Anti-Eviction Campaign. It held an annual summit, made efforts at national plans of action, and had a secretariat. However in 2006, there was a major controversy at the SMI summit in Durban, followed by a split as *Abahlali baseMjondolo* and the Western Cape Anti-Eviction Campaign withdrew. The details of this clash, and its legacies, would require a lengthy discussion that falls outside the scope and themes of this introduction. But an immediate outcome was that the Gauteng-based LPM sections (now the main LPM affiliates), *Abahlali baseMjondolo*, the Rural Network / *Abahlali basePlasini* (based in KwaZulu-Natal), and the Western Anti-Eviction Campaign formed their own Poor People's Alliance in 2008.

Despite initiatives like the CAWP, the SMI and the Poor People's Alliance, the new movements tended to remain stubbornly local and regional. Moreover, many – perhaps most – protests around housing, water and electricity, and municipal governments, took place outside these movements – many protests did not even involve formal, stable organisations.

The new movements all struggled to sustain themselves and grow. Despite high expectations, and the formation of new groups like the Unemployed People's Movement (UPM), which emerged in 2009, they never came near to the size of influence of earlier movements like the UDF. The CCF declined sharply by the late 2000s. The Western Cape Anti-Eviction campaign suffered a series of splits. The APF was formally closed down in 2010. By 2014, the LPM was down to a single active branch, in a squatter camp in Protea South, Soweto (see **LEKHETHO MTETWA, 2013, "THE LANDLESS PEOPLE'S MOVEMENT FIGHTS FOR THE PEOPLE'S RIGHTS,"** in this dossier).

What role, if any, was here for a "politics at a distance from the state" in this period? None of the new movements had common political positions and coherent praxes of the sort seen in FOSATU "workerism" or the UDF "people's power" project. A substantial sector in the APF was influenced by Trotskyism, and argued for launching a new workers' party. Others were more interested in immediate reforms than larger strategic issues.

There were elements that pointed in the direction of an autonomous and anti-statist popular politics. The Poor People's Alliance called for an election boycott in 2009. *Abahlali baseMjondolo* used direct actions, called election boycotts, and was presented in press statements as a movement based on self-managed and autonomous structures. However, the reality was messier. For example, *Abahlali baseMjondolo* made regular use of the courts, winning a major case in the Concourt against evictions (Abahlali baseMjondolo, 2009). Having regularly called for election boycotts in the past, in 2014 it controversially supported a vote for the centre-right Democratic Alliance. Then a year later, *Abahlali baseMjondolo* called for "democratic people's power from below," with a focus on moving from land occupations to efforts to "develop" the "lands that we have occupied and held" (see ***ABAHLALI BASEMJONDOLO*, 2015, "OCCUPY, RESIST, DEVELOP,"** in this dossier).

Groups like Bikisha Media Collective and the subsequent ZACF (which was also affiliated to the APF), and a layer of people influenced by autonomist Marxism and other ideas, tried to promote self-activity and a distance from the state in the APF and LPM. While the APF in Soweto was influenced by Trotskyism, it was also involved in organising illegal reconnections of electricity to households: one of the "guerrilla electricians" was a ZACF militant. The Soweto actions were praised by autonomists as a system of "working-class delivery" of services that did not require state mediation or intervention (Veriava and Naidoo, 2013: 85).

The Bikisha Media Collective argued for the use of direct action, building working class power, and its perspective was one of transforming the new movements into the basis of "a system of worker and community councils based on mandated delegates," through which "workers and communities" could "to take over and directly control the government companies and services (as well as the private companies and services)" (Bikisha Media Collective, 2001). The ZACF worked in APF structures, and in the LPM in Soweto (see **LEKHETHO MTETWA, 2013, "THE LANDLESS PEOPLE'S MOVEMENT FIGHTS FOR THE PEOPLE'S RIGHTS,"** in this dossier), and the anarchists set out to create new community structures as well, including a newsletter, library and garden in Motsoaledi squatter camp in Soweto. In 2005, they also initiated the Motsoaledi Concerned Residents group, an APF affiliate.

The anarchists were specifically opposed to using courts to try and force the South African government to provide socio-economic rights, and to reliance on the Concourt:

militants should focus on building an "independent, well organised and united movement that fights outside of and against the state: not bending to its rules or observing its self-appointed authority" (*Zabalaza*, 2010: 13). Their general approach is to build a revolutionary counter-power and counter-culture, including syndicalist unionism (see **WARREN MCGREGOR, 2014, "ANARCHIST-COMMUNISM: BUILDING BLACK WORKING CLASS COUNTER POWER AGAINST STATE, CAPITAL AND NATIONAL OPPRESSION,"** in this dossier). But they struggled to have much impact on the APF; their influence in the Motsoaledi Concerned Residents declined as well.

It is quite clear that unduly optimistic and celebratory academic analyses of the "mew social movements" downplayed their contradictions and limitations (Sinwell, 2011). The movements themselves were more self-critical, noting serious weaknesses in education and cadre development, and a difficulty linking up with new township-based struggles in the mid-2000s (e.g. Hlatshwayo, 2007).

Problems like factionalism, scarce resources and individual cases of corruption, all played a destructive role. The division between middle-class and working-class members (overlapping, to some extent, with race and education) was also important: each side in the 2006 SMI split accused the other of undemocratic practices and undue influence by NGOs, academics and (implicitly or explicitly) racial minorities.

Such challenges were not new: they had faced, for example, both FOSATU and the UDF. Despite operating in a far more repressive environment, both FOSATU and the UDF performed far better than the new movements. Other factors therefore also have to be noted in any assessment. SMI reports, for example, noted that weaknesses arose from the shaky "stepping stone" of weak "political education" (Hlatshwayo, 2007: 11). They also suggested that analyses were shallow, lacking a nuanced understanding of the South African state and capitalist class, and of the ability of the ruling class to reproduce its hegemony among larger layers of the working class and poor. (As an APF founder member, I found that formal APF policies, like building a socialist alternative to the ANC, co-existed with ongoing support for the ANC amongst the membership, as well as with other, quite conservative views; and that internal education was often centred on immediate issues – for example, exposing the aims of Igoli 2002 – rather than on developing critical thought or deeper theoretical or strategic reflections).

For some insiders, looking back, the APF remained trapped at "the moment of negativity and refusal ... anti-neo-liberal, anti-ANC," and in practice, it often ended up merely demanding better "service delivery" by the state (Veriava and Naidoo, 2013: 85). The court route came to take centre stage, and this reliance on the state, and its law, helped close down "the imagination of more locally driven, decentralised and collectivised approaches to service delivery" (Veriava and Naidoo, 2013: 84).

Conclusion: the 21st century

In the opening of this introduction, I noted the crisis of the main statist models championed by the left over the last century: the Keynesian welfare state, Marxist central planning, and import-substitution-industrialisation. This is the context on which modes of "at a distance" politics have assumed greater prominence and have seemed to promise a route out of the impasse.

What, then, of South Africa, now?

The period from 2012 has been marked by major social and political turbulence in South Africa. Major strikes, notably in mining, the Post Office and on wine farms, the shockwaves created by the massacre of platinum miners at Marikana, the decision by COSATU's largest blue-collar union, the National Union of Metalworkers of South Africa (NUMSA) to withdraw support from the ANC and SACP in 2013, and its expulsion from COSATU in 2014, and significant struggles by university students and workers in 2015–2016, are all part of this context. ANC support fell notably in the 2016 local elections.

The period has been described, in a key analysis, as a "turning point" in the country's history (Cottle, 2017). In 2013, NUMSA announced plans to initiate a "movement for socialism" and a United Front against neo-liberalism. This attracted the support of the Democratic Left Front (DLF), launched in 2011 by socialist currents and popular movements, including ZACF, in the wake of the APF. The UPM, a DLF affiliate, joined the United Front as well.

Future developments are less clear. NUMSA has, increasingly, defined its project as the revival of an orthodox Marxist-Leninist model, including the development of a new communist party. Relations between NUMSA and the United Front are not very strong, and the United Front is itself regionally uneven, host to a range of political views, and has faced serious reverses since its inauguration. African nationalism remains a powerful current, especially in the student movement, where the socialist left is a weak force. ANC and non-ANC nationalist currents vie for influence, with SASCO facing a challenge from the EFF's student wing and a resurgent Pan Africanist Student Movement of Azania (PASMA), linked to the PAC. NUMSA has criticised the EFF for having a militaristic and undemocratic structure and lack of a "clear class position" (Aboobaker, 2013).

On the other hand, elements of "at a distance" politics continue to exist. Like its immediate predecessor, the Conference for a Democratic Left (CDL, formed 2008), the early DLF included not just anarchists, but a current associated with "outside-but-with" the state politics. There is a growing interest in models of socialist politics that move beyond Marxism-Leninism and orthodox social democracy, arguing for "democracy from below" as a means to transform society and the state (e.g. Satgar and Zita, 2009; Satgar and Williams, 2013).

The UPM has argued for a "communist" and "popular" democracy akin to the Paris Commune, the early *soviets* in Russia and 1980s "people's power," and argued for the need to "deepen liberal democracy . . . into a politics of direct democracy where people live, work and study. We need to continually radicalise democracy from below" (**THE UNEMPLOYED PEOPLE'S MOVEMENT, "TEN THESES ON DEMOCRACY," GRAHAMSTOWN, 2011**, in this dossier).

Anarchists remained active in the LPM into recent years, and in propaganda and political education. Anarchism is also an influence on the Soundz of the South (SOS), a South African "anti-capitalist cultural resistance movement working with activists who use hip-hop and poetry to spread revolutionary messages, raise consciousness and critique neo-liberalism" (Bandcamp, 2013; see **SOUNDZ OF THE SOUTH (SOS), 2013, ANTI-CAPITALIST, ANTI-AUTHORITARIAN AFRICAN HIP-HOP AND POETRY**, in this dossier).

Based in Cape Town, SOS runs free concerts, including a "Don't Vote" series in Khayelitsha township ahead of the 2014 elections, calling on people to instead use direct action. The 2013 SOS album, "Freedom Warriors Volume 2," included tracks on the 2011 police murder of protestor Andries Tatane in Ficksburg, the 2012 Marikana massacre, the 2012 farmworkers' strikes in the Western Cape, and "the Mandela Betrayal and the Afrikan Revolution."

From below

In these ways, the same engagement with alternative political forms taking place globally is also taking place in South Africa, yet the same scope for populist, demagogic and statist forms of opposition that exists elsewhere is also very present – not least in the ANC, EFF and white conservative movements like Afriforum. Without a concrete class-based and internationalist project of building participatory democratic movements of struggle "at a distance from the state," ongoing economic crisis, racial inequality, political corruption and disenchantment with the ANC and other parties are as likely to generate a rightist backlash, as a progressive outcome.

Notes

1. Author contact: l.vanderwalt@ru.ac.za.
2. Materials are available at https://politicsatadistance.wordpress.com/ The programme is at https://politicsatadistance.wordpress.com/2016/10/12/programme-for-the-politics-at-a-distance-from-the-state-conference/. The concept and call are at https://politicsatadistance.wordpress.com/2016/10/08/cfp-politics-at-a-distance-from-the-state-conference-to-be-held-at-rhodes-university-grahamstown-south-africa-on-29th-30th-september-2012/.
3. The Fanny Klennerman Papers include copies of Alexander Berkman, 1942, *ABC of Anarchism*, London: Freedom Press, Emma Goldman, 1916, *Anarchism: What it Really Stands For*, New York: Mother Earth Publishing, and Emma Goldman, 1922, *The Crushing of the Russian Revolution*, London: Freedom Press, plus an undated edition of Mikhail Bakunin's *God and the State*: Fanny Klennerman Papers, Historical Papers, A2301, William Cullen Library, University of the Witwatersrand.
4. I do not include here state-run, compulsory bodies like the "All-China Federation of Trade Unions," which do not meet the most basic criteria of a union i.e. "a continuous association of wage earners for the purpose of maintaining or improving the conditions of their working lives" (Webb and Webb, 1920: 21–22).

References

Abahlali baseMjondolo, 14 October 2009, "Victory in the Constitutional Court!" Online at http://abahlali.org/node/5908/, accessed 1 September 2015.

Aboobaker, S. 29 December 2013, "NUMSA Wary of 'Capitalist' Malema," *Independent Online*. At http://www.iol.co.za/news/special-features/numsa-wary-of-capitalist-malema-1627179, accessed 1 September 2015.

Badat, M. S. 1999. *Black Student Politics, Higher Education and Apartheid: From SASO to SANSCO, 1968–1990*. Pretoria: HSRC Press.

Béliard, Y. 2016. "A 'Labour War' in South Africa: The 1922 Rand Revolution in Sylvia Pankhurst's *Workers' Dreadnought*." *Labor History*, 57 (1): 20–34.

Badiou, A. 2006. *Polemics*. London, New York: Verso.

Badiou, A., Del Lucchese, F. and J. Del Smith. 2008. "'We Need a Popular Discipline': Contemporary Politics and the Crisis of the Negative." *Critical Inquiry*, 34 (4): 645–659.

Bandcamp, 2013, "Freedom Warriors Vol. 2," online at https://sos1.bandcamp.com/album/freedom-warriors-vol-2, accessed 15 June 2014.

Bikisha Media Collective. 2001. *Evict the Bosses and Politicians: Stop Privatisation Now*. Leaflet. Johannesburg: Bikisha Media Collective/ Red and Black Forum.

Biney, A. 2011. *The Political and Social Thought of Kwame Nkrumah*. New York: Palgrave-Macmillan.

Bonefeld, W. and J. Holloway. 2014. "Commune, Movement, Negation: Notes from Tomorrow." *South Atlantic Quarterly*, 113 (2): 213–215.

Bray, M. 2013. *Translating Anarchy: The Anarchism of Occupy Wall Street*. Winchester, UK/Washington DC: Zero Books/ John Hunt Publishing.

Buhlungu, S. 2010. *A Paradox of Victory: COSATU and the Democratic Transformation in South Africa*. Pietermaritzburg: University Of KwaZulu-Natal Press.

Byrne, Sian. 2012. "'Building Tomorrow Today': A Re-examination of the Character of the Controversial 'Workerist' Tendency Associated with the Federation of South African Trade Unions (FOSATU) in South Africa, 1979–1985." Masters diss. University of the Witwatersrand.

Byrne, S. 2013. "Rethinking 'Workerism' and the FOSATU Tradition, 1979–1985." Paper presented at the Durban Moment Conference, Rhodes University, 21–23 February.

Byrne, S. and N. Ulrich. 2016. "Prefiguring Democratic Revolution? 'Workers' Control' and 'Workerist' Traditions of Radical South African Labour, 1970–1985." *Journal of Contemporary African Studies*, 34(3): 368–387, included in this volume.

Byrne, S., Ulrich, N. and L. van der Walt. 2017. "Red, Black and Gold: FOSATU, South African 'Workerism,' 'Syndicalism' and the Nation." In: E. Webster and K. Pampillas (eds.), *The Unresolved National Question in South Africa: Left Thinking Under Apartheid*. Johannesburg: Wits University Press, pp. 254–273.

Congress of South African Trade Unions (COSATU) and South African Communist Party (SACP). 1999. *Building Socialism Now: Preparing for the New Millennium*. Johannesburg: COSATU.

Cottle, E. 2017. "Is South Africa at a Turning Point?" *Global Labour Column*, 267: 1–2.

Drew, A. 2002. *Discordant Comrades: Identities and Loyalties on the South African Left*. Pretoria: University of South Africa Press.

Everatt, D. 1991. "Alliance Politics of a Special Type: The Roots of the ANC/SACP Alliance, 1950–54." *Journal of Southern African Studies*, 18(1): 19–39.

Fanny Klennerman Papers, Historical Papers, A2301, William Cullen Library, University of the Witwatersrand.

Fisher, R. 2003. "An Anarchist, That's What I Am." *Leading Architecture and Design*. March/April: 12.

Fitch, R. and M. Oppenheimer. 1968. *Ghana: End of an Illusion*. New York: Monthly Review Press.

Gool, R. 1990. *Cape Town Coolie*. Oxford: Heinemann.

Hattingh, S. and L. van der Walt. 2015. "The Kurdish Question: Nationhood or Autonomy." *Ndivhuwo: Journal for Intellectual Engagement*, 3: 70–72.

Heath, N. 2011. "Motler, Leonard Augustine, 1888–1967." *Libcom*. Online at http://libcom.org/history/motler-leonard-augustine-1888–1967

Helliker, K. and L. van der Walt. 2016. "Politics at a Distance from the State: Radical, South African and Zimbabwean Praxis Today." *Journal of Contemporary African Studies*, 34(3): 312–331, included in this volume.

Hirson, B. 1988. "Death of a Revolutionary: Frank Glass/Li Fu-Jen/ John Liang 1901–1988." *Searchlight South Africa*, 1 (1): 35–37.

Hirson, B. 1993. "The Trotskyist Groups in South Africa, 1932–1948." *Searchlight South Africa*, 3 (2): 72–100.

Hlatshwayo, M. 2007. *Outgoing Secretarial Report to SMI*. Presented at 5th Annual National Meeting of the Social Movements Indaba (SMI). Cape Town. December.

Holloway, J. 2005. *Change the World without Taking Power: The Meaning of Revolution Today*. London: Pluto Press. Revised edition.

Johns, S. W. 1995. *Raising the Red Flag: The International Socialist League and the Communist Party of South Africa, 1914–32*. Bellville: Mayibuye Books/ University of the Western Cape.

Johnson, K. 2012. "Sholem Schwarzbard: Biography of a Jewish Assassin." PhD diss. Harvard University.

Lenin, V. I. [1920] 1962. "The Trade Unions, the Present Situation and Trotsky's Mistakes." *Collected Works*, volume 32. Moscow: Progress Publishers, pp. 19–42.

"Lerumo" [M. Harmel]. 1971. *Fifty Fighting Years: The Communist Party of South Africa 1921–71*. London: Inkululeko Publications.

Leveson, M. 1981. "Introduction." In: M. Leveson, (ed.), *Vincent Swart: Collected Poems*. Johannesburg: A.D. Donker, pp. 7–24.

Lipman, A.R. 2009. *On the Outside Looking In: Colliding with Apartheid and Other Authorities*. Johannesburg: Architect Africa Publications.

Lodge, T. 1991. *All, Here, and Now: Black Politics in South Africa in the 1980s*. New York: Ford Foundation.

Lunn, H. 2009. "Hippies, Radicals and the 'Sounds of Silence': Cultural Dialectics at Two South African Universities, 1966–1976." PhD diss. University of KwaZulu Natal

From below

Maloka, E. 2013. *South African Communist Party: Exile and After Apartheid*. Johannesburg: Jacana.

Masquelier, C. and M. Dawson. 2016. "Beyond Capitalism and Liberal Democracy: On the Relevance of GDH Cole's Sociological Critique and Alternative." *Current Sociology*, 64 (1): 3–21.

McKinley, D.T. 2012. *Transition's Child: The Anti-Privatisation Forum (APF)*. Braamfontein: The South African History Archive.

McQueen, I. 2011. "Re-imagining South Africa: Black Consciousness, Radical Christianity and the New Left, 1967–1977." PhD diss. University of Sussex.

Mokonyane, D. [1979] 1994a. *Lessons of Azikwela: The Bus Boycott in South Africa*. London: Nakong Ya Rena. 2nd edition.

Mokonyane, D. 1994b. *The Big Sell-out by the Communist Party of South Africa and the African National Congress: Developments in South Africa and the Eclipse of the Revolutionary Perspective*. London: Nakong Ya Rena.

Morphet, T. 1980. "Richard Turner: A Biographical Introduction." In: R. Turner. [1972] 1980. *The Eye of the Needle: Towards Participatory Democracy in South Africa*. Johannesburg: Ravan Press, pp. vii–xxxiv.

Motler, L.A. 1923. "From Kraal to Goldmine." *Communist Review*, 4(1): 35–37.

Naidoo, J. 1986. "Building People's Power: A Working Class Perspective." Paper presented to a Grassroot Conference. 5 April.

Nash, A. 1999. "The Moment of Western Marxism in South Africa." *Comparative Studies of South Asia, Africa and the Middle East*, 19 (1): 66–82.

Ndamase, L., 2011, "Has Socialism Failed? 20 Years On – Contribution to the Critique – PART ONE," *The Red Spark: Theoretical Journal*, South African Students Congress, 2(1): 18–26.

Neocosmos, M. 1996. "From People's Politics to State Politics: Aspects of National Liberation in South Africa, 1984–1994." *Politeia*, 15(3): 73–119.

Phadu, T. 1997. "An Inside View of the Tembisa Struggles." *Debate: Voices from the South African Left*. 4: 28–30.

SASCO. 1996. *SASCO 5th Anniversary Statement: 5 Years of United and Militant Struggle*. 6 September.

Sachs, B. 1973. *Mist of Memory*. London: Valentine, Mitchell and Co.

Satgar, V. and L. Zita. (eds.). 2009. *New Frontiers for Socialism in the 21st Century*. Johannesburg: Cooperative and Policy Alternative Centre (COPAC).

Satgar, V. and M. Williams. (eds.). 2013. *Marxism in the 21st Century: Crisis, Critique and Struggle*. Johannesburg: Wits University Press.

Schechter, D. 1994. *Radical Theories: Paths beyond Marxism and Social Democracy*. Manchester: Manchester University Press.

Seekings, J. 1992. "Trailing Behind the Masses: The United Democratic Front and Township Politics in the Pretoria-Witwatersrand-Vaal Region, 1983–84." *Journal of Southern African Studies*, 18 (1): 93–114.

Semela, S., Thompson, S. and N. Abraham. 1979. *Reflections on the Black Consciousness Movement and the South African Revolution*. Berkeley, CA.

Shutes, C. 1974. *Phenomenology of the Subjective Aspect of Practical-Critical Activity. Chapter 1: Behindism*. Berkeley, CA.

Shutes, C. 1979. *Two Local Chapters in the Spectacle of Decomposition*. Berkeley, CA.

Shutes, C. 1983. *On the Poverty of Berkeley life: And the Marginal Stratum of American Society in General*. Berkeley, CA.

Thompson, S. and N. Abraham. 1985. *South Africa 1985: The Organisation of Power in Black and White*. London: BM Combustion.

Sinwell, L. 2011. "Is 'Another World' Really Possible? Re-examining Counter-hegemonic Forces in Post-apartheid South Africa." *Review of African Political Economy*, 127: 61–76.

Suttner, R. 2004. "Review Article: The UDF Period and its Meaning for Contemporary South Africa." *Journal of Southern African Studies*, 30 (3): 691–701.

Taylor, P.J. 1991. "The Crisis of the Movements: The Enabling State as Quisling." *Antipode*, 23 (2): 214–228.

The International. 1915. "The Wrath to Come." 3 December.

The International. 1918. "Industrial Unionism in South Africa." 22 February.

Thorpe, W. 1989. *"The Workers Themselves": Revolutionary Syndicalism and International Labour, 1913–23*. Dordrecht, Boston, London/ Amsterdam: Kulwer Academic Publishers/International Institute of Social History.

Trotsky, L. 1921. *The Defence of Terrorism (Terrorism and Communism): A Reply to Karl Kautsky*. London: George Allen & Unwin / The Labour Publishing Company.

Trotsky, L. ([1936] 2006. *The Revolution Betrayed: What is the Soviet Union and Where is it Going?* Delhi, Aakar Books.

Turner, R. 1972. *The Eye of the Needle: Towards Participatory Democracy in South Africa*. Johannesburg: SPROCAS.

Ulrich, N. 2007. " 'Only the Workers Can Free the Workers': The Origin of the Workers' Control Tradition and the Trade Union Advisory Coordinating Committee (TUACC), 1970–1979." MA diss. University of the Witwatersrand.

van der Linden, M. 2001. "The Prehistory of *Post-Scarcity Anarchism*: Josef Weber and the Movement for a Democracy of Content (1947–1964)." *Anarchist Studies*, 9: 127–145.

van der Walt, L. 2007. "Anarchism and Syndicalism in South Africa, 1904–1921: Rethinking the History of Labour and the Left." PhD diss. University of the Witwatersrand.

van der Walt, L. 2011. "Anarchism and Syndicalism in an African Port City: The Revolutionary Traditions of Cape Town's Multiracial Working Class, 1904–1924." *Labor History*, 52 (2): 137–171.

van der Walt, 2014. "Reclaiming Syndicalism: From Spain to South Africa to Global Labour Today." *Global Labour Journal*, 5 (2): 239–252.

van der Walt, L. 2016. "Back to the Future: Revival, Relevance and Route of an Anarchist/Syndicalist Approach for Twenty-First-Century Left, Labour and National Liberation Movements." *Journal of Contemporary African Studies*, 34(3): 348–367, included in this volume.

Veriava, A. and P. Naidoo. 2013. "Predicaments of Post-apartheid Social Movement Politics: The Anti-Privatisation Forum (APF)." In: J. Daniel, Naidoo, P., Pillay, D. R. Southall (eds.). *New South African Review 3: The Second Phase – Tragedy or Farce? Johannesburg: Wits University Press,* pp. 76–89.

Wainwright, H. 2004. "Change the World by Transforming Power: Including State Power!" *Red Pepper*. November.

Webb, S. and B. Webb. 1920. *The History of Trade Unionism, 1666–1920*. London: Longmans, Green and Co.

Wickens, P. L. 1973. *The Industrial and Commercial Workers' Union of Africa*. Cape Town: University of Cape Town.

Wilks, S. 1996. "Class Compromise and the International Economy: The Rise and Fall of Swedish Social Democracy." *Capital and Class*, 58: 89–111.

Zabalaza. 2010. "Conned by the Courts: How Working Class Movements are Diverted from Struggle." *Zabalaza: A Journal of Southern African Revolutionary Anarchism*. 11: 7–13.

International Socialist League, December 1917, "Industrial Unionism in South Africa" (extracts).

Formed in 1915, the International Socialist League was the lynchpin of the revolutionary syndicalist movement in 1910s South Africa. This was the main current on the revolutionary left, and influenced a section of the labour movement and some in the black African and Coloured nationalist groups of the time. The League founded syndicalist unions amongst black African, Coloured and Indian workers: the Clothing Workers Industrial Union, the Durban Indian Workers Industrial Union, the Horse Drivers Union, and the Industrial Workers of Africa. The document below, produced in support of a 1918 congress sponsored by the League, provides a sense of its project of counter-power: building revolutionary, bottom-up industrial unions to unite the working class, fight against racism and other forms of oppression, and take over, and self-manage, the means of production.

Source: *The International*, 22 February 1918, "Industrial Unionism in South Africa", described as the "manifesto of the Solidarity Committee, reprinted here by order of the I.S.L. Management Committee."

Industrial Unionism in South Africa

The Labour movement in South Africa is more dead than alive and is in dire need of reconstruction. This unfortunate position is due to the divisions in the ranks of the workers on the industrial field. Thousands upon thousands of white workers, and hundreds of thousands of black, are helpless against the tyranny of the employers, and live in misery because there is no provision made to organise them.

The employers organise in their various industries, the Master Builders, the Master Printers, the Chamber of Mines, the State Railways, all these have one organisation in their particular industry.

But the workers in these industries are divided into different sections with contrary aims. The employers' unions are thus able to deal with their employees in small units, fighting them in detail, ruling them by dividing them, and bossing it over the workers to their hearts content in consequence of our disunity ... thousands of workers who do not come under the crafts are left unorganised and at the mercy of the master class. The leading spirits of labour are drawn away into exclusive craft unions instead of standing by all the other workers in the particular industries where they work ...

We unhesitatingly declare that the Craft Union system is a great evil: that instead of being a menace to the masters, it is a bulwark of capitalism ... Trade Unionism, organisation by craft, is nothing more or less than organised disunity. Through this organised disunity the master class is able to retain undisputed control of the lives of hundreds of thousands of workers.

To this organised disunity of the Trade unions is due the beaten ragged arm of Labour. To this alone is due the increasing misery and poverty of the slums, the starvation wages of the labourers, the social cancer of illicit liquor and prostitution, and all social crimes. All these arise from the untrammelled exploitation of Labour by Capital, and all these evils are perpetuated by the cleavages in the ranks of the workers.

It is the mission of the working class alone to abolish poverty and crime. But it can only do this by organising on the industrial field to capture control of the machinery of production now in the hands of a few capitalists. It is our mission to usher in the rule of justice and common weal under the wing of the Industrial Republic of Labour. But how can the workers ever accomplish this great aim so long as they are torn asunder by divisions of craft and colour?

...The power of the workers lies solely in their capacity jointly to stop the wheels of industry. But the Craft Unions only organise a select few in each industry, and still worse, the Craft Unions organise a select few from many industries abstracting from them the cream of Labour, so that a Craft Union branch contains members from many industries, but commands no single industry...

The emancipation of Labour, nay, the present day amelioration of the lot of the workers' demands that the Trade Unions as at present constituted shall be swept away. Their narrow craft vanity, their still narrower colour prejudice, their exclusive benefit funds, their compromising with the robber system, their friendly agreements with their masters to the neglect of the bottom toiler, their scabbery on the unskilled and on one another, all this make them a delusion and a snare, serving only the purposes of the Capitalists.

Modern Capitalism demands the organisation of the workers along the line of industry irrespective of craft or colour. We demand for each industry one Union for all the workers in that industry. For the Mining industry one Union of all the Mine workers, surface, underground, black, white, reduction men, engine drivers, mechanics, office workers, etc., their place is in the Union for that industry and nowhere else. Just as Mineowners present one solid front in the Chamber of Mines, so should all the workers on those mines combine in one Union.

Thus organised, the individual Industrial Unions will link up into one National Industrial Union, which should regulate the transfer of cards as the workers migrate from one industry to another, so that the members are members of one great working class Union.

The working class is one, and the Workers Union must be one and indivisible. An injury to one worker, be he white or black, is an injury to all. Before the workers can discuss terms with the Capitalists they must settle accounts with one another and link up into One Big Union. In the commonwealth of labour, Labour is the only coat of arms. To those who toil shall all honour be due. The growing unity of the workers is the only victory. The dictatorship of the working class is the only "concession" worth fighting for.

Thus organised on the Industrial Field, we, the workers will learn to control industry and show the capitalist off the stage of human society. The one Industrial Union will become the Parliament of Labour and will form an integral part of the International Industrial Republic.

We commend the foregoing ideas to the workers and hope a practical organisation will be the result – an organisation capable as it grows, of fighting our every day battles, and of ultimately enabling the workers to control industry for themselves....

We call upon all workers who endorse these principles to co-operate towards their fulfilment by getting them discussed inside and out of the Trade Unions, so that the transformation from the old to the new may come, as come it must, if possible with the full consent of the present Trade Union membership.

Yours for Industrial Solidarity,
SOLIDARITY COMMITTEE, ANDREW WATSON, Hon. Sec., box 5493.

Industrial and Commercial Workers Union of Africa, 1925, Revised Constitution of the ICU (Preamble).

The Industrial and Commercial Workers Union of Africa, or ICU, was formed in Cape Town in 1919. That year, the ICU joined the revolutionary syndicalist Industrial Workers of Africa in organising a major strike by dockworkers. In 1920, the two unions merged with others in Bloemfontein under the ICU banner, with the intention of establishing One Big Union south of the Zambezi. In the years that followed, the ICU built up a substantial following in the cities – notably Durban, Cape Town, Port Elizabeth and Johannesburg – as well as a large base in the rural areas. It also spread into neighbouring Namibia, Zambia and Zimbabwe. ICU politics were an unstable mix of Christian, nationalist, liberal, Marxist and syndicalist influences, and its tactics and strategies were correspondingly incoherent. There is no doubt, however, that the ICU often envisaged the One Big Union dethroning the ruling class through a final, revolutionary strike, following which land would be returned to workers and tenant farmers, in an egalitarian commonwealth, free of racist and capitalist oppression.

Source: 1925 Constitution of the Industrial and Commercial Workers' Union of Africa, Section 2.

Whereas the interest of the workers and those of the employers are opposed to each other, the former living by selling their labour, receiving for its labour only part of the wealth they produce; and the latter living by exploiting the labour of the workers; depriving the workers of a part of the product of their labour in the form of profit, no peace can be between the two classes, a struggle must always obtain about the division of the products of human labour, until the workers through their industrial organisations take from the capitalist class the means of production, to be owned and controlled by the workers for the benefit of all, instead of for the profit of a few.

Under such a system, he who does not work, neither shall he eat. The basis of remuneration shall be the principle, from each man according to his abilities, to each man according to his needs. This is the goal for which the ICU strives along with all other organised workers throughout the world. Further this organisation does not foster or encourage antagonism towards other established bodies, political or otherwise, of African peoples, or of organised European labour.

Alan Lipman, "Two Conceptions of Democracy."

Alan Robert Lipman, born 1925 to a Jewish South African family, grew up in Johannesburg and Vrede. He served in the South African military in the Second World War, trained as an architect at the University of the Witwatersrand, joining the Communist Party of South Africa (CPSA) around 1948, then its underground successor, the South African Communist Party (SACP). He served as Durban editor of the SACP-linked Guardian, *worked in the anti-apartheid movement, including with African National Congress (ANC) leaders like Nelson Mandela, and helped draft the ANC's and SACP's 1955* Freedom Charter. *However, Lipman broke with the SACP over the 1956 Soviet invasion of invasion of Hungary, gravitated to the National Liberation Committee / African Resistance Movement, and was exiled in 1963. Working as an architect, then as a sociologist, in Britain, he moved towards anarchism, and also drew heavily on 19th century libertarian socialist William Morris (1834–1896). He returned to South Africa in 1990, was disillusioned with the ANC in government, and identified with the anarchists. He passed away in 2013, survived by his wife of sixty-four years, Beata; two children and three grandchildren.*

Source: Draft of A.R. Lipman. *On the Outside Looking In: Colliding with Apartheid and Other Authorities.* (later published in 2009, in Johannesburg by Architect Africa Publications).

... I take these commitments to be founded on a set of political ideas which centre on abolishing "the State," the seat of power and authority, in order to replace all forms of governmental order by freely associated, voluntarily co-operative groups and individuals. Free association and voluntary co-operation are essential, basic. State coercion is anathema, whether imposed by forceful action or authoritatively. In this sense, authority is legitimised social power, which rests on the ability of those who wield it to exact compliance, to call for and receive obedience which is independent of the will of the commanded ... Force, an underpinning concept, refers to the compulsion – often, but not necessarily physically violent – resorted to by those in power and/or authority ...

Anarchists disagree about how their preferred "society of the future," their utopia is to be brought about ... While the emphases differ, both marshal the same means of struggle. As, for example, the civil disobedience which Gandhi advocated. This demanded highly disciplined, mass ceremonial, illegal acts. Such action was intended to disrupt police and judicial procedures by overloading them. The State's machinery was peacefully to be stretched to breaking point. Second, there is direct action: radical acts taken outside the framework of parliamentary or constitutional legality. They can include "sit-ins," wild-cat strikes, prohibited "stay-aways," boycotts ... non-violent direct action ... Last, there is public resistance, a strategy that may well include direct action and civil disobedience ...

Taken together, this is the vision and means of realising a decent society, that I have long entertained. It has grown from my experiences of always potentially violent leadership in action as well as from the overall critique I have sought to apply ... If I have not fully incorporated its humane ideals, that has been due to a number of embedded issues.

First, anarchism, a customarily ridiculed or ignored theory, is a minority viewpoint, one whose opposition to authority has inhibited effective, large-scale organisation among its adherents. Second, most non-violent acts require sustained self-discipline on the part – of their proponents – not a readily obtained or applied quality. Third, those who engage in non-violent direct action cannot necessarily control the ensuing events, events that have tended all too often towards violence.

These and like factors go some way toward explaining the rarity – and, paradoxically, the frequently violent origins – of the short-term anarchist regimes established in the 20th century. To my knowledge, they have been confined to a small but influential grouping in post-revolutionary Russia (circa 1920), in Spain during the 1930s Civil War, and the short-lived French groups in 1968. As Russell Jacoby noted in his incisive history *The Dialectic of Defeat: Contours of Western Marxism* (1981), countervailing forces from the orthodox, authoritarian left and their counterparts on the right have been too powerful, malign, insidious, and eventually triumphant. Libertarian socialism – even the cautious "socialism with a human face" mooted during the Prague Spring of 1968 – has, yet, not prevailed.

Nationalism and internationalism

. . . Here, my standpoint is probably most succinctly conveyed by juxtaposing characteristic notions of nationalism with those of internationalism. I take the former to include feelings of group belonging, cohesion which commonly coalesce about cultural, linguistic, historical and frequently racial ties; they tend, in addition to be identified with particular territories. Nationalism of this nature has been a powerful drive in developing the arts and other cultural matters. It has also inspired resistance to imperialist and like attacks on many national groups; specifically on their territories.

There is, though, another form of nationalistic expression, one, which glorifies the nation, state as "the ideal form of political organisation with an overriding claim on the loyalty of its citizens" (*Fontana Dictionary of Modern Thought*, 1977) . . . This readily assumes the "aggressive, intolerant forms identified with military and trade rivalries, national expansion at the expense of other peoples . . ." (also the *Fontana Dictionary*). It has been integral to the authoritarian rule of Fascist, Nazi, Stalinist, colonial and similar regimes. I emphasise, this order of nationalism readily assumes aggressive intolerance, particularly in wartime conditions; it does not necessarily embrace such tendencies initially.

Internationalism posits quite different qualities: the so-called soft, non-aggressive, respectfully tolerant attributes, which committed, tough-minded nationalists tend impatiently to decry; characteristics they may well despise. It is rooted in the notion that, differences notwithstanding – indeed welcomed – there are common human interests, particularly among the *sans-culottes* of the world. It focuses on the ideals of commonality, fraternity, proclaimed by rebels across the planet, throughout known history. Such ideas animated, among many, many others, the slaves of the Spartacus rebellions, the 13th century peasants who were touched by the visionary monk John Ball, the "underclasses" of the French Revolution – the "common people." There, I trust with the humility due to this honourable tradition, I stand.

Two conceptions of democracy

There are . . . at least two central strands of democratic thought: indirect, representative and participatory, direct democratic governance. The first, the dominant notion, and its associated practices prevail in democratic states the world over. The other is an unarguably minority view with historically few examples – such as the Paris Commune of 1871 and the anarcho-syndicalism groups of mid-1930s Spain. There is, to my knowledge, but a single notable contemporary instance – the isolated Zapatista rebels of Mexico who, in their mountainous territory, have resisted repeated attacks through the 1990s into the 21st Century.

Ideally, and in the broadly painted brush-strokes . . . representative, indirect democracy calls for regular elections in which all eligible citizens vote by secret ballot for the political party, coalitions of parties or individuals who have successfully campaigned for their support. Such elections are, also ideally, required to offer effective choices between the contending parties; choices that may, and often do lead to changes of government. The elected representatives then meet in open assemblies – parliaments, congresses, chambers of deputies and the like – where they debate and vote for legislation that thereafter carries the stamp of democratic authority. In addition, customarily, citizens have the right, as individuals or in concert, to question and/or oppose these authoritative governing measures . . .

Proponents of the second, the far less widely received and acknowledged view . . . Direct, participatory democracy has been depicted by, among others, Karl Marx who founded much of his argument on the events of the Paris Commune. But the idea can be traced far further back; to, indeed, the classical Greek city states. There, we are told, democracy meant the rule of the *demos*, the entire body of citizens – excluding, as was then the case, women, children, slaves and people designated as being mentally deranged! It meant, in essence, the right – perhaps more honoured in the breach than in strict observance – of all sane, adult males openly to debate and decide by voting freely on matters of public concern. Such decisions had the imprimatur of legal and moral authority.

Those who have advocated this demos-like rule posit the idea that "true" democracy envisages a civil society in which the State has become redundant . . . they argue that "society is an organism of solidarity and homogeneous interests . . . the 'political' sphere of the 'general interest' vanishes along with the division between governors and governed – Colletti, *From Rousseau to Lenin* (1972). In my view, their arguments are sophisticated, updated, technically developed versions of William Morris' poetic depiction in his novelette *News from Nowhere* (1980) . . .

Generally, this view echoes Karl Marx's admiration of the Paris Commune, particularly the immediately pre-socialist measures that were implemented in its name — *The Civil War in France* (1871) . . . they included: the ruling that delegates could be recalled at any time by those who had elected them; that they were bound by the formally agreed instructions of their constituents; that they were paid at a level equivalent to the averaged salaries of skilled workers living in the Commune; that they were to resign at the end of their appointed periods to allow others to gain democratic experience. In summary, the measures represent a potentially insurrectionary politics of transition; one that foreshadows an eventual victory of popular, egalitarian, libertarian socialism . . .

Those who propose this type of democratic order are advocating participatory direct action for direct self-government: admittedly a clumsy phrase . . . As might be gleaned . . . Morris remains my always present, beloved mentor . . .

Socialist libertarianism: a further glimpse

An anarchist or, to call on the more polite synonym, libertarian socialist standpoint has permeated this chapter . . . Deep-seated, sustainable change, one notes, will not come as a result of apocalyptic events, of histrionic, usually violent confrontations which lead to final, pre-delineated ends. Such changes are, rather, part of drawn-out processes; they are part of long-term, historical continua. . . .

William Morris' 19th century proposal remains far, far more apposite. Paraphrased, he suggested that socialists relate immediately to others as they expect to do in their socialist futures, that they practice now so that will recognise the future when they get there – in more formal terms, that they adopt modes of organisation that consciously resemble the worlds they seek to bring about . . . And there are other lines; lines that tug as insistently at one's mind and heart. None is more compelling than Percy Bysshe Shelley's rallying cry from his *Masque of Anarchy*; a call that, despite over-use, carries its impassioned immediacy beyond the borders of any single state or node of oppression:

> Rise like Lions after slumber,
> In unvanquishable number,
> Shake your chains to earth, like dew,
> Which in sleep had fallen on you,
> Ye are many —they are few.

This I take to be an unmistakably cross-national call; one presently addressed to a world-wide, a distinctively varied 21st century audience – an ideologically and concretely imper-illed majority. Ye, indeed, are many, they, indisputably, are few. Your condition is ours: ours is yours. . . .

"The Worker in the Community," undated paper by panel of FOSATU shopstewards in Springs (extracts).

The Federation of South Africa Trade Unions (FOSATU) was formed in 1979. The largest formation in the emerging independent union movement, it was the strongest black working class organisation of the early 1980s. By 1985, when it helped found the Congress of South African Trade Unions (COSATU), it had over 140,000 members. FOSATU's independent left politics, often dubbed "workerism," distanced it from African nationalism, as represented by the African National Congress (ANC), and mainstream Marxism, as represented by the South African Communist Party (SACP).

FOSATU stressed working class autonomy and working class identity, democratic non-racial unions based on bottom-up "workers' control" as part of a larger working class movement, opposition to both capitalism and apartheid, and the extension of "workers' control" across economy and society. Its model of organising had an important influence on 1980s struggles in South Africa. The following text provides a glimpse of how FOSATU militants envisaged the extension of "workers' control" beyond the factories, and the mobilisation of union power behind township demands. It outlines an approach based on mandates, careful organising, member participation, direct action and winning steady gains. It also indicates FOSATU's creative and pragmatic approach.

Source: Xipu, Rolly, Amon Sibanyoni, Vincent Boshielo, Rusty Moagi, and D. Madupela, with Chris Dlamini. n.d. [?1984]. *The Worker in the Community*. Paper by panel of FOSATU shop stewards. Folder CD15.3. Taffy Adler Papers (AH2065): Historical Papers collection, University of the Witwatersrand. Minor corrections have been made to spelling, punctuation and capitalisation.

This panel is composed of the Shop Stewards from different factories and industries, in fact it is the local S/S Office Bearers [in the FOSATU Springs Local – LvdW] . . .

You will realise that the "Community" comprises . . . various organisations, being: church organisation, football organisation, Community Council, women societies, burial societies, AZAPO [Azanian People's Organisation, a nationalist group in the Black Consciousness tradition – LvdW] and of course the worker organisation . . . 99% of members of each of the above mentioned organisations and Societies belong to the Productive Class, and about

75% of these members are Workers . . . 10% of the total Community will be the Unproductive Class which is children and pensioners.

What has been happening . . . is that most of these organisations are led or controlled by non-workers i.e. "businessmen or intellectuals" who in in our experience as worker-leaders, have no in depth feeling or understanding of the down trodden masses, or worker day-to-day problems and sufferings, because, you cannot expect a businessman to complain over a 3c rise in bus fare, or R4.00 rise in house rentals. Same goes for the Intellectuals, you cannot expect them to complain or be involved in a fight against unfair dismissals, dispute or below breadline wages paid to the Shop Floor Worker, since these practices do not in most cases affect them.

In trade unions, a Shop Steward 'is responsible to workers his/her department, and will always take a mandate from these workers, and he/she is expected to report back to them of the outcome or any mandate or grievance, which means that he/she is always account-able to workers, and he/she always enjoys the support of the majority in that department, and that gives the S/S power to push for workers' demands as he can always mobilise them to take action if response is always negative from Management.

Just to put people in the picture, this procedure is put into practice by almost all FOSATU affiliates, and enshrined in FOSATU principle, that of Worker Control.

In some factories workers had begun to win fight about unfair dismissals, victimisation and wage increases . . . prior to the adoption of S/S in factories . . . foremen and supervisors especially white . . . would dismiss a worker for no apparent reason whatsoever, and nobody would challenge them . . . but after the introduction of S/S Committees, this practice was eliminated, and workers could see the direct effectiveness of the Shop Stewards' repre-sentativity, and this entrenched more confidence and trust from workers towards their Shop Stewards.

One should bear this in mind that we organise for power and support, and you may only achieve these provided you deliver the goods . . . for major issues, like collective grievances or wage proposal, we hold general meetings in the townships, and what has been happening is that when we report on previous mandates, workers would show satisfaction on most of the achievements . . . and would very much appreciate their Shop Stewards; effort, and that makes them . . . depend entirely on the Shop Stewards as their leaders, because of the obvious and practical results.

And what happen in these meetings is that: Workers would start raising other things that affect them, issues such as *incredible water bills, unannounced rent rise, unrealistic rental account* . . . shortage of school buses, bus routes, behaviour of the bus drivers and coupon system . . .

Now, if you look at these problems, you would say that the organisation in the commu-nity, for instance, the Community councillor or AZAPO in our area of Springs, should tackle these issues, but unfortunately, they did not. And we had problems . . . to find these organisation because the only place where you normally hear about them is in the *Sowetan* and *African Reporter* newspaper, and our experience tells us that it is only the offices of an organisation or in general meetings where complaints from people could be put across, and the leadership or anyone else with the knowledge or information on the problem would explain . . . relevant people would be delegated to take the matter up with a particular factory, Administration Board [unelected township governing bodies under apartheid – LvdW], PUTCO bus co. [Public Transport Corporation – LvdW] or whoever is responsible for it. So there are no such offices or general meetings of these organisations, all these problems could not be attended to, and they were escalating and affecting everybody in the township and especially the group with the lowest income.

So it goes without saying that almost 75% of the people living in Kwa-Thema [black working class township near Springs – LvdW] were faced with these problems, and the majority were workers.

We then had to devise some strategies of how to approach these problems, and what we decided was that we should involve Management in a bid to solve some of the problems.

Now some people may ask a question how is Management involved in issues that affect workers after working hours, and outside workplace.

The answer to that is simple, because you'll recall that employers initiated the creation of townships when they started opening factories, the reason was that they wanted labour to be nearby, so that if they wanted to operate on a 3-shift circle, they would be able to do so without any problem as workers would be travelling from nearby townships to work, the bosses also paid levies towards the provision of transport for workers to and from factories.

So with all this, we feel the bosses would be included in the problem-solving process.

They should deduct from weekly wages on pro-rata basis, an amount equalling to one's monthly rental and pay that to the Administration Board offices at the end of each month, for every worker. This would help in the monitoring of unrealistic rental accounts because it will now be checked by both the Shop Stewards and the bosses in each factory, so irregularities will be spotted by both parties and queried by the bosses to the Administration Board, because we have experienced that any individual worker going to these offices, he/she tries to argue the amount reflected on the accounts slip as being unrealistic and unacceptable, he/she will be threatened with eviction from his/her present dwelling. So the poor worker would end up paying.

... One instance where the local Shop Steward took a direct community problem ... was pertaining [to] the bus routes dissatisfaction, and also Coupon system which was changed by PUTCO local management ... In a local Shop Stewards meeting, a decision was taken that a delegation be sent to PUTCO, and an agenda was drawn, listing the items and the results of the meeting between PUTCO and the Shop Stewards delegation was that PUTCO would revert back to [the] old Coupon System which the people wanted.

Workers of Kellogg had already put the trick of involving management in solving the malpractice of Administration Board practice, and this had worked beautifully ... that is "setting a thief to catch a thief" but we don't mean exactly that ...

So it is clear that these exploitative practices can be controlled or combatted worker organisations (trade unions) and 75% of the population be free from the exploitation meted by the bosses, the Administration Board and the Bus Company. We may if possible start looking at the uncontrolled and fluctuating prices, especially on food at some [of] the township shops ...

So the Springs Shop Stewards' Local [FOSATU structure linking different affiliate unions at the local level – LvdW] has proposed that Zone Committees be established throughout the township, and discussion be held among the Shop Stewards and anybody living in the

Zone who could be interested, and more people should be encouraged, so that problems would be covered in a broader perspective, and the recommendation will be made to the local Shop Stewards Council which will then decide on a strategy of tackling the problems which we hope or believe that if the tactics or system mentioned on this paper were applied, the 75% or even 80% of Kwa-Thema inhabitants would be free from these exploitation and malpractices which are frustrating and destroying their happiness as well as their living in the township.

If people accept that workers are a majority in the community, then we should be led or controlled by the workers.

Remember that FOSATU and most . . . other people subscribe to the One Man One Vote principle. Therefore, we should not be evasive on the slogan "MAJORITY SHALL RULE."

. . . Community organisations do not exist in practices, it's only there to confuse people, because, truly speaking, an organisation without a clear programme of action cannot be effective, therefore:

"WORKER ORGANISATION SHOULD TAKE A LEAD."

"MAJORITY RULES" . . .

Murphy Morobe, May 1987, "Towards a People's Democracy: The UDF View" (extracts).

The United Democratic Front (UDF) was launched in Cape Town in 1983, a broad and non-racial anti-apartheid coalition. Although widely viewed as linked to the then-banned African National Congress (ANC), the UDF had its own dynamics, tensions and innovations, and was not politically monolithic. By the mid-1980s, a number of UDF-linked structures were involved in efforts to build participatory-democratic structures of "people's power" to supplant the apartheid state, a process closely linked to the massive struggles sweeping the country. The radicalism of sections of the UDF – as reflected in the speech below – is worth recalling in any discussion of a politics "at a distance from the state."

Source: Speech given on behalf of Murphy Morobe, Acting Publicity Secretary of the United Democratic Front (UDF), delivered to F. van Zyl-Slabbert's Institute for a Democratic Alternative for South Africa in May 1987. Spelling errors have been corrected.

We in the United Democratic Front are engaged in a *national* democratic struggle. We say we are engaged in a national struggle for two reasons. Firstly, we are involved in political struggle on a national, as opposed to a regional or local level.

This national struggle involves all sectors of our people – workers (whether in the factories, unemployed, migrants or rural poor), youth, students, women, and democratic-minded professionals. We also refer to our struggle as national in the sense of seeking to create a new nation out of the historical divisions of apartheid.

We also explain the *democratic* aspect of our struggle in two ways, and this is the main emphasis of my paper today. Firstly, we say that a democratic South Africa is one of the aims or goals of our struggle. This can be summed up in the principal slogan of the Freedom Charter: 'The People Shall Govern'. In the second place, democracy is the means by which we conduct the struggle. This refers to the democratic character of our existing mass-based organisations. It is useful to separate these two levels, but obviously they are also connected. By developing active, mass-based democratic organisations and democratic practices within these organisations, we are laying the basis for a future, democratic South Africa.

The creation of democratic *means* is for us as important as having democratic *goals* as our objective. Too often models of a future democratic South Africa are put forward which bear no relation to existing organisations, practices and traditions of political struggle in this country. What is possible in the future depends on what we are able to create and sustain now. A democratic South Africa will not be fashioned only after transference of political power to the majority has taken place, nor will it be drawn up according to blueprints and plans that are the products of conferences and seminars. The creation of a democratic South Africa can only become a reality with the participation of millions of South Africans in the process – a process which has already begun in the townships, factories and schools of our land.

I have argued that parliament and its related structures are *not* the starting point for a movement towards democracy in South Africa because of: 1) their basic illegitimacy, 2) their lack of real political power and 3) the narrow confines of the political debate that takes place within these structures, which more often than not runs counter to and opposes the political debate that is going on at broader levels. In addition, not only are we opposed to the present parliament because we are excluded, but because parliamentary-type representation in *itself* represents a very limited and narrow idea of democracy.

Millions of South Africans have for decades not only been denied political representation, but have also been oppressed and exploited. Our democratic aim therefore is control over every aspect of our lives, and not just the right (important as it is) to vote for a central government every four to five years.

When we speak of majority rule, we do not mean that black faces must simply replace white faces in parliament. A democratic solution in South Africa involves all South Africans, and in particular the working class, having control over all areas of daily existence – from national policy to housing, from schooling to working conditions, from transport to consumption of food. This for us is the essence of democracy. When we say that the people shall govern, we mean at all levels and in all spheres, and we demand that there be real, effective control on a daily basis.

This understanding of democracy tends to be fundamentally different from the various abstract constitutional models which tend to be put forward as solutions. Most of these are concerned with the question of how central political representation can be arranged so that 'groups' [racial or ethnic or party – LvdW] cannot dominate each other, or how what is referred to as the 'tyranny of the majority' can be avoided (many of these models are still unfortunately caught up in the paradigm which seeks to alter the basis of political representation to a more non-racial basis without any real transference of power away from the small elite which has the present monopoly). This debate gets stuck with the formula which says that democracy = political parties, each representing a different interest group, each jostling for political power.

Now it is important that a democracy contains a plurality of different viewpoints, and I wish to elaborate on this point later on. However, the essence of democracy cannot be limited to debate alone. The key to a democratic system lies in being able to say that the people in our country can not only vote for a representative of their choice, but also feel that they have some direct control over where and how they live, eat, sleep, work, how they get to work, how they and their children are educated, what the content of that education is; and that these things are not done for them by the government of the day, but the people themselves.

In other words, we are talking about direct as opposed to indirect political representation, mass participation rather than passive docility and ignorance, a momentum where ordinary people feel that they can do the job themselves, rather than waiting for their local MP to intercede on their behalf [. . .]

The rudimentary organs of *people's power* that have begun to emerge in South Africa (street committees, defence committees, shop-steward structures, student representative councils, parent/teacher/student associations) represent in many ways the beginnings of the kind of democracy that we are striving for.

These structures did not originate out of abstract ideas but out of the real political battles being fought against the existing undemocratic institutions that have traditionally sought to control people's lives. Originally, the slogan of "ungovernability" was popularised as a political weapon in the hands of people with no access to political power. As a speaker said at one of the rallies in the Transvaal during 1984: 'We must be difficult to control. We must render the instruments of oppression difficult to work. We must escalate all forms of resistance. We must make ourselves ungovernable'.

However, as Zwelake Sisulu has explained: "In a situation of ungovernability, the government does not have control. But nor do the people. While they have broken the shackles of direct government rule the people have not yet managed to control and direct the situation. There is a power vacuum ... No matter how ungovernable a township is, unless the people are organised, the gains made by ungovernability can be rolled back by state repression. Because there is no organised centre of people's power, the people are relatively defenceless and vulnerable ..."

It was out of the battles to wrest control of the townships from the state that the slogan 'Forward to People's Power' was taken up. In many townships, this was actually transferred from a slogan into a reality before the repressive tide of the second state of emergency took its toll.

There are countless details that I could narrate about the street committees of Cradock, New Brighton, Lamontville, Alexandra, Mamelodi, Soweto, the village committees in Sekhukhuneland and KwaNdebele, the shop-stewards committees of the East Rand. Never have our townships seen such debate, such mass participation, such direct representation, not just on the part of political activists, but on the part of ordinary South Africans who, throughout their whole lives, have been pushed around like logs of wood.

While details differ from area to area, the basic unit of people's power that emerged was the street or yard committee. This structure was an executive of ten to twelve people elected at a meeting of all the people on the street, not just those from one political tendency. These street committees, which would meet at least once a week and attend to the social, economic and political issues that cropped up in the street, sent representatives to zone, area or section committees that would represent upwards of twenty-five streets. Finally, a township civic executive would be chosen at a meeting of all the sections, and ratified at mass rallies, which in places like Mamelodi numbered over 25,000 people.

The tasks of these structures included 1) direct political representation, 2) two-way communication of ideas, from mass base to leadership and vice-versa, 3) education and information on what was happening in South Africa, 4) debate over the tactics and strategies of stayaways [community-based general strikes – LvdW], consumer and rent boycotts, 5) solving of social disputes through people's courts (as well as actively prohibiting any forms of kangaroo justice that the state has claimed forms the basis of our political practice), and 6) intervention in the running of the townships – building parks, clearing rubble, fighting crime, fixing roads, even collecting rent to build new houses and facilities for township residents. The street committees also began to work closely with the SRCs [Student Representative Councils – LvdW] in the schools in implementing people's educational programs, as well as with the trade unions and shop-stewards councils in building worker power in the factories. It is clear that one of the chief aims of the current state of emergency has been to smash these alternative forms of mass representation, given the direct and severe challenge they pose to the unrepresentative and undemocratic institutions of apartheid.

The difficulties of organising democratically at gunpoint under the state of emergency are surely obvious. Most of our meetings are banned, many of our officials are in jail, on trial or in hiding, and the need for tight security and secrecy obviously puts a strain on the development of a thorough-going, expanding mass-based democratic practice. However, the basic principles of our organisational democracy remain:

1) *Elected Leadership.* Leadership of our organisations must be elected (at all levels), and re-elections must be held at periodic intervals. No single individual must become irreplaceable. Elected leadership must also be recallable before the end of their term of office if there is indiscipline or misconduct.

2) *Collective Leadership.* We try and practice collective leadership at all levels. There must be continuous, ongoing consultation. Leadership skills, experience and knowledge must be spread, not hoarded.

3) *Mandates and Accountability.* Our leaders and delegates are not free-floating individuals.
   They always have to operate within the delegated mandates of their positions and delegated duties. This is not to say that we do not encourage individual views to be expressed. Nor that those elected to leadership positions can never take initiatives. On the contrary. We expect all the members of our organisations to think for themselves, to be able to raise and debate their ideas at any time, and have the right to differ with each other. We do not believe that there is only one single 'line' on any issue. However, once a decision has been voted on within an organisation, we expect all our members to act according to that decision, even if they originally voted against it.

4) *Reporting.* Reporting back to organisations, areas, units, etc. is an important dimension of democracy. We expect reports to be accurate, concise and well prepared. We feel very strongly that information is a form of power, and that if it is not shared, it undermines the democratic process. We therefore take care to ensure that language translations occur if necessary, and that reports and debates do not take place at a level of jargon beyond the reach of all our members.

5) *Criticism and Self-criticism.* We do not believe that any of our members are beyond criticism; neither are organisations and strategies beyond reproach. This means that regular evaluations must be held, questions must be asked and constructive criticism is encouraged. Our attitude is one of criticising a comrade as a friend rather than a victim.

Our emphasis on organisational democracy is therefore twofold – the constant need for organisational unity in the face of the enemy onslaught (our organisations cannot descend to the level of debating clubs or warring factions); within this organisational unity, there is the need to make space for differences of opinion, different options and different strategies.

We do not regard these democratic principles as luxuries; rather they are a fundamental weapon of our struggle. Without the fullest organisational democracy, we will never be able to achieve conscious, active and unified participation of the majority of people, and in particular the working class, in our struggle.

I have dealt at some length on the democratic methods that we have adopted within our organisations in order to demonstrate that there are tens of thousands of South Africans who are learning and practicing democracy today, despite the confines of an undemocratic society. Let me conclude by referring to our democratic goals in more detail.

It is clear to us that 300 years of minority rule has created gross inequalities at all levels of our society – not just at the level of political power, but also in terms of land, natural resources, income distribution, in the ownership and control of economic production and in areas of education, housing, transport, health, sport and culture. Thus for us, any democratic programme of demands cannot be solely concerned with government alone, but must address all the (unequal) relations of power in our society. In other words, both the dismantling of apartheid legislation *and the effects* of 300 years of minority rule must be addressed. A democratic system that does not recognise the need to right the historical injustices of apartheid cannot hope to succeed.

For many of us in the UDF, the Freedom Charter adopted at the Congress of the People in 1955 is one such democratic document that begins to answer some of these questions. The Freedom Charter was created through a democratic process, unprecedented in this country and probably in most other countries of the world. The character of the Charter is not the result of any one original thinker nor even a group of people with fine intellects. Its content derives from the conditions under which black people live in South Africa – in particular national oppression . . . I could go on to describe each clause at length, but I think the point is made, namely, that democracy in South Africa can only survive if it tackles the existing unequal relations of power and privilege as well as the issue of political representation and individual freedom . . .

[I]t is important to remember that Davids have defeated Goliaths before and will do so again. Few weapons are more powerful than mass participation and unity in action against the common enemy. These fundamental tenets of our struggle are only ensured through a commitment to the democratic process at all times.

The Unemployed People's Movement, "Ten Theses on Democracy," Grahamstown, 2011 (extracts).

The Unemployed People's Movement (UPM) emerged in 2009, and can be seen as part of the wave of post-apartheid social movements that began in the late 1990s. It has been active in Botshabelo in the Free State province, Durban in KwaZulu-Natal and Grahamstown in the Eastern Cape. It has been active in struggles against poverty, for access to water and electricity and jobs, and against anti-immigrant violence.

Its aims, however, go far beyond reforms or conventional politics, as the following text shows. It was prepared by the UPM in Grahamstown in the Eastern Cape as a contribution to a discussion at a Democratic Left Front (DLF) meeting in Johannesburg, Friday 2 September, 2011. The

DLF was launched early 2011 from the Conference for a Democratic Left (CDL), itself formed 2008, and aimed to unite various socialist currents and popular movements. The 2nd DLF conference in 2014 threw its weight behind the then-emerging United Front, loosely linked to the rebel National Union of Metalworkers of South Africa (NUMSA).

Source: UPM, Grahamstown.

. . . Thesis one: the discussion about democracy must be rooted in the realities of our struggles

If our movements have any chance of growing into a popular force that can win real victories against the state and capital then theory must speak to the realities of our struggles. We have to take the realities of our struggles very seriously because it is those realities that will determine whether or not we succeed or fail. We measure theory by how well it can speak to the realities of our struggles.

Thesis two: liberal democracy was not the final victory of the struggle

We are often told that this democracy [the parliamentary democracy opened in 1994 – LvdW] is the final fruit of the struggle against apartheid. That is not true. This democracy was a compromise in which the masses of the people were expelled from active participation in politics and returned to their allotted spaces in exchange for allowing the state to be placed under black management. As Frantz Fanon put it "the people were sent back to their caves." This is why Mandela told the people to stop struggling when he came out of jail. A radical leader will always encourage the people to keep organising and struggling even when he or she is in power.

Thesis three: liberal democracy must be defended

Liberal democracy is not democracy. It is just one very narrow and limited form of democracy that privileges elites and excludes ordinary people from active participation. But liberal democracy is much more democratic than the authoritarian and statist alternatives that the ANC [African National Congress – LvdW] is trying to entrench by rolling back media freedom, undermining the integrity of the courts and repressing social movements. Liberal democracy does give some space for debate and organisation and so we must defend it vigorously. However we must be very careful to avoid elitism and the domination of NGOs [Non-Governmental Organisations – LvdW] in this struggle to defend civil society.

Thesis four: liberal democracy must be extended

Communist democracy is popular democracy. It is the democracy of the Paris Commune, of the Soviets, of the people's power movement of the 1980s (which we must be careful not to celebrate uncritically due to the attacks on BC [Black Consciousness – LvdW] activists by UDF [United Democratic Front – LvdW] activists on the East Rand and here in Grahamstown too) and Tahir Square. We need to push wherever we can to deepen liberal democracy, with its dependence on a commodified legal system and the politics of representation by political parties and NGOs, into a politics of direct democracy where people live, work and study. We need to continually radicalise democracy from below.

Thesis four: politics comes before economics

There is a strong tendency in the left to put economics before politics. This is a mistake. It's all very well for people to propose alternative economic arrangements but without the force to implement them they are just ideas. Ideas can only be made a reality when people have the power to force progress forward. This is why politics (the political empowerment of the people) must come before economics (the creation of a just economy). We need to keep discussions about alternative economic models open at all times but our main task is the political empowerment of the people.

Thesis five: we are not struggling for service delivery

The struggles of the people are relentlessly described as "service delivery protests." Even many people on the left impose this meaning on our struggles. We reject this. Of course we do struggle for better services sometimes but this is always nested in a deeper struggle for control over our own lives, our own communities and development processes. We are struggling for the political empowerment of the people that can lead to a democratisation of decision-making which will lead to a more equal society.

Thesis six: the state is sometimes a threat to democracy

The state poses a serious threat to democracy. The attacks on the media, the judiciary, social movements and popular protest are all well known. At this point it is grossly irresponsible to see the ANC [African National Congress – LvdW] or the state as democratising forces. They are both actively trying to roll back the limited democratic gains that were made in 1994. We all need to be clear about this. We need to be clear that there can be no progressive resolution of our social crisis from within the ANC and that it is essential to build political alternatives outside of the ANC and the alliance [led by the ANC, and including the South African Communist Party and Congress of South African Trade Unions – LvdW]. We should take note of the different way that protests by organisations inside the alliance (e.g. SAMWU, ANC YL, TAC etc. [South African Municipal Workers Union, ANC Youth League, the Treatment Action Campaign, respectively – LvdW]) are treated by the police compared to how protests by organisations outside of the alliance (e.g. UPM, AbM, AEC, LPM [Unemployed People's Movement, Abahlali baseMjondolo, [Western Cape] Anti-Eviction Campaign, Landless People's Movement respectively – LvdW]) are treated by the police.

Thesis seven: civil society is sometimes a threat to democracy

It is a myth that civil society is always a democratic space. Civil society organisations are usually hierarchical, professional organisations which are not run democratically, have no democratic mandate and are often threatened by popular membership-based organisations. They are often white-dominated and always dominated by the middle class. They are often threatened by a politics that organises outside of the realm of professional civil society (the courts, conferences etc.). There have been many cases of civil society organisations being as hostile to popular politics as the state and maliciously and dishonestly presenting popular organisations as criminal, violent and irrational. . . .

Thesis eight: the criminalisation of our movements is a major threat to democracy

While we support the campaigns to protect media freedom and the independence of the courts they are often very elitist in how they are organised and in the way that they express their concerns. They usually leave out a major threat to our democracy which is the rampant criminalisation of popular movements. Both the state and the ANC on one side, and elements in NGO-based civil society on the other, (including its liberal and left streams), have a record of trying to misrepresent popular struggles as violent, irrational and criminal. It is essentially for all genuinely progressively forces to unite against this criminalisation of popular protest and popular organisation.

Thesis nine: we need to think democracy together with dignity

The indignity with which our people have to live every day is truly horrific. Today the brother of one of our comrades, a man who is 36 and has no job, is walking around Grahamstown with the body of his baby in his arms looking for someone to take the body. The hospital has turned him away. He is feeling useless and desperate. Democracy must not only be something technical. The way that we practice democracy must also contribute to defending and building the dignity of our people.

Thesis ten: we must all practice what we preach

All our organisations need to be rigorously democratic both internally and in how they relate to each other in forums like the DLF, Right2Know [an organisation promoting open access to information – LvdW] and so on. This means that people must be elected to all positions, accountable and recallable. It means that there must be equal representation of men and women. It also means that comrades from NGOs and Universities cannot assume an automatic right to leadership and that if a democratic process does not elect them or accept their views they must accept this process rather than trying to retain power by manipulating budgets behind the scenes or making wild allegations of criminality, conspiracy and so on.

Lekhetho Mtetwa, "The Landless People's Movement Fights for the People's Rights," 29–30 September 2013

The Landless People's Movement (LPM) was formed in 2001, much of the initial impetus coming from an NGO body called the National Land Committee (NLC). Although affiliated to Via Campesina, and linked to the Landless Workers Movement (MST) in Brazil, its activity has centred on the struggles of urban squatter communities, rather than on agrarian issues, farm occupations or organising alternative production systems. In 2004, LPM supporters protested the national elections declaring "No Land! No Vote!" In 2008, the Gauteng province-based LPM sections (now the main LPM affiliates) formed the Poor People's Alliance with the squatters' movement Abahlali baseMjondolo *and the Rural Network /* Abahlali basePlasini *(both in KwaZulu-Natal), and the Anti-Eviction Campaign (in the Western Cape). The Poor People's Alliance also took an anti-electoral position.*

In the texts provided below, Lekhetho Mtetwa, an activist in the LPM in Protea South in Soweto, and a member of the Zabalaza Anarchist Communist Front (ZACF), discusses the struggles of the LPM. Mtetwa was, at the time, LPM secretary in Protea South. It is important to note that by 2013 the LPM in Protea South in Soweto was the main LPM affiliate. Since Mtetwa's comments were made, this section has faced notable challenges. In 2010, a founder member and office-bearer sought to use the LPM to support her running for municipal office on a Democratic Alliance (DA)-linked ticket. This was defeated by Mtetwa and others, but a long-term schism resulted. From 2014, many in LPM-Protea South were (successfully) wooed by the new Economic Freedom Fighters (EFF) party: Mtetwa resigned in protest. Despite some subsequent disillusion in EFF, following the 2014 national elections, the section has not fully revived. It seems likely that it will be replaced by a branch of Abahlali baseMjondolo.

Sources: Two texts are provided below.

The first is a lightly edited transcript of an introduction to the LPM that Mtetwa gave on the 29 September 2013, at the "Politics at a Distance from the State" conference at Rhodes University, Grahamstown, South Africa. The second text is an interview with Mtetwa, at the same event, by Lucien van der Walt, on 30 September.

Lekhetho Mtetwa: the Landless People's Movement fights for the people's rights

I am from the Landless People's Movement (LPM), a movement that engages the people on land issues. People have been protesting for their right to land, while the state is trying to privatise and control land, and also push shack-dwellers away from the cities. The eviction of people is ongoing, so we fight for the "right to the city," and for the right to land and housing. Another issue we address is unemployment: land is not enough. The workers and the unemployed should occupy factories and workplaces, so that we can have jobs and meet our needs.

What does the word "state" mean? The state rests on violence against the working class.

At election times, politicians make empty promises, but after the elections they deploy violence against us, the working class. Our structures have been attacked by police and by vigilantes. In 2004, we had comrades who were arrested and tortured when they campaigned at election time, saying "No Land! No Vote!" In 2007, on the 3rd September, we were barricading roads, and we lost one comrade: he was knocked over by a van that rode away. The police attacked us, although we were exercising and demanding our rights.

I am involved in the LPM in Protea South, Soweto, where we are shack-dwellers. The state wants to remove all the shack dwellers, and to then use the land for houses for other people. This is a major issue that we are fighting. Forced removals are what we are facing. Housing is what we want: to be housed properly.

We also face a lack of consultation from our so-called elected municipal councillors: they do things, without consulting the community. The politicians rely on the votes of our grandparents: they use them to get elected, promising this and that to get at the end of the day more votes.

These are the problems that we are facing. To organise and fight for the things I have mentioned, we as LPM Protea South usually have a protest march or barricade the streets, so we can be seen by the state as fighting for our demands. Normally we make it a point that no-one from our community goes to work during the protests. There are shops in our area: we make it a point that no-one opens on that day also.

If each and every person joins the struggle, we can make changes. We need to fight the struggle together: even fighting for our rights in Protea South is not only a fight for LPM members only, but for everyone who lives in in this community and in this world. We are fighting for everyone who needs land and freedom.

All social movements should organise all the ordinary people to take direct action to defeat the state and the capitalists. If we always talk and talk without action, we are like an empty vessel. We need to be creative, and I push the idea of a poor people's summit, to build for big day of action and to allow struggles to be linked up.

Lekhetho Mtetwa: rebuilding the Landless People's Movement from below

Lucien van der Walt (LvdW): Thanks very much for agreeing to be interviewed. Can you tell me a bit about yourself and about the Landless People's Movement (LPM) and its work?

Lekhetho Mtetwa (LM): I am Lekhetho Mtetwa, secretary of the LPM in Protea South, from Chiawelo, in Soweto.

The LPM was set up in Protea South in 2001, and the person who introduced it was Maureen Mnisi. She became its chairperson for plus-minus 11 years, and was also Gauteng LPM chair.

How did I join? I raised issues in a public meeting, around land, and people said, "You know what, come and join us." And I was given light on how the LPM movement works, by word of mouth. Later I was given the documents of the movement. Eventually I was selected as a secretary, because I was politically strong. Initially I was co-opted onto the committee, later I was elected.

The LPM fights for the rights of the people, for housing, land, and jobs and against evictions. It fights so that the people may be able to support their families.

It doesn't support elections to the state, including to town councils. LPM focuses on the needs of the youth, and the community. We take the demands, and go to the local councillor, and present the demands. If nothing happens then, we take our demands to the top. And if nobody listens, then we march on government offices, and present a memorandum, and we barricade the roads, and stay-away from work.

LVDW: Can you can you tell me more about the current situation of the LPM? How is it doing these days?

LM: We are trying our best to rebuild the movement, and most of the support we have, we are getting from our community – and also from other social movements, which support us.

The LPM was, at one stage, claiming to be a country-wide organisation. Today, though, the main branch is in Protea South, Soweto. One of the issues is that there is not a structure linking different branches, even if they did exist. But as far as I know, the only other existing branch involves comrades in Durban. But there is nothing which I heard from that side for some time, about what they are maybe doing. We have contacts with them, but there is nothing we have planned together.

Understanding the problems, let us remember our branch of the LPM and other branches also, have faced repression. In our case has included arrests and assaults, and also attacks from vigilantes from nearby better-off areas in Soweto.

But there are also internal challenges. Recently there was a change in the leadership of the LPM branch in Protea South: I am the secretary of the new leadership. This change was linked to a fight against people who were using the movement for their own benefit, including trying to push it to join political parties, and provide votes. This is part of a bigger problem of nepotism, favouritism and opportunism that we see in some movements, and that we fight.

The earlier leadership tended to be top-down, not always even elected. We have changed that. What we are doing now is involving each and every person in our community, so that they can be part of us. What I am trying to say is that, as "leadership," we are not saying that, because we are the leaders or office-bearers, we will control and do everything. Instead, before we take things forward, we call a mass meeting wherein the community brings up suggestions and issues. Then we sit down as a committee, look at these matters, and then work out a way ahead. Then after that, we go back to the community: if they agree with everything, then we go further with everything; that is what we do; otherwise we again take the points and again change the plan, and again go back to the community.

Our focus is our branch's work, where we try our best to make the LPM movement go back to what it was before, but better. At this present moment we are trying to rebuild the movement within our community, and from there, we are planning to start other branches in other places.

LVDW: In the past, the LPM used the slogans "No Land! No Vote!" and then "No Land! No House! No Vote!" once it helped form the Poor People's Alliance along with *Abahlali baseMjondolo* and others in 2008. Do these slogans still get used?

LM: Yes, it doesn't end. It doesn't end as long as we are living under the circumstances under which we are living.

LVDW: And in the long-run what would be your vision of a new, a better South Africa? And what would be required to make this into reality?

LM: For me, I want to see everyone owning land and resources together, in common; everyone having a house, people living equal lifestyles and having useful jobs.

We should introduce the anarchist principles: all movements should come together and fight the system and in that way, build for revolution. We will then be able to defeat the state and the capitalists and thereafter the working class and poor people will be the ones controlling everything – everything which the bosses and politicians are owning and controlling at this present moment.

LVDW: How do you think we can create, solve the job problem in South Africa?

LM: By kicking out the bosses and taking over the factories and workplaces. That is the only way.

LVDW: Thanks very much for your time.

LM: Thanks a lot, com.

The Soundz of the South (SOS): Anti-Capitalist, Anti-Authoritarian African Hip-hop and Poetry, 29–30 September 2013

The Soundz of the South (SOS) is a South African "anti-capitalist cultural resistance movement working with activists who use hip-hop and poetry to spread revolutionary messages, raise consciousness and critique neo-liberalism" (Bandcamp, 2013). It has also described itself as "anarchist." Based in Cape Town, SOS runs free concerts, including a "Don't Vote" series in Khayelitsha township ahead of the 2014 elections, calling on people to instead use direct action. The 2013 SOS album, Freedom Warriors Volume 2, *included tracks on the 2011 police murder of protestor Andries Tatane in Ficksburg, the 2012 Marikana massacre of miners, the 2012 farm-workers' strikes in the Western Cape, and "the Mandela Betrayal and the Afrikan Revolution."*

Sources: Two texts are provided below.

The first text is a lightly edited transcript of an introduction to the group, given by collective member Mkhululi "Khusta" Sijora on the 29 September 2013 "Politics at a Distance from the State" conference at Rhodes University, Grahamstown, South Africa. The second text is an interview with SOS member Xholiswa Matakese. She was interviewed at the same event on the 30 September 2013 by Lucien van der Walt.

Sadly, Khusta passed away in 2016, following an illness. Tributes can be found at https://zabalaza.net/2016/07/28/comrade-mkhululi-sijora-obituary-1982-2016/ and http://www.ilrig.org/index.php/component/phocadownload/category/2-booklets?download=3: khusta-tributes

Mkhululi "Khusta" Sijora: introducing the Soundz of the South

My name is Khusta: I am from the movement called Soundz of the South, or SOS. Soundz of the South is a collective of cultural activists that is using the media of today to spread revolutionary messages. We are using, specifically, arts, which means poetry and hip-hop and other music and mediums. As SOS, we stand against all forms of exploitation, we stand against all forms of oppression, we stand against all forms of domination, and we are strongly against the hierarchical way of organising. We believe that it is only the people themselves that will free themselves. There is no political party or any representative that will bring freedom to the people. It is only the people that can know what it will take to free themselves.

Our movement is linked to the social movements within the communities that are organizing. We draw inspiration from the writings of the Zabalaza Anarchist Communist Front (ZACF). We draw inspiration from the struggles of the Mandela Park Backyarders [a

Khayelitsha-based movement of poor residents, also critical of voting – LvdW]. We draw inspiration from the likes of *Abahlali baseMjondolo*.

The reason why we are using music to spread these revolutionary messages is that we believe music played a very big role before 1994, in spreading a revolutionary consciousness amongst the youth, and other people. It was part of what saw the South Africans manage to overthrow the apartheid government.

But when we look at art and music today? Art and music have been commercialised and are not doing addressing the fight for justice in the society. Art is becoming collaborationist, and supporting the status quo, and misleading the youth and the rest of the people in the communities.

We believe that art has the potential to influence minds. We believe that art should be at the centre of the struggle in society, and we believe that a major reason why the society is the way it is, is because of the media. Artists should not collaborate with what is going on, they must fight the injustices that are happening.

We not only cultural activists in the sense that we just do music and we just write about it: we are involved in the struggles of our communities, we are part-and-parcel of each and every struggle that is going on within our communities. And we are trying to do whatever we can to change the minds of young artists, who think that in order for them to become successful in the music industry or in the arts industry they have to align with whatever is shown on SABC [the state-run TV and radio network – LvdW] or whatever is played on radio. We completely against this.

In terms of the way we organise: we have a space that we run every month in Khayelitsha where we gather young people and the community as well, where we gather artists together. We will have a certain theme or a topic that we will focus on, and then we will have different speakers talking on that particular theme, and then we have artists that will be performing on the theme, and then the public will engage the speakers and artists about the theme, and then there will be conversations amongst the crowd, as we move along with the programme.

We have been doing events around the upcoming elections to support the "No Land! No House! No Vote!" campaign together with the Symphony Way residents [also known as the Delft-Symphony Anti-Eviction Campaign, a movement of evictees – LvdW]. We have been doing events to motivate people not to vote, because by voting . . . well, we believe in the slogan that says *Amandla! Ngawethu!* This says that the power ("Amandla") is ours ("Ngawethu"). But immediately when people when go to the ballots and put their X's on the ballot papers, they are giving away the power that they have. They pass it onto a party. That is the reason why today, whenever we are faced with problems, and we are trying to resist, we are not heard: we have taken our power, and we have given it to somebody else! We are saying that it is high time that people claim back their power, and the only way of doing this, is through not voting at all but through organising within our communities.

We have also done events with the support of the Right2Know campaign against the censorship of information by the government. In 2010 we mobilised against the 2010 Soccer World Cup then being hosted in South Africa, because we believed that the World Cup was not for the people. It was there to maintain what is already going on, making the rich richer while the poor would not be going to benefit. Sadly, some of the people thought that we were crazy. But after 2010, people came back to us, they had realised that the World Cup was not theirs.

And at one point some of our members went to Brazil. Although the World Cup was over in South Africa, SOS got involved in efforts to counter the 2014 World Cup, mobilising with Brazilian communities. SOS members went there to share the experiences that we had in South Africa, as poor communities like Khayelitsha, to explain what the World Cup really meant to us, and that we have not benefited from it.

Two months past we were also here in Grahamstown. During the National Arts Festival [27 June-2 July 2013 – LvdW] we organised a smaller People's Resistance Festival together with the local Unemployed People's Movement (UPM). This festival was against the Grahamstown Festival because we believe that the Grahamstown Festival is here to maintain what is going on, to exploit the artists, benefitting the big corporations. Many artists come all the way to the Festival, incur many costs, and only to find themselves in deep debt. And most artists and most of the people in Grahamstown are not part-and-parcel of the Festival; and we are mobilizing against that exclusion.

Ngcwalisa Maqekeza: What "Soundz of the South" Means to Me

Lucien van der Walt (LVDW): Thanks very much for your time, comrade. Can you just start by giving me your name?

Ngcwalisa Maqekeza (NM): My name is Ngcwalisa Maqekeza, from Gugulethu, Cape Town, but I am everywhere!

LVDW: Can you tell me more about your involvement in SOS?

NM: I was introduced to Soundz of the South by comrade Anele Selekwa. I know him back from the days of the Social Movements Indaba [SMI: formed in 2002 as a national body involving movements like the Anti-Privatisation Forum, APF – LvdW]. We were working together there, but then I took a break. When I was trying to make my comeback into politics he invited me to come and check out SOS, and to see if it was my kind of vibe, and to join at some stage.

At SOS, we use media and art to conscientise our people. It is kind of hard to give political information and understanding to people, groom them and let them take the message outside, the way we, in the movements, have been doing things. This involves sitting in boardrooms in workshops and what not. But people there don't quite get everything: it's too much for them because they are not used to this kind of politics, and these ideas.

So what we do is create a song based on a certain issue, and that creates a certain awareness, and then we give it to people, and people can take it away with them. They can share it with everyone else, and that way, everyone gets the message, especially young people.

We do SOS events in the townships and we do them in the inner city as well. We will even invite other artists, who are not necessarily conscientising young people, artists who sing about cars, money . . . money they don't even have. We will invite them over: they come and we have a debate about general issues like the conditions we all live in. I mean, they live in the same conditions as us, regardless of what they sing or what kind of music they make. So we can reach a kind of common ground.

And during these sessions, we can also go into the crowd and find a person or two who want to ask questions. And this where you get a chance to do one-on-one sessions, because this is where you get deep into issues with a person. And they can ask anything. Not everyone can just raise their hands in a crowd full of people and say, "I want to know these things." So when you give a change to ask, they can ask what they want to ask.

LVDW: And many people come to your concerts from what I hear, they come in the hundreds.

NM: *Ja*, they do.

LVDW: And you also produce and sell CDs.

NM: Yes we do. On this coming Tuesday, we are launching a project by the women within SOS, called "Wordz of a Rebel Sistah(s)." It is a spoken word project, but not so strictly: there are some vocals. It is talking about who we are, about defining our, women's, place, about saying that women's place is not in the kitchen but in the struggle, at the forefront of the struggle.

So that is what we are doing, taking the power back, saying that we have got the power and we are taking action.

LVDW: Last: how can people help you? People that are not involved in SOS itself?

NM: We need materials. And we don't have office space. We want to create a social centre, a building, and reach more people. At the moment we are struggling to just find a piece of land where we can put the centre. We also want books because, you know, we want to circulate materials and because, if we had our centre, we would need more books. And obviously we want our centre to have a studio and recording equipment.

LVDW: That is excellent. Well, thank you for this. All strength to your struggle.

NM: My pleasure!

References

Bandcamp, 2013, "Freedom Warriors Vol. 2," online at *https://sos1.bandcamp.com/album/freedom-warriors-vol-2*, accessed 15 June 2014.

Warren McGregor, Zabalaza Anarchist Communist Front, "Anarchist-Communism: Building Black Working Class Counter Power against State, Capital and National Oppression," 16 December 2014

Warren McGregor is an activist born in the Coloured townships of the Cape Flats, now resident in Johannesburg, where he is involved in working class and union education. The ZACF, formed in 2003, is a revolutionary group that works primarily with township groups in Gauteng province. It rejects participation in elections, aiming to build a radical democracy, somewhat akin to the UDF's "people's power," but outside and against the state apparatus. This would involve an egalitarian society based upon collective ownership of the means of production, self-management, participatory planning, and production and distribution by need, in a stateless, socialist system.

Source: Interview with Warren McGregor by Leroy Maisiri, 16 December 2014, Johannesburg.

Leroy Maisiri (LM): First of all thank you so much for your time, and making room for me in your busy schedule. Please kindly begin stating your name and any political affiliations you have with organisations or movements within the left.

Warren McGregor (WM): It's a pleasure, but please call me "Warren." I am a member of the Zabalaza Anarchist Communist Front (ZACF), as well as of the Tokologo African Anarchist Collective (TAAC), and I identify myself politically as an anarchist.

LM: It appears there is a new interest in forming a "worker's party" in South Africa at present. Some people think the National Union of Metalworkers of South Africa (NUMSA) will be the heart of that party, given its recent separation from the Tripartite Alliance of the African National Congress (ANC), the Congress of South African Trade Unions (COSATU), and the South African Communist Party (SACP). Others place their hopes in formations like the new Workers and Socialist Party (WASP), or even in Julius Malema's Economic Freedom Fighters (EFF). And many people have great hopes that the ANC can be ousted by such parties in upcoming elections. Do you think that there is a need for a worker's party in South Africa?

WM: Do I think there is a need for it? No. Ultimately you have to look at what the purpose of the workers' party would be: obviously it would be the same as all other parties, to, in whatever way, access state power. Historically, ideas of a workers' party as a means for the working class to take power and change society come from the Marxist tradition and from social democracy, the desire being to access state power through revolutionary or (usually, these days) electoral means.

What we anarchists would say is that there is no need for a worker's party. And. in fact, that it would be very detrimental, not only here in South Africa but worldwide, to the workers' struggle.

Fundamentally for us, as anarchists, state power is part of the problem of why we have an unequal society.

The real, the hegemonic, power that is already dominant in society is the power of the ruling class. By "ruling class," we anarchists mean those dominating in the economic sphere as well as in the state sphere. And we include into the ruling class the bosses of big business, but also the bosses of the state: your top politicians, and those who run things like the military part of the state, your police and judiciary (all unelected by the way), as well as your top bureaucrats in the governing arm (all unelected).

So we would include them in the ruling class. Our analysis of the state includes the people who run the state, as part of the ruling class. Elites run corporations, elites run the state.

Because of our analysis of the state, we do not consider the state to be an instrument that can used to reconstruct society, or to construct an equal society, and thus we do not believe that socialism can be created through the state. And by "socialism" here, we mean a classless society and the equal redistribution of wealth and power in society, which means a stateless society, because the state centralises power.

I always say: if we want to create a stateless and equal society, how can we use the state? It's like saying: "In a year from now, I want to exist on a chocolate-less diet, so I do not want to eat chocolate – and to do that I will eat lots of chocolate! And then maybe the chocolate will start withering away!"

LM: Since you have said "no" to a worker's party, what is the alternative, according to you?

WM: It is to continue to work to build working class power in the country, but what we as anarchists, with the program of anarchism, would specifically build is "counter power." This is power that is *counter* the hegemonic power, essentially a power against, and outside and *counter* to, the power of the ruling class – and its states and corporations.

For us this means very specific things. It's about building the power of the working class to challenge the ruling class, and its capacity to reconstruct society from below at some point in the future. And the organs of counter power would include revolutionary (syndicalist) trade unions and community groups and other formations. By "working class" we do not include here just blue-collar workers. All people who work for others for wages and lack power are workers, no matter their jobs, and besides workers the working class includes workers' families, as well as the unemployed and, generally, the poor.

At the same time, the working class organisations of counter power must not only be fighting organisations, but must also be organisations of *education* as well. We need a radical education including the ability to critically analyse that which is around you, not just society but also yourself, and your organisation as well.

This is about building a revolutionary popular "counter culture" that also deals with ideas, and with issues like what we mean by "revolution" or "democracy," and the ideals we want for the future society, helping set in practice, now, in the development of our organisations, these ideals. So counter power and counter culture are linked fundamentally.

By "democracy" as an aim, we speak of a radical democracy, a direct democracy, where the people that form part of a particular project, community, factory, are involved in key decisions and are aware of the decisions, and share in the benefits that accrue from putting the decisions into action.

To get to a directly democratic society in all spheres, we need a revolutionary transformation in all spheres. But to get to a revolutionary transformation, we need to develop direct democracy right now in the organisations of counter power. And we also need to develop a revolutionary attitude, a revolutionary understanding and consciousness. At the end of the day, the ability of organs of counter power to develop towards revolutionary transformation is determined by the development of a revolutionary counter culture, of revolutionary consciousness.

LM: Thank you, very comprehensive. You say "revolutionary transformation," but are we just smashing the state here? How do reforms and immediate struggles fit? And what, specifically, is meant by "revolutionary transformation"?

WM: Anarchism aims at a revolutionary transformation of society, and by this, we mean a complete overhaul of the way that society is governed and organised, to "revolutionise" the economic, social and political arrangements. Anarchism is not about chaos, or a lack of rules: it asks for a different set of rules, a different order. We do not mean changing the people at the top of society, or the nationalisation of industry by the state: this still means a ruling class controlling an unequal system.

We mean a society where the means of production are commonly owned, a society that is self-managed and democratised, with no hierarchies, no oppression, and no ruling class. It means a self-managed, socialist society, egalitarian and democratic, with collective ownership and individual freedom.

This is what we mean by revolution.

But to get there you need to build working class revolutionary counter power to the point where it can take over society, replace the state and capital. This means building a mass base.

So in the process of developing counter power, you need to attract people to your organisations. That means being able to win reforms in the day-to-day, using day-to-day struggles, based on direct action, not elections and lobbying, so as to improve people's lives: to battle for higher wages, better housing conditions, and access to better conditions from capital and the state.

Being anti-statist does not necessarily mean that you do not use the battle for reforms within the revolutionary struggle. The idea is that the reforms are not the be-all and end-all of the struggle, and that the counter power remains *autonomous, outside and against* the state, and that fights for reforms are won through direct action by autonomous movements, and linked to the struggle to build revolutionary counter-power and counter-culture.

Reform struggles help to develop revolutionary capabilities, and lead to a sense of encouragement, and the victories and defeats in day-to-day struggles are educational tools not just for the popular organisations as a whole, but for the individuals within the organisations.

Victories help develop a sense of confidence in oneself as a militant in the organisation, as an organiser, and in the organisation itself. Defeats can be educational if we decide to study them as sites of critical analysis. Revolution is the goal, the end, and reforms are necessary, not decisive or ultimate, but steps on the road to revolutionary transformation.

LM: I want to get your general opinion of the state of the left and of anarchism, right now.

WM: Globally the left, for the last thirty years, has been on the back foot, the advent of neo-liberal globalisation and the restructuring of control in societies shifting the balance in favour of the ruling class all around the world, accompanied by attacks on working class formations. The collapse of the Soviet Union, which was basically the collapse of classical Marxism, has had a massive impact: you see it in a massive decline of authoritarian socialism.

But we have also seen, despite Francis Fukuyama calling the period "the end of history," various struggles, in particular, social movement struggles, struggles of the unemployed, and the rural population and peasants. All around the world we have seen upsurges, and these new movements have to a certain extent taken over where the trade unions used to be. Although the unions are far from dead.

We also see a resurrection of more libertarian socialism, in particular, anarchism. Now anarchism globally is still in a process of not necessarily defining itself, but of redefinition and rediscovery, of linking back to its historical roots, and recapturing parts of anarchist theory and history that have been lost or distorted. For example, from after the Second World War, writing about anarchist history has been focused on Northern Europe and America, relying on perspectives that discount the majority of anarchism that existed and exists globally and historically.

And we see that many of the struggles today, for example, the Occupy movements, also reflect the influence of more libertarian ideas and anarchist ideas without necessarily being purely anarchist. Many of those ideas are starting to find more space in the world.

However, there is a long way to go to reclaim the space that working class movements used to have a few decades ago, when they used to influence society, and also reclaiming the space for revolutionary left ideas, especially anarchism, which can radically change society.

The fact of the matter is that it is the radical right – in religious, fascist, populist and anti-foreigner variants – that is capturing the space opened by massive popular dissatisfaction with ruling elites.

LM: South Africa also has long tradition of left-wing and working class politics: where does anarchism fit here?

WM: Anarchism globally had its golden age in terms of influence from around 1870 to into the 1930s, and remained important after that, but less so than statist movements like anti-colonial nationalism and classical Marxism. But before that anarchism was certainly the most dominant socialist idea in the world, and its trade unionism, also known as "syndicalism," had a very big influence. It played a key role in the colonial and postcolonial world, including in anti-colonial and anti-imperialist struggles.

This included an important influence on South African black and white worker formations in the early part of the 1900s. But it's only in the latter part of the 1990s that we have a rekindling of an anarchist presence in South Africa, and an organised attempt to get re-involved in working class struggles. This all means that anarchism here is still quite a small force, first of all in the left, and secondly, even smaller in terms of influence among the working class and poor.

But on the other hand we are growing not only as an organisation and organised force, but, more importantly, the ideas of anarchism, when engaged with in a proper and honest way, find favour with black working class people here. More important than sitting on committees in coalitions like the new United Front, promoted by NUMSA, or chasing political party dreams, is systematic back-to-basics work with grassroots working class people, to win influence and to develop a black working class cadre of anarchists who are involved in everyday struggles, community struggles, union struggles etc.

LM: And the left in South Africa?

WM: I have tons of respect, despite any ideological disagreements and differences in tactical and strategic choices, for others in the left and in the progressive movement.

There are real differences in terms of strategy and tactics. But we are not sectarians: our history shows this. I have been involved in the anarchist movement for about six-and-a-half years, and it's clear anarchists have a long tradition of involvement in struggle with working class organisations, and this has included working with a variety of socialist and non-socialist groups.

We absolutely do not reject working with other political organisations, but we draw the line when it comes to what we are working for: if something goes against our principles or goes against the working class, we draw the line and do not cooperate.

We promote structured, democratic, mandate-based approaches to organising and reject the South African "populist" style. This is closely linked to the ANC and its offshoots, and centres on unelected and unaccountable leaders and self-appointed demagogues directing the actions of crowds who have no real say.

Fundamentally, there is no way we would consider a political party, whether left or right, to be of any use to revolutionary transformation or even reforms. This does not preclude the possibility that we will work, where needed, with political party people – and not just with independent or revolutionary socialists, because we would work with ordinary SACP and ANC members in struggles. These organisations have a big rank-and-file working class membership and those members can be engaged.

But as vehicles for a radical change? The SACP and ANC and indeed, all the other parties, including the EFF, cannot be these vehicles. Elections won't and don't help. To get anywhere in elections, the left would need to pour resources, resources that could have been used in building working class organisation and education, into getting people to vote, and even if seats are won, the representatives just become part of the problem, part of the state apparatus and ruling class. If militancy is funnelled into elections or a workers' party, it eventually means the subjugation of working class militancy to elections.

We will support any initiative that mobilises people and has a potential to become counter power or a space to win people to our ideas, and to build counter culture. But a workers' party and electioneering are a dead end, a grave yard for left, democratic and working class politics.

What is going to change society is a groundswell of working class organisation, structured, democratic and able to develop in the direction of counter culture and counter culture, not a unity of the left, which is not really possible. And this groundswell requires not just organising people but also changing the ideas that they have.

We, anarchists, are not messiahs who are going to bring about change the actual change, the revolutionary transformation. It is the working class that will, through a long, hard struggle with both victory and defeat, by building organisation and consciousness, despite suffering many losses, that will change the world. It's not a quick-fix, it's not a politics of election promises or freedom from above. State power and elections have never worked for the working class: that is the quick fix that fixes nothing.

Take the EFF: in power it has gone back on its promises and it reproduces many features of ANC populism.

LM: Thank you once again, for your input and your time

Abahlali baseMjondolo, 18 December 2015, "Occupy, Resist, Develop"

The Abahlali baseMjondolo ("shack dwellers'") movement was formed in 2005, part of the wave of post-apartheid social movements from the late 1990s. Centred on Durban in the eThekwini municipality, the movement has gained attention for its use of direct action tactics like road blockades, its election boycotts, stress on democratic organising, and history of repression at the hands of local party political machines. Although it stresses the importance of self-activity and fights for dignity, the movement has also made some use of the state's courts and in 2014, controversially supported a vote for the centre-right Democratic Alliance.

Source: press statement.

Press statement:

The year 2015, the tenth year of the existence of our movement, has almost come and gone. On the 3rd of October we gathered at the Curries Fountain Stadium to celebrate ten years of struggle. More than four thousand comrades participated in the celebration. We have survived years of serious repression – including arrests, assaults, torture, imprisonment, the destruction of our homes, slander and assassination. In these ten years we have won many victories in the struggle for land and dignity.

We are committed to putting the social value of land before its commercial value. We are committed to land reform from below. We have successfully occupied and held many new lands during the last ten years. This was the most difficult struggle to wage. It needed courage and *inkani*. It needed the ability to move from the land, into the streets and the courts. We are proud that we have been able to occupy land and build our own homes and develop our own communities for our own families.

Many of our comrades have paid a very high price for their commitment to this struggle. This is the year in which we commemorated all our comrades who have lost their lives in the struggle. The Annual Thuli Ndlovu Lecture was launched on the 24th September in honour of this courageous, fearless and radical woman who, in the midst of death threats, continued with the struggle for the betterment of the people of KwaNdengezi and *Abahlali* in general. Thuli was a fighter, a strong woman who did not back down even when she was receiving death threats from the ANC local councillor. Thuli refused to be silenced by those who abuse the rights of the people. She was shot seven times.

Two ANC ward councillors (Mduduzi Ngcobo known as "Nqola" and Velile Lutyeku) were charged with murder and will be appearing at the Durban High Court on the 26th January for her death. This is the first time that those who oppress us have been held accountable for their actions.

The Thuli Ndlovu Lecture will held annually in honour of all our comrades who had fallen in the struggle for land, housing and human dignity. We call on all our members, progressive forces and all women's rights organisations to come in numbers on the 26th of January to support Thuli's family and *Abahlali* in the Durban High Court where the accused councillors will appear before the judge.

We have continued to struggle against xenophobia working closely with migrant organisations, including the Congolese Solidarity Campaign. We have worked hard to tie the struggles of oppressed South Africans and migrants together. We are proud that we have stood strong against xenophobia and that we have been willing to take real risks to stand with our comrades from other countries. We have also continued to take a clear and strong position in support of our LGBTI comrades.

Joining our movement is a serious commitment. It is a slow process and one that must be collectively undertaken. This year we have launched a number of new branches in Durban and Pietermaritzburg. We are also preparing to launch three new branches (Good Hope, Driefontain and Protea South) in Gauteng.

We do not only struggle to occupy land. We also struggle to occupy space in the media, in universities and in important debates. Land is often won and lost in local struggles but we also struggle for a just country and a just world. This year we have been able to meet with comrades in America, Brazil, India, Ireland, Nigeria, Norway and Zimbabwe. We were very pleased to be able to send one comrade to the MST [Landless Workers Movement – LvdW] political school for militants in Brazil.

We are very pleased that membership based grassroots organisations are slowly starting to be able to occupy a space in the international solidarity networks that used to be completely dominated by NGOs. We have also been able to win space in discussions from which we have previously been excluded. We were surprised but pleased to be able to participate in the South African Human Rights Commission's National Hearing on Access to Land, Housing and Service Delivery. We are very pleased that we were part of this historic and strategic contribution to building democracy and our country for the better.

The struggle for land reform from below will continue in 2016. The struggle to build democratic people's power from below will continue in 2016. But after careful discussion we have decided that our main focus in 2016 will be to improve the conditions on the lands that we have occupied and held.

We have occupied. We have resisted. Now is the time to develop.

Nelson Mandela said that "If the ANC does to you what the apartheid government did to you, then you must do to the ANC what you did to the apartheid government". We do not want our children to suffer the way we have suffered. It is better to die a martyr than to die in vain. It is better to die with dignity than to live in humiliation. As those who gathered in Kliptown for Congress of the People in 1955 said "THESE FREEDOMS WE WILL FIGHT FOR SIDE BY SIDE, THROUGHOUT OUR LIVES, UNTIL WE HAVE WON OUR LIBERTY".

Issued by Thapelo Mohapi, T.J. Ngongoma and Zandile Nsibande

Index

Index

PM Press is an independent, radical publisher of books and media to educate, entertain, and inspire. Founded in 2007 by a small group of people with decades of publishing, media, and organizing experience, PM Press amplifies the voices of radical authors, artists, and activists. Our aim is to deliver bold political ideas and vital stories to all walks of life and arm the dreamers to demand the impossible. We have sold millions of copies of our books, most often one at a time, face to face. We're old enough to know what we're doing and young enough to know what's at stake. Join us to create a better world.

PM Press
PO Box 23912
Oakland CA 94623
www.pmpress.org

PM Press in Europe
europe@pmpress.org
www.pmpress.org.uk

FRIENDS OF PM

These are indisputably momentous times—the financial system is melting down globally and the Empire is stumbling. Now more than ever there is a vital need for radical ideas.

In the many years since its founding—and on a mere shoestring—PM Press has risen to the formidable challenge of publishing and distributing knowledge and entertainment for the struggles ahead. With hundreds of releases to date, we have published an impressive and stimulating array of literature, art, music, politics, and culture. Using every available medium, we've succeeded in connecting those hungry for ideas and information to those putting them into practice.

Friends of PM allows you to directly help impact, amplify, and revitalize the discourse and actions of radical writers, filmmakers, and artists. It provides us with a stable foundation from which we can build upon our early successes and provides a much-needed subsidy for the materials that can't necessarily pay their own way. You can help make that happen—and receive every new title automatically delivered to your door once a month—by joining as a Friend of PM Press. And, we'll throw in a free T-shirt when you sign up.

Here are your options:
- $30 a month: Get all books and pamphlets plus 50% discount on all webstore purchases
- $40 a month: Get all PM Press releases (including CDs and DVDs) plus 50% discount on all webstore purchases
- $100 a month: Superstar—Everything plus PM merchandise, free downloads, and 50% discount on all webstore purchases

For those who can't afford $30 or more a month, we have Sustainer Rates at $15, $10, and $5. Sustainers get a free PM Press T-shirt and a 50% discount on all purchases from our website.

Your Visa or Mastercard will be billed once a month, until you tell us to stop. Or until our efforts succeed in bringing the revolution around. Or the financial meltdown of Capital makes plastic redundant. Whichever comes first.

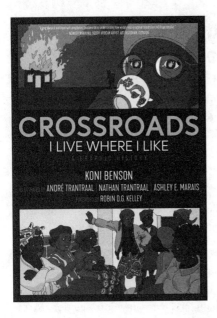

Crossroads
I Live Where I Like: A Graphic History

Koni Benson • Illustrated by André Trantraal, Nathan Trantraal, and Ashley E. Marais
Foreword by Robin D.G. Kelley
$20.00 • ISBN: 978-1-62963-835-5
7x10 • 168 pages

Drawn by South African political cartoonists the Trantraal brothers and Ashley Marais, *Crossroads: I Live Where I Like* is a graphic nonfiction history of women-led movements at the forefront of the struggle for land, housing, water, education, and safety in Cape Town over half a century. Drawing on over sixty life narratives, it tells the story of women who built and defended Crossroads, the only informal settlement that successfully resisted the apartheid bulldozers in Cape Town. The story follows women's organized resistance from the peak of apartheid in the 1970s to ongoing struggles for decent shelter today. Importantly, this account was workshopped with contemporary housing activists and women's collectives who chose the most urgent and ongoing themes they felt spoke to and clarified challenges against segregation, racism, violence, and patriarchy standing between the legacy of the colonial and apartheid past and a future of freedom still being fought for.

Presenting dramatic visual representations of many personalities and moments in the daily life of this township, the book presents a thoughtful and thorough chronology, using archival newspapers, posters, photography, pamphlets, and newsletters to further illustrate the significance of the struggles at Crossroads for the rest of the city and beyond. This collaboration has produced a beautiful, captivating, accessible, forgotten, and in many ways uncomfortable history of Cape Town that has yet to be acknowledged.

Crossroads: I Live Where I Like raises questions critical to the reproduction of segregation and to gender and generational dynamics of collective organizing, to ongoing anticolonial struggles and struggles for the commons, and to new approaches to social history and creative approaches to activist archives.

> "*Crossroads* is, quite simply, beautiful. It is intellectual and appealing and everything one could hope for from this kind of project. It is a meaningful engagement with a deeply troubling and enormously significant past. Not only does it weave text and images together to their best effect, but this is also one of the most insightful studies of urban history and social movements in any medium."
> —Trevor Getz, professor of African history, San Francisco State University; author of *Abina and the Important Men: A Graphic History*; and series editor of the Oxford University Press's Uncovering History series

IN, AGAINST, AND BEYOND CAPITALISM

The San Francisco Lectures

JOHN HOLLOWAY

Preface by Andrej Grubačić

In, Against, and Beyond Capitalism

The San Francisco Lectures
John Holloway
Preface by Andrej Grubacic
$14.95 • ISBN: 9781629631097
5 x 8 • 112 pages

In, Against, and Beyond Capitalism is based on three recent lectures delivered by John Holloway at the California Institute of Integral Studies in San Francisco. The lectures focus on what anticapitalist revolution can mean today—after the historic failure of the idea that the conquest of state power was the key to radical change—and offer a brilliant and engaging introduction to the central themes of Holloway's work.

The lectures take as their central challenge the idea that "We Are the Crisis of Capital and Proud of It." This runs counter to many leftist assumptions that the capitalists are to blame for the crisis, or that crisis is simply the expression of the bankruptcy of the system. The only way to see crisis as the possible threshold to a better world is to understand the failure of capitalism as the face of the push of our creative force. This poses a theoretical challenge. The first lecture focuses on the meaning of "We," the second on the understanding of capital as a system of social cohesion that systematically frustrates our creative force, and the third on the proposal that we are the crisis of this system of cohesion.

"His Marxism is premised on another form of logic, one that affirms movement, instability, and struggle. This is a movement of thought that affirms the richness of life, particularity (non-identity) and 'walking in the opposite direction'; walking, that is, away from exploitation, domination, and classification. Without contradictory thinking in, against, and beyond the capitalist society, capital once again becomes a reified object, a thing, and not a social relation that signifies transformation of a useful and creative activity (doing) into (abstract) labor. Only open dialectics, a right kind of thinking for the wrong kind of world, non-unitary thinking without guarantees, is able to assist us in our contradictory struggle for a world free of contradiction."—Andrej Grubacic, from his Preface

"Holloway's work is infectiously optimistic."
—Steven Poole, the *Guardian*

WE

A

ARE

John Holloway

THE

~

CRISIS

Reader

OF

JOHN HOLLOWAY

CAPITAL

We Are the Crisis of Capital

A John Holloway Reader

John Holloway

$22.95 • ISBN: 9781629632254

6 x 9 • 320 pages

We Are the Crisis of Capital collects articles and excerpts written by radical academic, theorist, and activist John Holloway over a period of forty years. This collection asks, "Is there a way out?" How do we break capital, a form of social organisation that dehumanises us and threatens to annihilate us completely? How do we create a world based on the mutual recognition of human dignity?

Holloway's work answers loudly, "By screaming NO!" By thinking from our own anger and creativity. By trying to recover the "we" buried under the categories of capitalist thought. By opening those categories and discovering the antagonism they conceal and by discovering that behind the concepts of money, state, capital, crisis, and so on, there moves our resistance-and-rebellion.

An approach sometimes referred to as Open Marxism, it is an attempt to rethink Marxism as daily struggle. The articles move forward, influenced by the German state derivation debates of the 1970s, by the CSE debates in Britain, and the group around the Edinburgh journal *Common Sense*, and then moving on to Mexico and the wonderful stimulus of the Zapatista uprising, and now the continuing whirl of discussion with colleagues and students in the Posgrado de Sociología of the Benemérita Universidad Autónoma de Puebla.

"Holloway's thesis is indeed important and worthy of notice."
—Richard J.F. Day, *Canadian Journal of Cultural Studies*

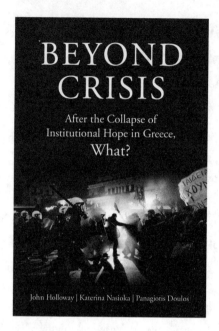

Beyond Crisis
After the Collapse of Institutional Hope in Greece, What?

Edited by John Holloway, Katerina Nasioka, and Panagiotis Doulos

$21.95 • ISBN: 9781629635156

6 x 9 • 256 pages

The government led by Syriza in Greece, elected in January 2015, at first seemed to be the most radical European government in recent history. It proclaimed itself the "Government of Hope" and throughout the world symbolized the hope that radical change could be achieved through institutional politics. The referendum of July 2015 rejected the austerity imposed by the banks and the European Union but was followed by a complete reversal of the government's position and its acceptance of that austerity.

The collapse of hope that accompanied the failure of the institutional Left opened the way to the return of the right-wing New Democracy Party, with a more aggressive program than ever. The essays collected in *Beyond Crisis*, among other things, form a case study of the "Greek experiment" that points to deeper implications concerning the global upsurge of disillusioned anger that has spurred the rise of far-right populism and support for strong leaders, exclusion of ethnic minorities, and greater "racial purity."

The Syriza government's dramatic crash showed the limits of institutional politics, a lesson apparently overlooked by the enthusiastic followers of Jeremy Corbyn and Bernie Sanders. But it also poses profound questions for those who reject state-centered politics. The anarchist or autonomist movement in Greece has been one of the strongest in the world, yet it has failed to have a significant impact in opening up alternative perspectives.

So how do we pick up the pieces? What direction should we follow from now on? How do we understand what happened and learn from it? The essays in this collection do not point to a single conclusion or path forward but rather raise questions that remain open about how to move beyond the current crisis amid a darkening sky of seeming impossibility.

> "*Beyond Crisis* does not look on the bright side. It looks straight into the eye of the storm and unfolds the hopelessness of conventional left politics in Greece and how it became part of the unfolding cycle of state violence and austerity. And it unfolds the community of hope, its courage of resistance and negativity, that has come to fore in Greece, and elsewhere too, as the direct democracy of a society of the free and equal."
> —Werner Bonefeld, professor of politics, University of York, England

No Gods, No Masters, No Peripheries

Global Anarchisms

Edited by Raymond Craib and Barry Maxwell

$27.95 • ISBN: 9781629630984

6 x 9 • 408 pages

Was anarchism in areas outside of Europe an import and a script to be mimicked? Was it perpetually at odds with other currents of the Left? The authors in this collection take up these questions of geographical and political peripheries. Building on recent research that has emphasized the plural origins of anarchist thought and practice, they reflect on the histories and cultures of the antistatist mutual aid movements of the last century beyond the boundaries of an artificially coherent Europe. At the same time, they reexamine the historical relationships between anarchism and communism without starting from the position of sectarian difference (Marxism versus anarchism). Rather, they look at how anarchism and communism intersected; how the insurgent Left could appear—and in fact was—much more ecumenical, capacious, and eclectic than frequently portrayed; and reveal that such capaciousness is a hallmark of anarchist practice, which is prefigurative in its politics and antihierarchical and antidogmatic in its ethics.

Copublished the with Institute for Comparative Modernities, this collection includes contributions by Gavin Arnall, Mohammed Bamyeh, Bruno Bosteels, Raymond Craib, Silvia Rivera Cusicanqui, Geoffroy de Laforcade, Silvia Federici, Steven J. Hirsch, Adrienne Carey Hurley, Hilary Klein, Peter Linebaugh, Barry Maxwell, David Porter, Maia Ramnath, Penelope Rosemont, and Bahia Shehab.

> "Broad in scope, generously ecumenical in outlook, bold in its attempt to tease apart the many threads and tensions of anarchism, this collection defies borders and category. These illuminating explorations in pan-anarchism provide a much-needed antidote to the myopic characterizations that bedevil the red and black."
> —Sasha Lilley, author of *Capital and Its Discontents*

The Art of Freedom
A Brief History of the Kurdish Liberation Struggle

Havin Guneser

Introduction by Andrej Grubacic

Interview by Sasha Lilley

PAPERBACK $16.95 • ISBN: 9781629637815

HARDCOVER $39.95 • ISBN: 9781629639079

5 x 8 • 192 pages

The revolution in Rojava captured the imagination of the left, sparking a worldwide interest in the Kurdish Freedom Movement. *The Art of Freedom* demonstrates that this explosive movement is firmly rooted in several decades of organized struggle.

In 2018, one of the most important spokespersons for the struggle of Kurdish Freedom, Havin Guneser, held three groundbreaking seminars on the historical background and guiding ideology of the movement. Much to the chagrin of career academics, the theoretical foundation of the Kurdish Freedom Movement is far too fluid and dynamic to be neatly stuffed into an ivory-tower filing cabinet. A vital introduction to the Kurdish struggle, *The Art of Freedom* is the first English-language book to deliver a distillation of the ideas and sensibilities that gave rise to the most important political event of the twenty-first century.

The book is broken into three sections:

- "Critique and Self-Critique: The rise of the Kurdish freedom movement from the rubbles of two world wars" provides an accessible explanation of the origins and theoretical foundation of the movement.
- "The Rebellion of the Oldest Colony: Jineology—the Science of Women" describes the undercurrents and nuances of the Kurdish women's movement and how they have managed to create the most vibrant and successful feminist movement in the Middle East.
- "Democratic Confederalism and Democratic Nation: Defense of Society Against Societycide" deals with the attacks on the fabric of society and new concepts beyond national liberation to counter it. Centering on notions of "a shared homeland" and "a nation made up of nations," these rousing ideas find deep international resonation.

Havin Guneser has provided an expansive definition of freedom and democracy and a road map to help usher in a new era of struggle against capitalism, imperialism, and the State.

> "Havin Guneser is not just the world's leading authority on the thought of Abdullah Öcalan; she is a profound, sensitive, and challenging revolutionary thinker with a message the world desperately needs to hear."
> —David Graeber, author of *Debt: The First 5,000 Years* and *Bullshit Jobs: A Theory*

Their Blood Got Mixed

Revolutionary Rojava and the War on ISIS

Janet Biehl

$27.95 • ISBN: 9781629639444

7 x 10 • 256 pages

In the summer of 2012 the Kurdish people of northern Syria set out to create a multiethnic society in the Middle East. Persecuted for much of the 20th century, they dared to try to overcome social fragmentation by affirming social solidarity among all the region's ethnic and religious peoples. As Syria plunged into civil war, the Kurds and their Arab and Assyrian allies established a self-governing polity that was not only multiethnic but democratic. And women were not only permitted but encouraged to participate in all social roles alongside men, including political and military roles.

To implement these goals, Rojava wanted to live in peace with its neighbors. Instead, it soon faced invasion by ISIS, a force that was in every way its opposite. ISIS attacked its neighbors in Iraq and Syria, imposing theocratic, tyrannical, femicidal rule on them. Those who might have resisted fled in terror. But when ISIS attacked the mostly Kurdish city of Kobane and overran much of it, the YPG and YPJ, or people's militias, declined to flee. Instead they resisted, and several countries, seeing their valiant resistance, formed an international coalition to assist them militarily. While the YPG and YPJ fought on the ground, the coalition coordinated airstrikes with them. They liberated village after village and in March 2019 captured ISIS's last territory in Syria.

Around that time, two UK-based filmmakers invited the author to spend a month in Rojava making a film. She accepted, and arrived to explore the society and interview people. During that month, she explored how the revolution had progressed and especially the effects of the war on the society. She found that the war had reinforced social solidarity and welded together the multiethnic, gender-liberated society. As one man in Kobane told her, "Our blood got mixed."

> "A spirited portrayal of the everyday life of a revolution at its most basic levels of societal organization and political mobilization. Janet Biehl beautifully shows the interactions, face-to-face negotiations, and debates between the people who come from different ethnic backgrounds in citizens' councils in neighborhoods and villages. Despite the trauma of war, Biehl shows that these people insist on building a new life and an alternative society to make a break from histories of injustice that have torn apart the people from each other."
> —Sardar Saadi is director of The Rojava Institute of Social Sciences (RISS) at the University of Rojava

A History of Pan-African Revolt

C.L.R. James
Introduction by Robin D.G. Kelley
$16.95 • ISBN: 9781604860955
5.5 x 8.5 • 160 pages

Originally published in England in 1938 (the same year as his magnum opus *The Black Jacobins*) and expanded in 1969, this work remains the classic account of global black resistance. Robin D.G. Kelley's substantial introduction contextualizes the work in the history and ferment of the times, and explores its ongoing relevance today.

"*A History of Pan-African Revolt* is one of those rare books that continues to strike a chord of urgency, even half a century after it was first published. Time and time again, its lessons have proven to be valuable and relevant for understanding liberation movements in Africa and the diaspora. Each generation who has had the opportunity to read this small book finds new insights, new lessons, new visions for their own age…. No piece of literature can substitute for a crystal ball, and only religious fundamentalists believe that a book can provide comprehensive answers to all questions. But if nothing else, *A History of Pan-African Revolt* leaves us with two incontrovertible facts. First, as long as black people are denied freedom, humanity and a decent standard of living, they will continue to revolt. Second, unless these revolts involve the ordinary masses and take place on their own terms, they have no hope of succeeding."
—Robin D.G. Kelley, from the Introduction

"I wish my readers to understand the history of Pan-African Revolt. They fought, they suffered—they are still fighting. Once we understand that, we can tackle our problems with the necessary mental equilibrium." —C.L.R. James

"Kudos for reissuing C.L.R. James's pioneering work on black resistance. Many brilliant embryonic ideas articulated in *A History of Pan-African Revolt* twenty years later became the way to study black social movements. Robin Kelley's introduction superbly situates James and his thought in the world of Pan-African and Marxist intellectuals."
—Sundiata Cha-Jua, Penn State University

State Capitalism and World Revolution

C.L.R. James, Raya Dunayevskaya, and Grace Lee Boggs
Introduction by Paul Buhle
Preface by Martin Glaberman
$16.95 • ISBN: 9781604860924
5.5 x 8.5 • 160 pages

Over sixty years ago, C.L.R. James and a small circle of collaborators making up the radical left Johnson-Forest Tendency reached the conclusion that there was no true socialist society existing anywhere in the world. Written in collaboration with Raya Dunayevskaya and Grace Lee Boggs, this is another pioneering critique of Lenin and Trotsky, and reclamation of Marx, from the West Indian scholar and activist, C.L.R. James. Originally published in 1950, this definitive edition includes the original preface from Martin Glaberman to the third edition, C.L.R. James' original introductions to three previous editions and a new introduction from James' biographer Paul Buhle.

> "When one looks back over the last twenty years to those men who were most far-sighted, who first began to tease out the muddle of ideology in our times, who were at the same time Marxists with a hard theoretical basis, and close students of society, humanists with a tremendous response to and understanding of human culture, Comrade James is one of the first one thinks of."
> —E.P. Thompson

Autonomy Is in Our Hearts

Zapatista Autonomous Government through the Lens of the Tsotsil Language

Dylan Eldredge Fitzwater
Foreword: John P. Clark

$19.95 • ISBN: 9781629635804
6 x 9 • 224 pages

Following the Zapatista uprising on New Year's Day 1994, the EZLN communities of Chiapas began the slow process of creating a system of autonomous government that would bring their call for freedom, justice, and democracy from word to reality. *Autonomy Is in Our Hearts* analyzes this long and arduous process on its own terms, using the conceptual language of Tsotsil, a Mayan language indigenous to the highland Zapatista communities of Chiapas.

The words "Freedom," "Justice," and "Democracy" emblazoned on the Zapatista flags are only approximations of the aspirations articulated in the six indigenous languages spoken by the Zapatista communities. They are rough translations of concepts such as *ichbail ta muk'* or "mutual recognition and respect among equal persons or peoples," *a'mtel* or "collective work done for the good of a community" and *lekil kuxlejal* or "the life that is good for everyone." *Autonomy Is in Our Hearts* provides a fresh perspective on the Zapatistas and a deep engagement with the daily realities of Zapatista autonomous government. Simultaneously an exposition of Tsotsil philosophy and a detailed account of Zapatista governance structures, this book is an indispensable commentary on the Zapatista movement of today.

> "This is a refreshing book. Written with the humility of the learner, or the absence of the arrogant knower, the Zapatista dictum to 'command obeying' becomes to 'know learning.'"
> —Marisol de la Cadena, author of *Earth Beings: Ecologies of Practice across Andean Worlds*

Liberating Sápmi
Indigenous Resistance in Europe's Far North

Gabriel Kuhn

$17.00 • ISBN: 9781629637129
5.5 x 8.5 • 220 pages

The Sámi, who have inhabited Europe's far north for thousands of years, are often referred to as the continent's "forgotten people." With Sápmi, their traditional homeland, divided between four nation-states—Norway, Sweden, Finland, and Russia—the Sámi have experienced the profound oppression and discrimination that characterize the fate of indigenous people worldwide: their lands have been confiscated, their beliefs and values attacked, their communities and families torn apart. Yet the Sámi have shown incredible resilience, defending their identity and their territories and retaining an important social and ecological voice—even if many, progressives and leftists included, refuse to listen.

Liberating Sápmi is a stunning journey through Sápmi and includes in-depth interviews with Sámi artists, activists, and scholars boldly standing up for the rights of their people. In this beautifully illustrated work, Gabriel Kuhn, author of over a dozen books and our most fascinating interpreter of global social justice movements, aims to raise awareness of the ongoing fight of the Sámi for justice and self-determination. The first accessible English-language introduction to the history of the Sámi people and the first account that focuses on their political resistance, this provocative work gives irrefutable evidence of the important role the Sámi play in the resistance of indigenous people against an economic and political system whose power to destroy all life on earth has reached a scale unprecedented in the history of humanity.

The book contains interviews with Mari Boine, Harald Gaski, Ann-Kristin Håkansson, Aslak Holmberg, Maxida Märak, Stefan Mikaelsson, May-Britt Öhman, Synnøve Persen, Øyvind Ravna, Niillas Somby, Anders Sunna, and Suvi West.

> "I'm highly recommending Gabriel Kuhn's book *Liberating Sápmi* to anyone seeking to understand the world of today through indigenous eyes. Kuhn concisely and dramatically opens our eyes to little-known Sápmi history, then in the perfect follow-up brings us up to date with a unique collection of interviews with a dozen of today's most brilliant contemporary Sámi voices. Bravo."
> —Buffy Sainte-Marie, Cree, singer-songwriter

Reassessing the Transnational Turn

Scales of Analysis in Anarchist and Syndicalist Studies

Edited by Constance Bantman and Bert Altena

$24.95 • ISBN: 9781629633916

6 x 9 • 256 pages

This edited volume reassesses the ongoing transnational turn in anarchist and syndicalist studies, a field where the interest in cross-border connections has generated much innovative literature in the last decade. It presents and extends up-to-date research into several dynamic historiographic fields, and especially the history of the anarchist and syndicalist movements and the notions of transnational militancy and informal political networks.

Whilst restating the relevance of transnational approaches, especially in connection with the concepts of personal networks and mediators, the book underlines the importance of other scales of analysis in capturing the complexities of anarchist militancy, due to both their centrality as a theme of reflection for militants, and their role as a level of organization. Especially crucial is the national level, which is often overlooked due to the internationalism which was so central to anarchist ideology.

In the context of resurgent populist nationalism across the global North, especially Europe, as well as parts of the Global South, *Reassessing the Transnational Turn* is a timely and welcome exploration focusing on the high point of the historical anarchist movement, approximately between the 1870s and 1939. In it, some of the more problematic, politically ambiguous, and underexplored relationships between anarchist movements and (trans)nationalism are interrogated by a range of historians and political scholars.

Contributors include Davide Turcato, Ruth Kinna, Isabelle Felici, Kenyon Zimmer, Pietro Di Paola, Raymond Craib, Nino Kühnis, and Martin Baxmeyer.

> "A compelling series of interventions. They speak not only to their direct disciplinary peers but also to broader currents and concerns across the social sciences. Anarchists, and Left academia more generally, tend to occupy a comfortable space in which it is easy to feel like our intellectual development and ideas are somehow immune from the gritty realities of social life and the various dimensions of nationalism, parochialism, and localism that run through it. On the contrary, *Reassessing the Transnational Turn* asks us to delve deeply and honestly into the canon and mythology of radicals past and reconsider their lived ambiguities and complexities, including the darker sides which we might prefer to ignore."
>
> —Anthony Ince, *Antipode*